7

BUSINESS ECONOMICS IN A RAPIDLY-CHANGING WORLD

CONTEMPORARY ISSUES IN ISLAMIC FINANCE

PRINCIPLES, PROGRESS AND PROSPECTS

BUSINESS ECONOMICS IN A RAPIDLY-CHANGING WORLD

BUSINESS ECONOMICS IN A RAPIDLY-CHANGING WORLD

CONTEMPORARY ISSUES IN ISLAMIC FINANCE

PRINCIPLES, PROGRESS AND PROSPECTS

ANDREW C. WORTHINGTON
EDITOR

nova publishers
New York

For permission to use material from this book please contact us:
Telephone 631-231-7269; Fax 631-231-8175
Web Site: http://www.novapublishers.com

Library of Congress Cataloging-in-Publication Data

Contemporary issues in Islamic finance : principles, progress and prospects / editor, Andrew C. Worthington.
pages cm
Includes index.
ISBN 978-1-62948-905-6 (hardcover)
1. Finance--Islamic countries. 2. Finance--Religious aspects--Islam. I. Worthington, Andrew C.
HG187.4.C663 2014
332.0917'67--dc23

2013048013

Published by Nova Science Publishers, Inc. † New York

CONTENTS

In: Contemporary Issues in Islamic Finance
Editor: Andrew C. Worthington
ISBN: 978-1-62948-905-6

Chapter 1

Introduction to Contemporary Issues in Islamic Finance

Andrew C. Worthington[*]
Griffith University, Australia

Islamic finance—financial institutions, products, and services designed to comply with the central tenets of *Shariah* (or Islamic law)—is one of the most rapidly growing segments of the global finance industry. While the widespread practice of Islamic finance in the modern world only commenced with savings institutions in 1963 (in Egypt and Malaysia), it has now spread to many other types of financial products and services, including banking, funds management (including mutual funds), *Takaful* (Islamic insurance) and *Sukuk* (Islamic bonds). Islamic financial products have now proliferated across almost every aspect of contemporary financial services, with comparable products complimenting and competing with those found in the conventional finance sector. Consequently, the number of financial institutions offering Islamic financial products and services has also dramatically increased, from only a few hundred in the mid-2000s to nearly a thousand with operations in more than 75 countries and a total value of *Shariah*-compliant assets exceeding $1.6 trillion.

Though initially concentrated in the Middle East (especially Bahrain) and Southeast Asia (particularly Malaysia), Islamic finance principles are now increasingly found elsewhere. This includes developing economies where the financial sector is almost entirely Islamic (Iran and Sudan) or where Islamic and 'conventional' financial systems coexist (Indonesia, Malaysia, Pakistan and the United Arab Emirates). It also includes developed economies where a small number of Islamic financial institutions have been established and where large conventional banks have opened Islamic financing windows (such as in Europe and the United States).

While practiced for many centuries, it is important to recall that only in the last thirty years have the Islamic financial institutions offering *Shariah*-compliant products and services become more widespread and substantial. Indeed, even in Muslim countries, it is only very recently that analogous Islamic finance products and services have evolved in direct competition with the financial products and services offered by conventional financial

[*] Department of Accounting, Finance and Economics, Griffith University, Nathan QLD 4111, Australia. Email. a.worthington@griffith.edu.au.

institutions. Unfortunately, research into Islamic finance has lagged behind this rapid growth, with academic, industry and government researchers hard-pressed to make up the deficiency. This is important for the future of this still emerging industry, given the need for research to fill the gap in addressing the consumer, financial market, regulatory and other implications of Islamic finance. For example, while Islamic financial institutions and instruments share many features with their conventional counterparts, there is still much to learn about the difference in other features impact upon, among other things, pricing and other market-related behavior. Similarly, there is a need to consider what impediments remain to o the adoption of Islamic financial products and services in many contexts, including the role of regulatory and supervisory regimes in banking law, constraints present in legal systems more broadly, and those relating to the knowledge of consumers and financial professionals. The purpose of this volume is to address this need, at least in part, by presenting eleven very recent studies of contemporary Islamic finance.

In Chapter 2, Alsadek Gait and Andrew Worthington provide a succinct and accessible analysis of the definition, sources, principles, and methods of Islamic finance. This serves as a suitable starting point for further work into Islamic finance and many of the pressing regulatory, supervisory and competitive issues that remain yet unaddressed. They define Islamic finance as a financial service principally implemented to comply with the main tenets of *Shariah* (or Islamic law). In turn, the main sources of *Shariah* are the *Holy Quran*, *Hadith*, *Sunna*, *Ijma*, *Qiyas* and *Ijtihad*. The *Holy Quran* is the book of revelation given to the Prophet Muhammad; Hadith is the narrative relating the deeds and utterances of *Muhammad. Sunna* refers to the habitual practice and behavior of Muhammad during his life. *Ijma* is the consensus among religion scholars about specific issues not envisaged in either the *Holy Quran* or the *Sunna*. *Qiyas* is the use of deduction by analogy to provide an opinion on a case not referred to in the Quran or the *Sunna* in comparison with another case referred to in the *Quran* and the *Sunna*. Finally, *Ijtihad* represents a jurists' independent reasoning relating to the applicability of certain Sharia rules on cases not mentioned in ether the *Quran* or the *Sunna*.

Following this, Gait and Worthington identify the main principles of Islamic finance as the prohibition of *Riba* and the removal of debt-based financing from the economy, the prohibition of *Gharar*, encompassing the full disclosure of information and removal of any asymmetrical information in a contract. The principles also include the exclusion of financing and dealing in sinful and socially irresponsible activities and commodities such as gambling, casinos, production of alcohol, etc., risk-sharing, the provider of financial funds and the entrepreneur share business risk in return for shares of profits and losses.

Lastly, Islamic financial contracts should encompass materiality, a financial transaction needs to have a 'material finality', that is a direct or indirect link to a real economic transaction and justice, a financial transaction should not lead to the exploitation of any party to the transaction. Employing these principles, the main financial instruments they identify in Islamic finance are *Mudarabah*, the provision of capital in a partial-equity partnership, *Musharakah*, full equity partnerships, *Murabaha*, an instrument for financing the purchase of goods, *Bai muajjall*, deferred payments on products, *Bai Salam*, advance sale contracts, *Istisna*, or manufacturing contracts, *Ijarah*, lease financing and *Quard Hassan*, the system of benevolent loans.

In Chapter 3, Yahia Baej and Andrew Worthington discuss Islamic banking more specifically. Islamic banking is one of the fastest growing industries in global finance. New institutions are adapting Islamic financial products and services with increasing attention from academics and practitioners all over the world. Similar to conventional banks and other financial institutions, Islamic banks are private profit-seeking enterprises. Nevertheless, the *Shariah* principles guide the latter, which strictly prohibits dealing with interest (*Riba*), uncertainty (*Gharar*), gambling (*Maysir*) and some other financial products and services. Baej and Worthington first provide a detailed assessment of the religious sources underpinning Islamic banking, comprising the primary sources of the *Holy Quran* and the *Sunnah* of the Prophet (collectively known as *Al-Wahyain* or the Two Revelations), and the secondary sources subsequently derived from the work of Muslim scholars, namely, the *Al-Ijma'* (or scholarly consensus) and *Al-Qiyas* (or analogy). The chapter then outlines the key financial products and services commonly practiced by Islamic banks, including *Murabahah* (cost-plus sales), *Musharakah* (full partnership), *Mudarabah* (silent partnership), *Ijarah* (Leasing), *Istisna'* (contract of manufacture), and *Al-Qard Al-Hassan* (benevolent loans). The final part of the chapter discusses the evolving definition of Islamic banking, the fundamental differences between conventional and Islamic banks, and the process of transformation to Islamic banking as experienced by new and existing banks.

In Chapter 4, Ainulashikin Marzuki and Andrew Worthington consider the growth of Islamic mutual funds in Malaysia. Islamic mutual funds (IMFs) continue to grow as an alternative investment vehicle for investors wishing to integrate Islamic values and secular financial objectives in their investments. The most distinctive feature of IMFs lies in screening strategies based on the application of *Shariah*. Conventionally, this mainly involves the application of exclusionary screening, whereby fund managers screen out companies involved in certain activities, including *Riba* (interest), *Gharar* (uncertainty), and *Maysir* (gambling), and prohibited products from their portfolios as prescribed by the *Quran*, *Sunnah* and related Islamic texts. The central outcome is that the managers of IMFs, unlike those of conventional mutual funds (CMFs), necessarily access only a subset of the population of investments available. This has dramatic implications for many conventional dimensions of mutual fund behavior, including performance, the flow of funds, and the fund selection behavior of investors. This chapter provides a comprehensive overview of the development of Islamic managed funds in Malaysia and discusses the historical, regulatory framework, financial reporting, benchmark indices and operational aspects of Islamic managed funds.

In Chapter 5, Md. Narul Kabir and Andrew Worthington discuss credit risk in Islamic banking as one of the most important aspects of bank management. Whether Islamic banks have higher or lower credit risk than conventional banks depends on two important elements. First, the nature of credit risk in Islamic financial products. Second, the suitability of credit risk measurement techniques for Islamic banks. They review and critically evaluate the available literature relating to the credit risk of Islamic banks. This enables practitioners and regulators alike to gain a comprehensive awareness of the nature of credit risk in Islamic banking products from several different perspectives. They also identify the measurement techniques currently available for Islamic banks along with the pros and cons of each of the measurement techniques.

In Chapter 6, Alsadek Gait and Andrew Worthington discuss the consumer prospects for Islamic finance in Libya. While commercial Islamic finance is not yet widely practiced in Libya, most businesses have at least some knowledge about Islamic methods of finance. They partly attribute this awareness to both knowledge of developments in other Muslim countries and to the fact that many commercial products and services offered by Islamic financial institutions bear close relation to informal financing and business arrangements already practiced among Muslims. These include *Musharakah* (full partnerships) and *Quard Hassan* (interest-free loans), with the latter practiced personally by about one-fifth of all business respondents. Gait and Worthington find that many firms are predisposed to Islamic finance, but those that do generally have less business experience, are smaller in terms of both assets and the number of employees, have lower levels of outstanding debt and fewer owners. In fact, only 5.1% of potential user firms have assets in excess of LYD500,000 compared to 73.0% of firms that are not potential users, and no potential user has liabilities exceeding LYD200,000. This would immediately suggest that while Islamic finance could potentially play a major role in business financing in Libya, it would primarily be for small and medium-sized enterprises.

In Chapter 7, Md. Narul Kabir and Suzuki Yasushi focus on the risk management practices of Islamic banks, especially in managing credit risk. They do this by considering both macroeconomic and bank specific variables affecting the credit risk of Islamic banks in Bangladesh and Malaysia. Using least squares techniques, they find three significant determinants of credit risk in Islamic banks in Bangladesh, namely, the loan to deposit ratio, cost inefficiency, and size. In contrast, two additional variables significantly affect the credit risk of Islamic banks in Malaysia, namely, credit growth and the returns on assets. Overall, they find that macroeconomic factors do not exert any significant impact on the nonperforming loans of Islamic banks in either of these countries.

In Chapter 8, Yahia Baej and Andrew Worthington assess the challenges and prospects for Islamic finance in Libya, an overwhelmingly Muslim-populated country but one without a formal system of Islamic finance and banking. However, since independence, the principles of *Shariah* have at least partly applied in the state, and successive Libyan governments have shown a willingness to implement a dual system comprising Islamic and conventional banking institutions in the future. Nonetheless, the country's financial and banking system remains largely conventional, unlike many other countries with large Muslim populations, including Egypt, Saudi Arabia, the United Arab Emirates, Turkey, Bahrain, and Malaysia, which have witnessed the development of banking systems with a substantial Islamic component. They conclude that the weakness of the Libyan economy due to long periods of international sanctions, isolation, and systematic corruption, the absence of an Islamic monetary market, the uncertain relationship between the Central Bank of Libya and the newly introduced banks, and the lack of suitable human resources in banking are the major challenges facing Islamic banking in Libya.

In Chapter 9, Ainulashikin Marzuki and Andrew Worthington evaluate the performance of Islamic mutual funds (IMFs) in Malaysia during the period February 1996 to December 2009. In doing so, they respond to the following two questions. First, how does the performance of IMFs compare with conventional mutual funds (CMFs) in Malaysia? Second, do IMFs perform better during bear markets? They find that IMFs generally outperform CMFs during the sample period. However, even though the results suggest that IMFs generally outperform CMFs during downward market trends, they do not appear to exhibit any significant investment hedging function during periods of market crisis.

In Chapter 10, Zurina Shafii, Supiah Salleh and Nurazalia Zakaria Shariah evaluate the role of audit as the third line of defense in ensuring that the operations of Islamic financial institutions (IFIs) align with *Shariah* principles. These operations refer to not only day-to-day operations, processes, procedures and management records, but also financial statements.

Shariah audit thus provides information to the market that the IFIs are complying fully with the *Shariah* guidelines. This is especially important, as the market is keen on knowing this information as it provides the foremost rationale for Islamic finance and banking. The authors conclude that the growth of Islamic finance over the past three decades plus the subprime crisis has provided greater emphasis for IFIs to be ever more Shariah-compliant. The chapter also usefully provides suggested auditable areas for the audit scope of *Shariah* audit in the financial statements of IFIs.

Finally, in Chapter 11 Yahia Baej and Andrew Worthington evaluate the various types and degrees of risk associated with Islamic banks in their every-day activities. However, even though Islamic and conventional banks are superficially similar, the nature and role of these risks can vary widely. The objective of this chapter is then to compare various aspects of risk management in conventional and Islamic banks including the concept of risk, the types of risk, the various risk measurement and management approaches and techniques, and capital adequacy. Baej and Worthington find that *Shariah* considers some conditions for risk to be acceptable, such as the objective of taking the risk, the value that taking risk would add to the economy, and the degree of risk taken. On this basis, a number of conventional risk measurement and banks management approaches and techniques are fully available to Islamic banks as they are in essence *Shariah*-compatible. However, adopting and developing tools that evaluate the unique risks associated with the nature of Islamic banking is crucial. For example, alongside the international capital adequacy guidelines, a number of supervisory bodies and auditing and accounting bodies have developed special guidelines.

The topics addressed in this volume are broad and range across a large number of different contexts. However, they share a common focus in addressing the needs of academic, professional and industry researchers, policymakers, monetary authorities, consumer groups, and other interested in better understanding Islamic finance in all its complexity as it continues to grow and develop as a valid alternative to conventional finance and banking systems throughout the world.

In: Contemporary Issues in Islamic Finance
Editor: Andrew C. Worthington
ISBN: 978-1-62948-905-6

Chapter 2

A PRIMER ON ISLAMIC FINANCE

Alsadek Gait and Andrew C. Worthington*
Griffith University, Australia

ABSTRACT

Islamic finance is one of the most rapidly growing segments of the global financial system. However, despite the increasing importance of Islamic finance, particularly in developing economies in the Middle East and South-East Asia, religious and social complexity has acted against a fuller understanding by regulators, policymakers, researchers, and practitioners. This chapter provides a succinct and accessible analysis of the definition, sources, principles, and methods of Islamic finance. This serves as a suitable starting point for further work into Islamic finance and many of the pressing regulatory, supervisory and competitive issues that remain yet unaddressed.

1. INTRODUCTION

Islamic finance—financial institutions and products designed to comply with the central tenets of *Shariah* (or Islamic law)—is one of the most rapidly growing segments of the global finance industry. Starting with the Dubai Islamic Bank in 1975 (and operations in the United Arab Emirates, Egypt, the Cayman Islands, Sudan, Lebanon, the Bahamas, Bosnia, Bahrain and Pakistan), the number of Islamic financial institutions worldwide now exceeds over three hundred, with operations in seventy-five countries and assets in excess of US$400 billion (El-Qorchi 2005).

Though initially concentrated in the Middle East (especially Bahrain) and South-East Asia (particularly Malaysia), Islamic finance principles are now increasingly found elsewhere. This includes developing economies where the financial sector is almost entirely Islamic (such as Iran and Sudan) or where Islamic and 'conventional' financial systems coexist (including Indonesia, Malaysia, Pakistan and the United Arab Emirates) (El-Qorchi

* Corresponding author: Department of Accounting, Finance and Economics, Griffith University, Nathan QLD 4111, Australia. Email. a.worthington@griffith.edu.au.

2005). It also includes developed economies where a small number of Islamic financial institutions have been established and where large conventional banks have opened Islamic financing windows (such as in Europe and the United States) (Archer and Rifaat 2002).

The global proliferation of Islamic financial institutions has accompanied parallel developments in Islamic financial products. Starting with simple prohibitions on usury, investment in tobacco, alcohol, gambling and armaments and a requirement that all financial transactions be based on real economic activity, Islamic financial products now cover a broad range of financial services, including funds management, asset allocation, payment and exchange settlement services, insurance and reinsurance, and risk management. For almost all conventional financial products, there is nearly always an analogous Islamic finance product. For example, Islamic securities now account for 42 percent of outstanding private debt securities and 25 percent of outstanding bonds in Malaysia and the sovereign (and quasi-sovereign) and the German State of Saxony–Anhalt tapped the corporate *Sukuk* (Islamic medium-term note) market in a €100 million issue in 2004. In addition, the Dow–Jones Islamic Market Index and the Financial Times Stock Exchange Global Islamic Index provide benchmarks for the more than 130 Islamic equity mutual funds worldwide (El-Qorchi 2005).

Unfortunately, this rapid development and the substantial cultural and language barriers that exist have acted against a fuller and more widely held understanding of Islamic finance. This is problematic in a number of respects. To start with, regulators worldwide are now faced with the need to standardize and harmonize regulation and supervision in systems that may include Islamic institutions and products (Choudhry and Mirakor 1997; Kahf 1997; El-Hawary et al. 2004). While a number of specialised Islamic organisations assist in this process—the Accounting and Auditing Organization for Islamic Financial Institutions (2007), the Islamic Finance Services Board (2007), the International Islamic Financial Market (2007), the Islamic Development Bank (2007) and the International Islamic Rating Agency (2007), amongst others—yet other national and international regulators also need to be involved. This is especially so considering the differences in behavioural assumptions between Islamic and conventional financial institutions, firms, and products. As examples of this wider interest in Islamic finance, the International Organisation of Securities Commissions (2004) commissioned a recent taskforce on Islamic capital markets, while the World Bank (2007) recognizes that "…to enhance its expertise on Islamic financial services, the Bank is engaged in the analysis of their corporate governance, transparency, market discipline and risk management features". Moreover, the International Monetary Fund's (2007) *Finance and Development* series frequently deals with topics of interest in Islamic banking [see also Errico and Mitra (1998)].

Concomitantly, there is ongoing debate over the fact that Islamic banks do not separate fund management and investment activities from commercial banking. This may cause technical difficulties for supervisors and regulators (Sundararajan and Errico 1997). Likewise, the risk-sharing nature of liability contracts has raised concerns on the definition of capital and capital adequacy ratios: some have argued that the appropriate regulatory framework for Islamic banking must place a greater emphasis on operational risk management and information disclosure than is normally the case with conventional banks (El-Qorchi 2005). Moreover, many developing economies are grappling with the design of better supervisory and regulatory regimes, and thus how they should treat Islamic finance within these regimes (Wilson 2002). A better understanding of Islamic finance is called for in all respects.

At the same time, researchers in conventional finance have been restricted in their efforts to investigate these and other important issues by the strong interface between religion, finance, and the social and cultural barriers that act against the acquisition of this knowledge. This necessarily impairs research into Islamic finance, its role, and potential impacts. In a similar manner, practitioners in conventional finance firms may find it difficult to gain an understanding of Islamic finance necessary for the design of compliant products and an awareness of the competitive position of Islamic finance firms and products.

Accordingly, the purpose of this chapter is to introduce the definition, sources, principles, and methods of Islamic finance. While several publications are already available concerning Islamic finance concepts [see, for example, Anwar (1995), Haron (1995), El-Gamal (2000), Warde (2000), Lewis and Algaoud (2001), Iqbal and Llewellyn (2002), Abdul-Gafoor (2003), Obaidullah (2005)] in nearly all cases these deal with specific aspects and/or abstract from the basic principles necessary for the first-time reader. This article starts with the religious and social underpinnings of Islamic finance and links this with the principles and methods of contemporary Islamic products. It therefore provides guidance to those conducting empirical research in Islamic finance as well as an aid for policymakers, managers, and practitioners interpreting the outcomes of Islamic finance studies.

The remainder of the chapter is divided into six main sections. Section 2 offers some definitions of Islamic finance. Section 3 highlights the historical background and religious context of Islamic finance. Section 4 outlines the main principles of Islamic finance. Section 5 presents the main methods of Islamic finance, and Section 6 briefly focuses on Islamic banking. The final section concludes.

2. Definition of Islamic Finance

Islamic finance is defined as a financial service principally implemented to comply with the main tenets of *Shariah* (or Islamic law). In turn, the main sources of *Shariah* are the *Holy Quran, Hadith, Sunna, Ijma, Qiyas,* and *Ijtihad.* The *Holy Quran* is the book of revelation given to the Prophet Muhammad. *Hadith* is the narrative relating the deeds and utterances of Muhammad. *Sunna* refers to the habitual practice and behaviour of Muhammad during his lifetime. *Ijma* is the consensus among religion scholars about specific issues not envisaged in either the *Holy Quran* or the *Sunna. Qiyas* is the use of deduction by analogy to provide an opinion on a case not referred to in the *Quran* or the Sunna in comparison with another case referred to in the *Quran* and the Sunna. Finally, *Ijtihad* represents a jurists' independent reasoning relating to the applicability of certain *Shariah* rules on cases not mentioned in ether the *Quran* or the *Sunna.*

A large number of Islamic finance definitions are found in the literature, ranging from the relatively simple definitions for specific aspects (say, Islamic banking) to more complex definitions covering all financial operations. Warde (2000, p. 5), for example, defines Islamic finance as follows: "Islamic financial institutions are those that are based, in their objectives and operations, on Quran's principles (principles of the Muslims' holy book)". This particular definition suggests that Islamic financial firms are not just banks, but also other types of financial intermediaries that employ *Shariah* principles. The other point of departure is that the *Shariah* ostensibly requires the adjustment of all aspects of Muslims' lives and the formation of a complete moral system. According to Iqbal (1997), while the prevailing Western financial system focuses on the capitalistic features of economic and financial processes, Islamic finance aims to make an actual moral and equitable distribution in resources and social fairness in all (Muslim) societies.

3. Historical and Religious Context

The development process of Islamic finance commenced at the beginning of the 7th century when Muhammad professedly received revelations directly from *Allah* (the God of Islam). Moore (1997 p.3) regards the actual date as 613AD when Muhammad was about forty years old. At the time, the doctrine of financial operations during Muhammad's era was derived directly from the *Holy Quran* and the *Sunna* (traditions) of Muhammad. Since then, while Islamic *Shariah (Quran and Sunna)* has ostensibly coordinated all financial transactions between Islamic persons, there has been a continuing process of mutual adjustment between *Shariah* and the actual financial practices of Muslim societies.

In Muhammad's lifetime, Islamic methods of finance often drew upon examples from the Prophet's experiences. Kahf and Khan (1993), for example, have pointed out that Muhammad was the first to use the M*udarabah* (silent partnership) in trade with a rich women named Khadijah (who latter became his wife). At the time, Muslims used to practice *Musharakah* (full partnership) when operating large commercial enterprises under a profit/loss sharing principle. In addition, Muhammad made it permissible for people to use sale on credit (*bai salam*) which was to finance consumption or production without usury and he encouraged Muslims to provide benevolent loans (*Quard Hassan*) (Kahf and Khan 1993). The ongoing Islamisation of Arabic countries meant that *Shariah* rapidly spread to both Muslims and non-Muslims at this time.

After the death of Muhammad in 632AD, a great expansion of Islam occurred throughout the Arabic states and in large parts of the non-Arab world. The Islamic state in this 'golden age' was dominant in three continents, Asia, Africa, and Europe. According to Moore (1997) the Islamisation of economic systems during the four centuries following Muhammad's death reached Morocco and Spain to the west, India and China to the east, central Asia to the north and Africa to the south. Historical records of contracts registered between businesspersons at the time, including Mudarabah and Musharakah, also indicate the extension of Islamic tools of finance. Islamic finance practices continued largely unchanged until the beginning of the 19th Century (Warde 2000).

From the nineteenth century, nearly all Muslim countries fell under the control of the Western colonial powers (France in North Africa, Britain and France in the Middle East, Britain in the Indian sub-continent and Britain and The Netherlands in South-East Asia), effectively dividing the Islamic world into many small states. Anwar (1995) argues that by the mid-nineteenth century almost all Muslim-controlled areas fell to the Western colonial powers and thus the existing financial scheme which complied with *Shariah* was effectively replaced by the capitalist system. From then until the second half of the twentieth century, most Muslim economies were dominated by the economic traditions and systems of Western Europe (Moore 1997). However, while commercial banks, insurance companies and other types of intermediary firms employed conventional methods of finance (mostly as braches or agents of institutions in the colonising country), Islamic methods of finance were still often practised between individual Muslims.

With the independence of the Arabic countries from the colonial powers by the second half of the twentieth century, many Islamic economies also became more independent. As a result, Muslim economists started reconsidering the application of Islamic finance into a formal banking industry. Iqbal and Molyneux (2005) suggest the first attempt to establish an Islamic bank was in 1971 when the Egyptian government established the Nasser Social Bank. This bank provided a number of Islamic financial products, including interest-free loans to the poor, student scholarships, and small business credit on a profit/loss sharing basis, closely followed by the Dubai Islamic Bank in 1975. El-Qorchi (2005) attributes the rapid growth in the last thirty years to several key developments. First, the strong demand from immigrant and non-immigrant Muslims for *Shariah*-compliant financial services and transactions; second, the growing oil wealth found in the Middle East; and third, the increasing competitiveness of Islamic finance products vis-à-vis their conventional counterparts. Other factors likely include the rise of fundamentalism and resurgence of strident Muslim practice in many communities and the incentives offered by governments in some Muslim countries to encourage the establishment of Islamic banks.

4. Principles of Islamic Finance

Islamic finance is controlled by *Shariah,* the legal framework of Islam and its Quranic interpretation, along with the teachings of *Sunna.* This framework provides guidelines for people to follow the principles of the *Holy Quran* and the *Sunna* in their decision-making in all aspects of life. Financial transactions are one of the more important dealings controlled by *Shariah,* ostensibly to ensure the more equitable distribution of income and wealth among Muslims in Islamic economies.

The principles of Islamic finance have been extensively studied by Muslim and non-Muslin scholars alike (Wilson 2006; Metwally 2006; Iqbal and Molyneux 2005; Siddiqi 2004; Akacem and Gilliam 2002; Zaher and Hassan 2001; Lewis and Algaoud 2001; Al-Jarhi and Iqbal 2001; Warde 2000; El-Gamal 2000; Dar and Presley 1999; Dumale and Sapcanin 1999; Abdul-Gafoor 1999; Moore 1997; Iqbal 1997; Haron 1995; Kahf and Khan 1993; Metwally 1993). The general principles are as follows: (i) the prohibition of *Riba* (usury or excessive interest) and the removal of debt-based financing from the economy; (ii) the prohibition of *Gharar*, encompassing the full disclosure of information and removal of any asymmetrical information in a contract; (iii) the exclusion of financing and dealing in sinful and socially irresponsible activities and commodities such as gambling and the production of alcohol; (iv) risk-sharing, the provider of financial funds and the entrepreneur share business risk in return for shares of profits and losses; (v) materiality, a financial transaction needs to have a 'material finality', that is a direct or indirect link to a real economic transaction; and (vi) justice, a financial transaction should not lead to the exploitation of any party to the transaction.

Prohibition of *Riba* (Usury or Interest)

Al-Jarhi and Iqbal (2001) and Siddiqi (2004) argue that *Riba* is an Arabic word that means any increase or growth in a loan paid by the debtor to the lender, regardless of whether the increase is large or small. Metwally (2006, p. 17) links the concept more closely to usury: "Usury is translated to mean *Riba* which literally means an excess or addition above the principle lent. Since interest, however small, is an excess over the capital lent". Of course, *Riba* (usury or interest), while historically practiced by many Near East populations such as the Mesopotamians, Hittites, Phoenicians and Egyptians, had also been condemned by other religions before the establishment of Islam. For example, the Jewish Torah and later sections of the Hebrew Bible criticize interest taking, but interpretations of the Biblical prohibition vary. One common understanding is that Jews are forbidden to charge interest upon loans made to other Jews, but are allowed to charge interest on transactions with Gentiles. Similarly, the prohibitions against usury in Christian theology have ranged between straight prohibitions on interest to papal edicts against excessive interest.

It is generally argued that the prohibition of *Riba* (usury or interest, whether small or large) is the most important principle of Islamic finance. Any interest or predetermined payment over and above the actual amount of principle is strongly prohibited by the *Holy Quran* and the *Sunna.* Metwally (2006, p.16-17) translates the evidence from the *Holy Quran* and the *Sunna* as follows:

> Those who devour usury will not stand except as stands one whom The Evil One by his touch hath driven to madness. That is because they say: Trade is like usury. But Allah hath permitted trade and forbidden usury (2:275).
>
> O Ye who believe! Fear Allah and give up what remains of your demand for usury, if Ye are indeed believers. If Ye do it not, take notice of war from Allah and His Apostle. But if Ye turn back, Ye shall have your capital sums: Deal not unjustly and Ye shall not be dealt with unjustly (2:278–279).
>
> The Prophet has condemned both the receiver and the giver of usury. It is claimed that the prophet said: Sell not gold for gold except in equal quantity, nor sell silver for silver except in equal quantity, nor sell anything present, for that which is absent.

In this tradition, gold and silver were used as money in Muhammad's era when usury on these materials was forbidden. In addition, El-Gamal (2000, p.3) translates another *Hadith* (or message) from the *Sunna* where it is very clear that *Riba* (usury or interest) is strictly forbidden:

> Muslim narrated on the authority of Abou Said Al-Khudriy: Bilal visited the Messenger of Allah with some high quality dates, and the prophet inquired about their source. Bilal explained that he traded two volumes of lower quality dates for one volume of higher quality. The Messenger of Allah said: "this is precisely *Riba!* Do not do this. Instead, sell the first type of dates, and use the proceeds to buy the other.

Even though there are no specific verses in the *Quran* or messages from the *Sunna* providing reasons for the forbidding of R*iba,* some studies argue these may be inferred [see, for instance, Moore (1997), Siddiqi (2004) and Iqbal and Molyneux (2005)]. Moore (1997), for example, observes that *Riba* contradicts the principles of profit/loss sharing which aims to create a proper balance between the lender and the borrower. Siddiqi (2004) provides other reasons for the prohibition of *Riba*. First, *Riba* is a form of social corruption referred to by Arabic scholars as *Fasad*. Siddiqi (2004, p. 42) translates the following from the *Holy Quran* (30:38-41):

> That which you give in usury in order that it may increase in other people's property has no increase with Allah; but that which you give in charity, seeking Allah's countenance, has increase manifold. Allah is He Who created you and then sustained you, then causes you to die, then gives life for you again. Is there any of your (so-called) partners (of Allah) that does aught of that? Praised and exalted be He above what they associate with him. Corruption does appear on land and sea because of (the evil) which men's hands have done, that He may make them taste a part of that which they have done, in order that they may return.

Here the giving or taking usury can be related to the appearance of corruption, which in a society results from men's wicked behaviours on earth. Second, *Riba* implies the wrongful appropriation of other people's property without justification. In other words, usury or interest is a property right claimed outside the lawful framework of identified property rights that create a balance between rich and poor people. In Islam, people who affect the property rights of others will face punishment from Allah at the day of the judgment. The *Holy Quran* (4:161) supports this contention: "And of their taking usury when they were forbidden it, and of their devouring people's wealth by false pretences. We have prepared for those of them who disbelieve a painful doom". Third, *Riba* decreases the resources of states through a negative effect on the growth of economies. The *Holy Quran* (2: 276) states, "Allah has blighted usury and made almsgiving fruitful. Allah loves not the impious and guilty" (Siddiqi 2004, p.36). This verse suggests that the usury or interest creates unfairness. On the other hand, a better way to create growth in the economy is by giving to charities or providing interest-free loans.

Fourth, *Riba* demeans and diminishes the humanity of individuals. Siddiqi (2004, p. 43) inferred this meaning from Allah that those who receive or pay usury are affected by the touch of the Evil (2:275). Persons so affected become mad with greed because they need to obtain more and more interest and usury without stopping. Fifth, *Riba* leads to money being made from money: an unacceptable practice in Islamic finance. In Islam, money is an exchange instrument that has no value in itself. It is argued that those who place their money as a deposit in a bank or lend it to gain interest earn money without effort or risk. According to *Shariah,* people should be productive and useful, but only by investing their money in useful trade and economic enterprise (Siddiqi 2004).

Finally, the most essential reason for the prohibition of *Riba* is that it is unfair in that it affects borrowers and lenders alike. Iqbal and Molyneux (2005) argue that the borrower must pay interest and repay the capital, as well as bearing any losses from the use of these funds (a form of 'double charging': that is, charging for both the funds and the use of the funds). In addition, *Riba* is also regarded as being unjust to the lender. This is because the real rate of interest may become negative if, say, the rate of inflation is higher than rate of interest. Therefore, lenders who wish to earn a profit from lending money could make a loss. Once again, the loss incurred would be unrelated to the actual use of the funds.

Prohibition of *Gharar* (Risk and Uncertainty)

The second significant prohibition in Islamic finance is *Gharar*, generally translated as risk, hazard, or uncertainty. Al-Dareer (1997, p.10) defines *Gharar* in jurisprudential terms under three headings:

> First, *Gharar* applies exclusively to cases of doubtfulness or uncertainty, as in the case of not knowing whether something will take place or not. The definition by Ibn Abidin is a case in point: *Gharar* is uncertainty over the existence of the subject matter of sale. A second view holds that *Gharar* applies only to the unknown, to the exclusion of the doubtful. This view is adopted by the Zahiri School. Thus, according to Ibn Hazm, *Gharar* in sales occurs when the purchaser does not know what he has bought and the seller does not know what he has sold. The third view is a combination of the two categories above; *Gharar* here covers both of the unknown and the doubtful, as exemplified by the definition proposed by Al-Sarakhsy who states that *Gharar* obtains where consequences are concealed. This is the view favoured by most scholars.

More simply, El-Gamal (2000, p.7) defines *Garar as* "... the sale of probable items whose existence or characteristics are not certain, due to the risky nature which makes the trade similar to gambling". However, Al-Saati (2003) counters that there is no agreement among Muslim jurists about the degree of uncertainty in commercial transactions to be considered as *Gharar*. Iqbal and Molyneux (2005, p.14), for instance, suggest "*Gharar* refers to acts and conditions in exchange contracts, the full implications of which are not clearly known to the parties. This is something very similar to asymmetric information". Metwally (2006) also argues that *Gharar* are speculative transactions harmful to society.

Metwally (2006), Iqbal and Molyneux (2005), Al-Saati (2003) and El-Gamal (2000) agree upon some basic features of Gharar in exchange contracts. To start with, *Gharar* can be any contract for sale or purchase that includes uncertainty in genus, species, quantity of the object, price, time of payment in deferred sales, existence of object, and identity of object. Although there is no explicit statement known in the *Quran* forbidding *Gharar*, it is well-accepted that it is forbidden. For example, Al-Saati (2003, p. 7) has inferred the prohibition of *Gharar* from two Quranic verses (2:188; 4:29) as follows: "And do not eat up your property among yourselves for vanities, nor use it as bait for the judges". "O ye who believe! Eat not up your property among yourselves in vanities; but let these be amongst you traffic and trade by mutual good will". In addition, he adds that there is a consensus between some scholars about the meaning of *Al-batil* (vanity) which is *Gharar*.

However, there are many *Hadiths* (traditions) banning *Gharar* sales narrated by Muslims. For instance, "Ahmad and Ibn Majah narrated on the authority of Abu-said Al-khudriy: Muhammad has forbidden the purchase of the unborn animal in its mother's womb, the sale of the milk in the udder without measurement, the purchase of spoils of war prior to their distribution, the purchase of charities prior to their receipt, and the purchase of the catch of a diver" (El-Gamal (2000, p.7). Metwally (2006, p.15) also argues that the Muhammad said "One who imports from outside and sells at the market rate for his maintenance is blessed, while he who withholds transactions in view of estimated dearness in future, is thrown away from God's pleasure".

Prohibition of *Maysir* (Gambling and Other Games of Chance)

Most Islamic scholars regard *Maysir* as gambling or any games of chance (including lotteries, lotto, casino-type games and betting on the outcomes of animal races). Together, these share a desire for obtaining return through deliberate risk-taking (Al-Saati 2003). Both games of chance and gambling are banned by *Shariah.* Iqbal and Molyneux (2005, p.15) provide evidence from the *Holy Quran* (5:90) as follows: "O, you who believe! Intoxicants (all kinds of alcoholic drinks), and gambling, and *Al-Ansab* (animals that are sacrificed in the name of idols on their altars) and *Al-Azlam* (arrows thrown for seeking luck or decision) are an abomination of Satan's handiwork. So avoid that (abomination) in order that you may be successful".

Further, Metwally (2006, p.15) argues that "*The Holy Quran* says (Ch. 2, Verse 219); they question thee about alcoholic drinks and games of chance (speculation). Say: in this is great sin and some utility for men; but its sin is greater than its usefulness". Even though there is a general consensus among Muslims who believe in the tenets of *Shariah* and therefore do not question the reasons for forbidding the *Maysir,* Iqbal and Molyneux (2005) provide some reasons underlying the prohibition of games of chance and gambling. They argue that because of the high risk available in these types of transactions, some people win a large amount of money, but others suffer from a loss of their money, and sometimes face bankruptcy. This could lead to greater financial and societal problems. In addition, these games and gambling are unnecessary for society because they cannot add any surplus to societal wealth.

Prohibition of Using or Dealing in Forbidden Commodities

Islamic finance encourages people to invest their money, but this general encouragement is expected to comply with the rules set by *Shariah.* According to Islamic doctrine, some commodities, such as alcohol, drugs, and pork, are strictly forbidden. Thus, people should not use or exchange items banned by the *Holy Quran.* Lewis and Algaoud (2001) have pointed out that neither individuals or institutions can trade or finance enterprises dealing in forbidden items. The aim of *Shariah* in this regard is to promote 'ethical' investments that again do not affect people and society adversely through the violation of religious prohibitions.

The Sharing of Business Profits and Risks

Islamic finance encourages people to invest their money effectively without any injustice for those who are either lenders or borrowers. According to this principle, lenders should share with borrowers the profits or losses from the funded enterprise. Usually this is taken as they should equally distribute the risk of their business, consistent with their sharing of the capital contributed to the enterprise. Kahf and Khan (1993) explain this in two parts: a profit-sharing principle and a profit/loss sharing principle. According to the former, both the owner of the capital and the entrepreneur share in the profits of the enterprise, referred to as *Mudarabah.* In this method of finance, the owner of the funds provides capital to an entrepreneur who provides experience and effort as a working partner. However, they only share the profits of the business. In the case of a loss, the owner of the funds bears the risks of loss and the entrepreneur losses their time and effort. The latter principle is a full partnership in capital and management, as well as in the profit and loss, of a particular enterprise. For instance, the *Musarakah* (full partnership) in Islamic finance allows partners to share specific percentages of capital in their working partnership and any profit/loss earned from the enterprise is divided according to the proportion of capital invested.

Paying and Collecting of *Zakah* (Payments to the Poor)

Ahmed (2004) defines *Zakah* as "...a due right on specific items of assets or properties, in specific percentages with considerations of the passage of a year and satisfaction of the condition of *nisab". Nisab* is the minimum amount of assets that is *zakat*able according to *Shariah* that considers Zakah as one of the five pillars of Islam identified by the *Holy Quran.* Metwally (2006, p.14) provides a comprehensive definition as follows:

> *Zakah* is the cornerstone of the financial structure in an Islamic economy. It is one of the fundamental tenets of Islam. Literally, *Zakah* means purification. Technically it means a contribution of a proportion of wealth for the use of the poor and needy as sanctification for the remainder of the property. Hence, in modern terminology, *Zakah* is a tax collected from the relatively richer Muslims and distributed (mainly) among the poorer Muslims.

The *Holy Quran* in a number of instances includes references to "...keep up prayer and pay *Zakah*" (Metwally 2006, p.14). Sometimes, *Zakah* is also referred to as S*adqa* (charity or alms) in verses of the *Holy Quran.* For instance, "...alms are for the poor, and the needy, and those employed to administer the funds, and those whose hearts have been reconciled to truth, and those in debt and those in the cause of Allah, and the Wayfarer" (9:60 cited in Metwally 2006). This verse indicates the categories of needs to which *Zakah* could be paid. Even though there is no doubt in Islamic teaching that Allah created people equally, it is equally recognised that people live in income inequality, with many individuals unable to obtain enough money to meet their needs. Paying *Zakah* represents a financial way to support those who suffer from poverty or those who become debtors without having the ability to repay their debts.

Clearly, Islam also makes it mandatory for the rich to support the poor and needy. The *Holy Quran* states: "And those in whose wealth there is a recognized right, for the beggar who asks and for the unlucky who has lost his wealth" (70:24-25 cited in Ahmed 2004, p 21). Interestingly, the amount of *Zakah* should not deplete the resources of the rich. Although, there are no specific verses from the *Holy Quran* that observe the correct amount of the *zakah*, Muhammad indicated a number of ratios for different assets. For example, for all 'idle assets' (like gold, silver and money) 2.5 percent should be imposed (Metwally 2006). In Ahmad's (2004) definition this percentage is payable annually. This effective approach could achieve many goals at the same time that have important social and economic objectives such as reductions in poverty, crime and the creation of social and economic equity. However, to achieve these goals efficiently, the collection and distribution of *Zakah* requires special administration that provides good management for the funds. Peerzade (2005) claims that

Zakah that is payed should be transferred to the public coffers for spending. One implication is that governments should institutionalize *Zakah* to ensure the minimisation of poverty.

Takaful (Islamic Insurance)

The commercial insurance industry is one of the most widespread financial industries (Billah 2001b). However, most Muslim jurists argue that commercial insurance involves *Gharar,* and is thus prohibited. According to El-Gamal (2000), this point of view arises because commercial insurance contracts have a substantial *Gharar* component that affects the outcome of an insurance contract. In brief, the insurance contract represents a sale contract and the amount of the insurance which may be collected by the insurer and the insured is potentially unknown. It is the unknown payoffs implicit in an insurance contract that leads to *Gharar.* One means of overcoming this is Islamic insurance or *Takaful.* This is a mutual self-help scheme between those who wish to support each other in difficult times. El-Gamal (2000) introduces Islamic insurance as a cooperative insurance scheme that could be established with a pool of funds by a specific group of people who do not aim to obtain profit from the pool, but may invest its funds in permissible activities in Islam to increase the fund's wealth. In turn, the *Takaful* provides members with financial help in the instance of specific events.

Muslim scholars derived T*akaful* from the *Holy Quran* where it says: "Help you one another in righteousness and piety, but help you not one another in sin and rancour" (5:2 cited in Billah 2001a, p. 4). Billah (2001a, p. 2) further supports the permissibility of *Takaful* by citing two traditions from the *Sunna* as follows:

> Narrated by Anas bin Malik, the Holy Prophet told a Bedwin Arab who left his camel untied trusting to the will of Allah said: Tie the camel first and then leave it to Allah".
>
> Narrated by Abn Huraira, the Holy Prophet said: whosoever removes a worldly hardship from a believer, Allah will remove from him one of the hardships of the day of the judgment. Whosoever alleviates from one, Allah will alleviate his lot in this world and the next.

Maysami and Williams (2006) also argue that *Takaful* is a permissible tool which complies with the principle of joint guarantee in *Shariah* encouraging mutual self-help. However, Islamic insurance should help policyholders only, not for the earning of profits, although using the funds in permissible activities to increase its wealth is acceptable. Consequently, Islamic insurance institutions have been established in Muslim and non-Muslim countries to offer its services for those in need of financial assistance. Metwally (2006) has observed that the *Takaful* funds can potentially be administrated by an Islamic bank which collects *Takaful* insurance premiums, provide financial assistances for policyholders, and invests these funds in permissible enterprises according to the wishes of the participants and in compliance with *Shariah.*

5. Islamic Methods of Finance

As discussed in the previous section, Islamic finance is designed according to fundamental principles that comply with *Shariah.* This section focuses on the most common Islamic finance methods as practiced by Islamic banks and other financial institutions. The principal instruments take the following forms: (i) *Mudarabah*, the provision of capital in a partial-equity partnership; (ii) *Musharakah*, full equity partnerships, (iii) *Murabaha*, an instrument used for financing the purchase of goods; (iv) *Bai muajjall*, deferred payments on products; (v) *Bai Salam*, advance sale contracts; (vi) *Istisna*, or manufacturing contracts; (vii) *Ijarah*, lease financing; and (viii) *Quard Hassan*, a system of benevolent loans.

Mudarabah (Capital Trusts)

The *Mudarabah* (or capital trust) is a form of profit or loss (equity-based) sharing used by tradesmen in Mecca before Islam. The best evidence for its existence is Muhammad employed *Mudarabah* with a rich woman named Khadijah about fifteen years prior to the establishment of Islam (Abdul-Gafoor 2006). *Mudaraba*, in jurisprudence, is "...a mode of financing through which the bank (the owner of the capital or *rabb-al-mal*) provides capital finance for a specific venture indicated by the customer (the entrepreneur or *mudarib*)" (Obaidullah 2005, p.57). In other words, *Mudarabah* is a contract between two parties: an investor (individual or bank) who provides a second party, the entrepreneur, with financial resources to finance a particular enterprise. Profits are then shared between the two parties (*rabb-al-mal and mudarib*) according to some pre-agreed ratio, but if there are losses the investor bears all financial losses and the entrepreneur the operating losses; principally the opportunity cost of their own efforts. The flows of funds are depicted in Figure 1. This distribution of profits and losses is an equitable approach that conforms to Islamic principles.

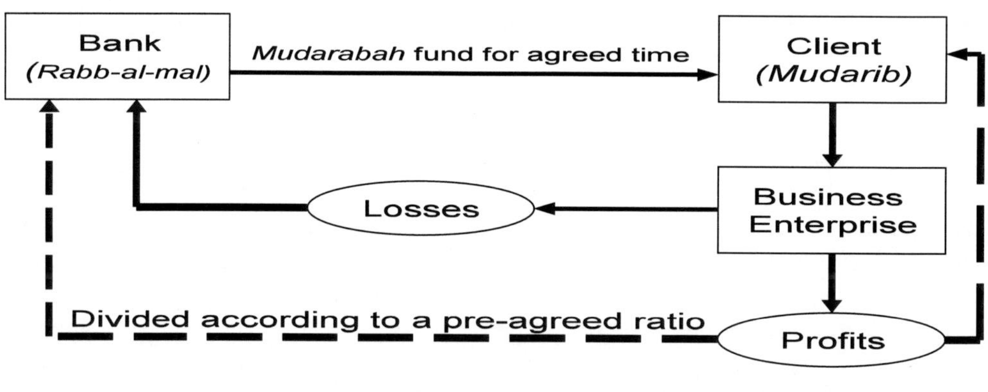

Figure 1. Bank Finances *Mudarabah* for Client.

In an alternative form, the *rabb-al-mal* is a customer who deposits capital in a bank, representing the *mudarib,* to invest according to *Mudarabah.* In addition, Aljarhi and Iqbal (2001) suggest that *Mudarabah* deposits could be compounded in a public pool for investment, which is a permissible way for the manager (bank) to mix *Mudarabah* deposits with its own funds. In this case, profits would again be distributed according to an agreed formula, but losses once again remain the liability of the capital providers as shown in Figure 2. Although *Mudarabah* may be applied in various economic activities, the majority of Islamic jurists and scholars hold the view that *Mudarabah* contracts are only suitable for commercial activities.

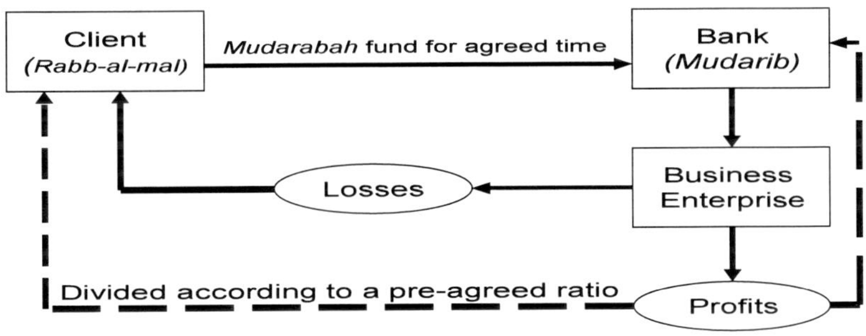

Figure 2. Client Finances Mudarabah for Bank.

Musharakah (Full Partnerships)

Musharakah (or full partnership) is "...an arrangement where two or more parties establish a joint commercial enterprise and all contribute capital as well as labour and management as a general rule" (Iqbal and Molyneux 2005, p. 20). The profits and losses that flow from the *Musharakah* are again shared among the parties on a pre-agreed ratio. Generally, *Musharakah* is most suited for financing private or public companies and project financing. In the context of Islamic banking, *Musharakah* is described as a joint venture between an Islamic bank and a customer or business firm. The Islamic bank can potentially act as the fund provider to finance industry, trade and almost all legal enterprises through either equity investment or direct participation.

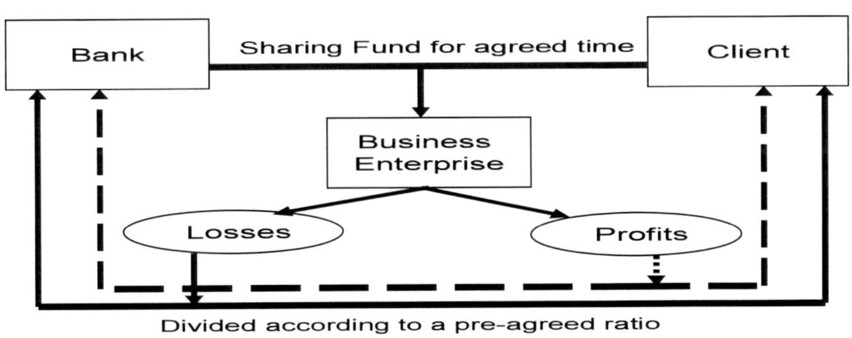

Figure 3. Musharakah between Bank and Client.

Lewis and Algaoud (2001) suggest that *Musharakah* contracts can be established in one of two ways. The first way of these is a permanent contract that ensures for all its parties (the investor, bank, and entrepreneur) an equitable share in the annual profit/loss on pre-agreed terms. This kind of permanent contract holds constant for a limited or unlimited period according to the original agreement as shown in Figure 3. The second type of *Musharakah* is a diminishing contract preferred by bankers because it allows the bank to reduce its share of equity each year and receive periodic profits based on the reducing equity balance. In this form, the equity share of the customer in the capital of enterprise increases over time until he or she becomes the sole owner of the enterprise. The relationships are depicted in Figure 4. As shown, *musharakah* has many advantages that provide equal benefits for all parties and there is a consensus among Islamic scholars of its validity under *Shariah*. However, El-Gamal (2000) has observed that most of the parties in *Musharakah* contracts usually require the help of legal experts to ensure that any potential *Riba* or *Gharar* is carefully avoided.

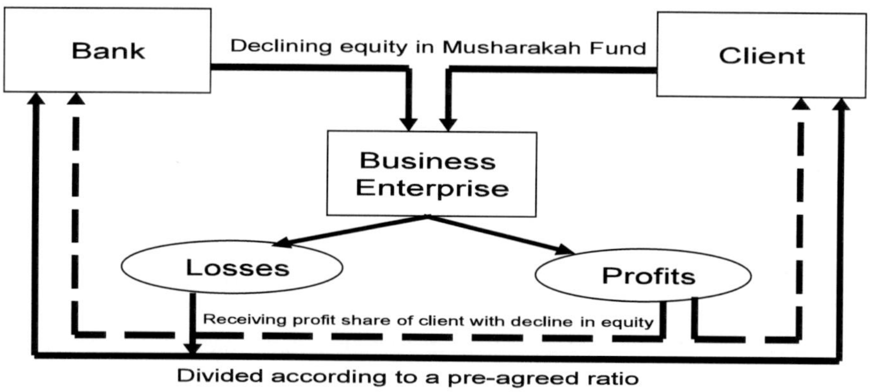

Figure 4. Declining *Musharakah* between Bank and Client.

Murabaha (Mark-Ups on Sale)

Murabaha is an Islamic instrument for buying and reselling the purchase or import of capital goods and other commodities by institutions, including banks and firms. Under the *Murabaha* contract, the customer provides the bank with the specifications and prices of the goods to be purchased or imported. The Islamic bank studies the application, collects information about the specifications and prices of the goods, and focuses especially on the price and conditions for payment. When the bank and its client agree on the terms of the deal, the bank purchases the goods or commodities and resells them to the customer. The profit that accrues to the bank is mutually agreed upon as a profit margin (mark-up) on the cost of purchase (Metwally 2006). The fundamental principles attached to *Murabaha* can be summarised as follows: (i) goods must be classified, clearly identified according to commonly accepted standards and must exist at the time of sale; (ii) goods for sale must be in the ownership of the bank at the time of sale; (iii) the cost price must be known at the time of sale and this should be declared to the client. This is especially the case when the bank succeeds in obtaining a discount where the profit margin is calculated on the net purchase price (this means discounts also provide benefits to the client); and (iv) the time of delivery of the goods and the time of payment must be specified. (Obaidullah 2005; Iqbal and Molyneux 2005; Lewis and Algaoud 2001; El-Gamal 2000; Kahf 1997).

In fact, the *Murabaha* contract is merely a two-party buying and selling contract between bank and customer involving no financial intermediation or financing. In other words, the bank offers this service to clients who should pay the cost of the goods plus a profit margin to the bank immediately following receipt. In addition, the client can pay for the goods and the bank's profit margin by deferred instalments or a deferred lump sum without an increase over the original value. This type of contract is referred to as *Bai muajjall-Murabbah* or *Bai bithaman ajjal* (Obaidullah 2005).

Bai muajjall (Deferred Payments)

The term *Bai muajjall* is a sale on a deferred payment basis that allows business or individuals to receive products now and pay for their value in the future. Lewis and Algaoud (2001) consider that credit sales could include *Bai muajjall-Murabaha* since all deferred payments are in instalments or a lump sum. However, there is a significant difference between *Bai muajjall* and *Bai muajjall-Murabaha* in that in any kind of *Murabaha* the buyer must know the cost price of the commodity as a prerequisite to an acceptable contract (Obaidullah 2005). There is a consensus among Islamic jurists and scholars about the permissibility of credit sales (*Bai muajjall*) as a form of finance that includes no *Riba*. El-Gamal (2000), for example, suggests Islamic jurists have generally permitted sales where the price has increased with deferment, but have forbidden sales where the amount of the debt increased with deferment. For example, in a credit sale both the buyer and seller agree to defer the sale price until payable in one month and increase the sale price to cover. This sort of agreement would be permissible. However, it is not permitted if they defer the lending that proceeds from the sale now for one month and increase the amount by interest. The first example is a trading transaction accepted by the *Holy Quran* and the *Sunna,* but the second example is a lending transaction involving *Riba.*

Bai salam (Prepaid Purchases)

Bai salam is a form of advance payment or forward buying defined by Iqbal and Molyneux (2005, p. 25) as follows: "S*alam* is a sale contract in which the price is paid in advance at the time of contracting against delivery of the purchased goods/services at a specified future date". Even though the sale and purchase of nonexistent goods are prohibited because of *Gharar*, the *Bai salam* is a permissible activity that is adopted by the *Sunna* to facilitate certain activities in agriculture and industry. As one example, El-Gamal (2000, p. 17) cites the following *Hadith* narrated on the authority of Ibn Abbas:

> The Messenger of Allah came to *Madinah* and found its inhabitants entering *salam* contracts (with the price paid in advance) in fruits for one, two, and three years. He said: Whoever enters into a *salam* contract, let him specify a known volume or weight, and a known term of deferment.

In addition, the Messenger of Allah said: "Whoever enters into *Salaf,* should stipulate a determined weight and measurement, and a determined date of delivery", the word (*Salaf*) of the *Hadith* has meaning of *salam* (cited in Al-Masri (2003, p.29). The main legal requirements for *Bai salam* contracts to be permissible are: (i) the commodities sold should not be available at the time of contracting; (ii) the quality and quantity of goods must be known; (iii) the date and place of delivery for these commodities should be defined; and (iv) the purchase cost price should be paid completely at the time of the contract.

Istisna (Manufacturing Contracts)

Istisna is a relatively new method in Islamic banking, defined as a manufacturing contract which allows one party to obtain industrial goods with either an upfront cash payment and deferred delivery or deferred payment and delivery. It has been translated by El-Gamal (2000, p 17) as a "...commission to manufacture" usually used to cover work progress in the manufacturing and building industries. This method has a significant advantage in that the cost price is prepaid or is deferred as instalments to create a product at a lower price than the cost of buying the complete product or building. In the context of Islamic banking, individuals or firms request their bank to facilitate a contract of production for a good, and the bank concludes an *Istisna* contract with a third party (the manufacturer) to produce and deliver the specific item under particular requirements (Lewis and Algaoud 2001). The permissibility of *Istisna* is adopted by the use of analogy (*Qyas*) among most Muslim jurists with the permissibility of *Bai salam* (El-Gamal 2000). However, *Istisna* differs in many ways from *Bai aslam. For example, the Istisna*'s subject is usually a commodity or item which demands manufacturing, the payment in *Istisna* could be a lump sum or instalments which can be deferred; and the time of delivery in an *Istisna* contract could be unknown (Iqbal and Molyneux 2005).

Ijarah (Lease Financing)

Ijarah is the reward or recompense that proceeds from a rental contract between two parties, where the lessor (the owner of the asset) leases capital asset to the lessee (the user of the asset). *Ijarah* literally means "...to give something on rent" (Lewis and Algaoud 2001). The use of *Ijarah* was known before Islam and is evidenced by the *Holy Quran* and the *Sunna*. For example, (28:26-27 cited in El-Gamal 2000 p, 13)

> ...Said one of them: O father, hire him on wages, for truly the best to employ is a strong and trust worthy man. He said: I intend to wed one of my daughters to you, on condition that you work for me for eight years, and if you complete ten full years, that will be a grace from you.

It is also adopted in the following *Hadith* narrated by Ahmad Abu Dawud and Al-Nasai cited in El-Gamal (2000 p. 13):

> The farmers during the time of the Prophet used to pay rent for the land in water and seeds. He forbade them from doing that, and ordered them to use gold and silver (money) to pay the rent.

In Islamic finance, there are two forms of leasing: (1) direct leasing finance (*Ijarah*), whereby the lessor (either an individual or a firm) allows the lessee to use capital assets owned by the lessor for a specified period of time ranging from a few days to years depending on the type of asset. In return, the lessee pays the rental fee monthly or annually. However, the ownership of the capital assets cannot transfer to the lessee in this type of leasing (as in finance leases) and insurance on the capital assets remains the responsibility of the lessor (Zaher and Hassan 2001). In contemporary Islamic banking, *Ijarah* has been adapted to provide a form of hire purchase (*Ijarah wa-Iqtina*), whereby an institution or individual customer requests the bank to purchase equipment with the intention of leasing it to the customer. In turn, the Islamic bank rents the asset to the client who pays a certain fixed rent and promises to purchase the asset within a specified period to transfer ownership from the bank to the customer (Al-Jarhi and Iqbal 2001). Furthermore, this could be transformed as a decreasing-value lease that allows the client to pay an instalment of the value of the asset plus its rent each period to reduce the lessor's share of ownership until the lessee becomes the owner (Metwally 2006).

Quard Hassan (Benevolent Loans)

The act of lending money is not forbidden in *Shariah*, only *Riba* is prohibited in the process of lending. *Quard Hassan* is a benevolent loan without interest to assist the needy in an attempt to alleviate hardship. Consequently, individuals and firms may lend money on an interest-free basis to any number of beneficiaries for many purposes, including expenses relating to education and marriage. The amount paid by the lender is considered an interest-free loan from the time of payment until the date of the settlement. Metwally (2006) and Lewis and Algaoud (2001) add that the borrower's payment of any amount over and above the principal to the lender is permissible so long as it is at the borrower's discretion. It is also permissible for the lender to request assets as collateral and charge administrative expenses on the loan (Obaidullah 2005).

6. Islamic Banking

As discussed earlier, Islamic banking is a relatively recent phenomenon dating only from the early 1970s. Al-Jarhi and Iqbal (2001, p. 23) define an Islamic bank as follows:

> An Islamic bank is a deposit-taking banking institution whose scope of activities includes all currently known banking activities, excluding borrowing and lending on the basis of interest. On the liabilities side, it mobilizes funds on the basis of *Mudarabah* contract. It can also accept demand deposits which are treated as interest-free loans from the clients to the bank, and which are guaranteed. On the assets side, it advances funds on a profit-and-loss sharing or a debt-creating basis, in accordance with the principles of the

Shariah. It plays the role of an investment manager for the owners of time deposits, usually called investment deposits. In addition, equity holding as well as commodity and asset trading constitute an integral part of Islamic banking operations. An Islamic bank shares its net earnings with its depositors in a way that depends on the size and date-to-maturity of each deposit. Depositors must be informed beforehand of the formula used for sharing the net earning with the bank.

Clearly, an Islamic banking system can only be made operational by incorporating two fundamental principles: namely, the prohibition of interest and the introduction of profit-and-loss sharing methods with strict conformance to *Shariah.*

A Brief Review of Developments in Islamic Banking

The first Islamic social bank was established in Pakistan in the 1950s to help poor farmers. At about the same time, Malaysian Muslims established funds that helped pilgrims gather their savings for the pilgrimage to *Makkah* (Mecca) The Mit Ghamer savings bank in Egypt was established in 1963 and the Nasser Social Bank in 1971 (Lewis and Algaoud 2001). The public sector promotion of Islamic banking began with the Islamic Development Bank in 1975 (Iqbal and Molyneux 2005). Islamic banking spread dramatically during the final decades of the last century. Currently, these are more than 200 Islamic banks and financial institutions operating worldwide with over $200 billion in assets (Wilson 2002, p. 373). In fact, the number of Islamic banks' is currently increasing by about 15 percent annually (Taylor 2003, p.400).

The overriding objective of Islamic banks is to promote economic development in Muslim societies by mobilizing financial resources in accordance with *Shariah*. However, there are many other objectives that have also been suggested. Haron (1995) finds that Islamic banking objectives also potentially include the following: (i) provide contemporary Islamic financial services to people and protecting them from financial deals that involve *Riba*; (ii) develop banking services and products based on *Shariah*; (iii) create acceptable yields as legitimate profits to the shareholders and investors deposits; (iv) achieve moral consciousness side-by-side with profitable transactions; and (v) serve Muslims and other nations through benevolent lending to promote fraternal bonding.

Types and Examples of Islamic Banks

While it is possible to classify Islamic banks according to their ownership structures (state, jointly, and privately owned) an alternative classification based on their purpose is also found in the literature. This taxonomy of Islamic banking includes Islamic social banks, development banks, commercial banks and holding banks.

First, the main feature of an Islamic social bank is its emphasis on objectives that embrace the mobilization of savings between individual consumers. This is generally considered more important than an increase in bank profits. This kind of bank also often offers other social services such as the collection and distribution of *Zakah* and the provision of interest-free loans. An example is the Mit Ghamer savings bank in Egypt. Second, Islamic development banks usually aim to enhance and promote social and economic development in the state more broadly. This can be an institution that also aims to finance public sector development projects in other (mostly Muslim) countries. The concept is accepted to have started in Saudi Arabia with the creation of the Islamic Development Bank in 1975 by the governments of Saudi Arabia, Kuwait, Libya, Turkey, the United Arab Emirates, Iran and Egypt. This particular institution aims to foster economic development, social progress and economic relations of member countries and Muslim communities in conformity with the principles of *Shariah*.

Third, an Islamic commercial bank is defined as a financial institution that accepts deposits from depositors and makes them available to entrepreneurs either at mark-up or via profit-and-loss sharing methods of finance. These banks usually engage in all types of commercial activities and may invest directly in across sectors in the economy. Most modern Islamic banks are examples of commercial banks that offer deposit accounts and financing instruments derived from Islamic principles. Examples include Bank Muamalat (Indonesia), Islamic Bank Brunei, Bahrain Islamic Bank, Bank Melli Iran, Al-Baraka Bank Lebanon, Bank Al-Jazeera (Saudi Arabia), Abu Dhabi Islamic Bank, Al-Amanah Islamic Bank (Philippines), Grindlays Modaraba (Pakistan) and Islamic Bank of Britain. Finally, an Islamic holding bank is a holding institution established to assist existing Islamic banks to identify investment opportunities in the international market along with possible financing projects in Muslim states. Currently, there are three groups of Islamic holding banks: the Islamic Banking System International, the Dar al-mal al Islami Trust and the Al-Baraka Group.

Islamic Banking Operations

Islamic banking operations have developed over the time to modify the operations of conventional banks to meeting individual and firm needs under *Shariah*. Islamic banks depend on shareholders' capital as well as deposits from depositors and funds invested by investors. The sources of Islamic banks and their uses of these funds have been investigated in a number of studies, particularly Abdul-Gafoor (2003), Alam (2000) and Haron (1995).

The three main types of Islamic deposit accounts are as follows. First, Islamic current accounts are a service offered to depositors to process bank transfers and pay cheques through existing transfer and settlement systems. These accounts are payable on demand and no interest or profits are paid to depositors. Current accounts can also be held in a foreign currency to facilitate international trade. Second, as with comparable products offered by conventional banks, Islamic savings accounts offer flexible deposits, withdrawal on demand, and a guarantee of capital. However, unlike conventional bank savings accounts, interest is forbidden on account balances. However, depositors can obtain benefits in the form of 'prizes' that depend, in part, on the value of the deposit and the bank's profitability. These services are also often offered fee-free to depositors.

Third, Islamic investment deposit accounts are designed for customers who wish to invest their funds using profit/loss sharing principles. In practice, there are two main types of investment accounts, specified and unspecified. In the first category, the depositor empowers the bank to invest funds in conditional or limited investments: that is, specific enterprises or sectors. In the second category, the depositor gives the bank an unconditional authorisation to invest the deposited sum according to the wishes of the bank in any suitable project.

Investment accounts are usually administrated under the principles of *Mudarabah* and *Musharakah* that establish the bank as the entrepreneur (*mudarib*) or a participant and the depositor as an investor or a participant. Within this, they share profits and losses according to some pre-agreed ratio.

In the Islamic banking system the using of offered funds is rather more complicated. Unlike conventional banks, in Islamic banks money should not earn returns without evidence of a direct collaboration between capital and effort. Therefore, Islamic banks cannot act as a financial intermediary in the strictest sense since this would involve accepting deposits from individuals or firms and lending them to borrowers who are also individuals or firms. However, according to the principles of Islamic finance many financing or participating instruments can be used to meet financial needs in the market and to provide short-, medium- and long-term funds. These include *Mudarabah, Musharakah, Murabaha, Bai muajjall, Bai Salam, Istisna, Ijarah* and *Quard Hassan*.

Outside retail services, Islamic banks offer many similar services to conventional banks in the form of performance bonds, letters of guarantee, letters of credit, travellers' cheques, money transfers, foreign exchange transactions and safe deposits. In these situations, the Islamic bank can collect a service or administration fee corresponding to the expense incurred on the service rendered under *Shariah*. Moreover, the bank can charge commission when transactions involves the sale and purchase of metals (such as gold) on behalf of a customer because the bank serves as an agent. This is likewise permitted under *Shariah*.

CONCLUSION

Islamic finance is defined as a financial service principally implemented to comply with the main tenets of *Shariah* (or Islamic law). In turn, the main sources of *Shariah* are the *Holy Quran*, *Hadith*, *Sunna*, *Ijma*, *Qiyas* and *Ijtihad*. The *Holy Quran* is the book of revelation given to the Prophet Muhammad; *Hadith* is the narrative relating the deeds and utterances of Muhammad; *Sunna* refers to the habitual practice and behaviour of Muhammad during his life; *Ijma* is the consensus among religion scholars about specific issues not envisaged in either the *Holy Quran* or the *Sunna*; *Qiyas* is the use of deduction by analogy to provide an opinion on a case not referred to in the *Quran* or the *Sunna* in comparison with another case referred to in the *Quran* and the *Sunna*; and *Ijtihad* represents a jurists' independent reasoning relating to the applicability of certain *Shariah* rules on cases not mentioned in ether the *Quran* or the *Sunna*.

The main principles of Islamic finance include the prohibition of *Riba* and the removal of debt-based financing from the economy, the prohibition of *Gharar*, encompassing the full disclosure of information and removal of any asymmetrical information in a contract, the exclusion of financing and dealing in sinful and socially irresponsible activities and commodities such as gambling, casinos, production of alcohol, etc., risk-sharing, the provider of financial funds and the entrepreneur share business risk in return for shares of profits and losses, materiality, a financial transaction needs to have a 'material finality', that is a direct or indirect link to a real economic transaction and justice, a financial transaction should not lead to the exploitation of any party to the transaction.

Employing these principles, the main financial instruments in Islamic finance are *Mudarabah*, the provision of capital in a partial-equity partnership, *Musharakah*, full equity partnerships, *Murabaha*, an instrument for financing the purchase of goods, *Bai muajjall*, deferred payments on products, *Bai Salam*, advance sale contracts, *Istisna*, or manufacturing contracts, *Ijarah*, lease financing and *Quard Hassan*, the system of benevolent loans.

References

Abdul-Gafoor, A. (1999). *Islamic Banking and Finance: Another Approach.* Paper presented to the Islamic Hinterland Conference on Critical Debates among Canadian Muslims, Toronto.

Abdul-Gafoor, A. (2003). *Islamic Banking.* Kuala Lumpur: A.S. Noor Deen.

Abdul-Gafoor, A. (2006). Mudaraba-Based Investment and Finance. *Journal of Islamic Banking and Finance* 23(4), 78–98.

Accounting and Auditing Organization for Islamic Financial Institutions (2007) Available at http://www.aaoifi.com/. Accessed May 2007.

Ahmed, H. (2004). Role of Zakah and Awqaf in Poverty Alleviation. Occasional Paper No. 8, Islamic Research and Training Institute, Islamic Development Bank, Jeddah. Available at http://www.irtipms.org/PubAllE.asp Accessed October 2006.

Akacem, M. and Gilliam, L. (2002). Principles of Islamic Banking: Dept versus Equity Financing. *Middle East Policy* 9(1), 124–138.

Alam, M. (2000). Islamic Banking in Bangladesh: A Case Study of Ibbl. *International Journal of Islamic Financial Services* 1(4), 10–29.

Al-Dhareer, S. (1997). Al-Gharar in Contracts and Its Effects on Contemporary Transactions. Eminent Scholars' Lecture Series No.16, Islamic Research and Training Institute, Islamic Development Bank, Jeddah. Available at http://www.irtipms.org/PubAllE.asp. Accessed November 2006.

Al-Jarhi, M and Iqbal M. (2001). Islamic Banking: Answers to Some Frequently Asked Questions. Occasional Paper No.4, Islamic Research and Training Institute, Islamic Development Bank, Jeddah. Available at http://www.irtipms.org/PubAllE.asp. Accessed October 2006.

Al-Masri, R. (2003). Market Price of Salam on the Date of Delivery: Is It Permissible. *Islamic Economics* 16(2), 29–32.

Al-Saati, A. (2003). The Permissible Gharar (Risk) in Classical Islamic Jurisprudence. *Islamic Economics* 16(2):, 3–19.

Anwar, A. (1995). *Riba and Common Interest.* Karachi: Shafiq Press.

Archer, S. and Rifaat, A.K. (2002). *Islamic Finance: Growth and Innovation.* London: Euromoney Books.

Billah, M. (2001a). Sources of Law Affecting Takaful (Islamic Insurance). *International Journal of Islamic Financial Services* 2(4), 24–29.

Billah, M. (2001b). Takaful (Islamic Insurance) Premium: A Suggested Regulatory Framework. *International Journal of Islamic Financial Services* 3(1), 1–8.

Choudhry, N. and A. Mirakhor (1997). Indirect Instruments of Monetary Control in an Islamic Financial System, *Islamic Economic Studies*, 4(2): 27–66.

Dar, H. and Presley, J. (1999). Islamic Finance: A Western Perspective. *International Journal of Islamic Financial Services* 1(1): 3–11.

Dhumale, R. and Sapcanin, A. (1999). An Application of Islamic Banking Principles to Microfinance. Technical Note, Rural Finance Learning Center, World Bank Group, Washington. Available at http://www.gdrc.org/icm/country/wana/wb-bnkprinciples.pdf Accessed October 2006.

El-Gamal, M. (2000). *A Basic Guide to Contemporary Islamic Banking and Finance.* Rice University, Houston.

El-Hawary, D., W. Grais, and Z. Iqbal, 2004, Regulating Islamic Financial Institutions: The Nature of the Regulated, World Bank Working Paper 3227, Washington: World Bank.

El-Qorchi, M. (2005) Islamic Finance Gears Up, *Finance and Development*, 42(4), 46–50.

Errico, L. and Mitra F. (1998). Islamic Banking: Issues in Prudential Regulation and Supervision, IMF Working Paper 98/30, Washington: International Monetary Fund.

Haron, S. (1995). The Framework and Concept of Islamic Interest-Free Banking. *Journal of Asian Business* 11(1), 26–39.

International Islamic Financial Market (2007) Available at http://www.iifm.net/ Accessed May 2007.

International Islamic Rating Agency (2007) Available at http://www.iirating.com/ Accessed May 2007.

International Monetary Fund (2007) *Finance and Development.* Available at http://www.imf.org/external/pubs/ft/fandd/2007/03/index.htm Accessed May 2007.

International Organization of Securities Commissions (2004). Islamic Capital Market: Fact Finding Report. *Report of the Islamic Capital Market Task Force of the International Organization of Securities Commissions* (Madrid).

Iqbal, M. and D. Llewellyn (eds.) (2002). *Islamic Banking and Finance: New Perspectives on Profit-Sharing and Risk* (Cheltenham, UK: Edward Elgar).

Iqbal, M. and Molyneux, P. (2005). *Thirty Years of Islamic Banking: History, Performance, and Prospects.* Palgrave Macmillan, Houndmills: New York.

Iqbal, Z. (1997). Islamic Financial System. *Finance and Development* 34(2), 42–45.

Islamic Development Bank (2007) Available at http://www.isdb.org Accessed May 2007.

Islamic Finance Services Board (2007) Available at http://www.ifsb.org/ Accessed May 2007.

Kahf, M and Khan, T. (1993). Principles of Islamic Finance. Research Paper No. 16, Islamic Research and Training Institute, Islamic Development Bank, Jeddah. Available at http://www.irtipms.org/PubAllE.asp. Accessed May 2007.

Kahf, M. (1997). Instruments of Meeting Budget Deficit in Islamic Economy Research Paper N.42, Islamic Research and Training Institute, Islamic Development Bank, Jeddah. Available at http://www.irtipms.org/PubAllE.asp. Accessed May 2007.

Lewis, M. and Algaoud, L. (2001). *Islamic Banking.* Edward Elgar, Cheltenham.

Maysami, R and Williams, J. (2006). Evidence on the Relationship between Takaful Insurance and Fundamental Perception of Islamic Principles. *Applied Financial Economics Letters* 2(4): 229–232.

Metwally, M. (1993). *Essays on Islamic Economics.* Academic Publishers, Calcutta.

Metwally, M. (2006). Economic Consequences of Applying Islamic Principles in Muslim Societies. *Journal of Islamic Banking and Finance* 23(1), 11–33.

Moore, P. (1997). *Islamic Finance: A Partnership for Growth.* Euromoney, London.

Obaidullah, M. (2005). *Islamic Financial Services*, Islamic Economics Research Centre, Jeddah.

Peerzade, S. (2005). Towards Self-Enforcing Islamic Tax System: An Alternative to Current Approaches. *Islamic Economics* 18(1), 3–12.

Siddiqi, M. (2004). Riba, Bank Interest and the Rationale of Its Prohibition. Islamic Research and Training Institute, Islamic Development Bank, Jeddah.

Sundararajan, V. and Errico, L. (2002) Islamic Financial Institutions and Products in the Global Financial System: Key Issues in Risk Management and Challenges Ahead International Monetary Fund Working Paper No. 02/192.

Taylor, J. (2003). Islamic Banking - the Feasibility of Establishing an Islamic Bank in the United States. *American Business Law Journal* 40(2): 385–416.

Warde, I. (2000). *Islamic Finance in the Global Economy*. Edinburgh: Edinburgh University Press.

Wilson, R. (2002). Islamic Banking Reviews. *The Economic Record* 79(242), 373–374.

Wilson, R. (2006). Islam and Business. *Thunderbird International Business Review* 48(1): 109–123.

World Bank (2007) *Islamic Finance*, Available at: http://go.worldbank.org/21MOO8XYV0 Accessed May 2007.

Zaher, T. and Hassan, M. (2001). A Comparative Literature Survey of Islamic Finance and Banking. *Financial Markets, Institutions, and Instruments* 10(4), 155–199.

In: Contemporary Issues in Islamic Finance
Editor: Andrew C. Worthington

ISBN: 978-1-62948-905-6

Chapter 3

THE ORIGINS AND FUNDAMENTALS OF ISLAMIC BANKING

Yahia M. Baej [*] ***and Andrew C. Worthington***
Griffith University, Australia

ABSTRACT

Islamic banking is one of the fastest growing industries in global finance. New institutions are adapting Islamic financial products and services with increasing attention from academics and practitioners all over the world. Similar to conventional banks and other financial institutions, Islamic banks are private profit-seeking enterprises. Nevertheless, the latter is guided by the principles of Islamic law (*Shariah*) which strictly prohibits dealing with the interest (*Riba*), uncertainty (*Al-Gharar*), gambling (*Al-Maysir*) and some other financial products and services. This chapter first provides a detailed assessment of the religious sources underpinning Islamic banking, comprising the primary sources of the *Holy Qur'an* and the *Sunnah* of the Prophet PBUH (collectively known as *Al-wahyain* or the Two Revelations), and secondary sources subsequently derived from the work of Muslim scholars, namely, the *Al-Ijma'* (or scholarly consensus) and *Al-Qiyas* (or analogy). The chapter then outlines the key financial products and services commonly practiced by Islamic banks, include *Murabahah* (cost-plus sales); *Musharakah* (full partnership); *Mudarabah* (silent partnership); *Ijarah* (Leasing); Istisna' (contract of manufacture); and *Al-Qard Al-Hassan* (benevolent loan). The final part of the chapter discusses the evolving definition of Islamic banking, the fundamental differences between conventional and Islamic banks, and the process of transformation to Islamic banking as experienced by new and existing banks.

[*] Corresponding author: Department of Accounting, Finance and Economics, Griffith University, Nathan QLD 4111, Australia. Email. yahia.baej@griffithuni.edu.au.

1. Sources of Islamic Law

The *Holy Qur'an* and the *Sunnah* of the Prophet, which known as *Al-wahyain* (the two revelations), are the only primary sources of Islamic law (Shafi'i, 1940). In addition to these two original sources and based on them, Muslim scholars derived *Al-Ijma'* (scholarly consensus) and *Al-Qiyas* (analogy) that are called the sources of *Shariah* or the sources of Islamic legislation (Al-Ghazali, 1993). Although the classification of these sources as well as the level of acceptance of them may vary among the *Shariah* scholars of Islamic schools[1] (Malik, shaffi'i, Ibn Hanbal, and Abu Hanifa), all schools regard the first two resources as the most important sources of Islamic law. According to Al-Munajjid (2010), there are some other sources such as the opinions of the companions (*Sahabah*), *Sadd Al-Dharaa'i'* (blocking the means that lead to evil), *Istihsaan* (discretion), *Istishaab*, *'Urf* (custom), the laws of those who came before us, *Al-Masaalih Al-Mursalah* (things that serve the general interests of the Muslims). However, there is no consensus agreement among the scholars with regard to their validity and the degree of acceptance. Therefore, the *Holy Qur'an*, the *Sunnah* of the Prophet Muhammad PBUH, *Al-Ijma'* and *Al-Qiyas* are the four sources that Muslim scholars agreed upon them. Thus, these sources are being discussed respectively in the following sections. In addition, *Al-Ijma'* and *Al-Qiyas* will be also discussed as secondary sources.

The Holy Qur'an

The first and foremost origin of Islamic Finance is the *Holy Qur'an* (or *Al-Qur'an Al-Karim* means: the noble *Qur'an*). Muslims consider the *Holy Qur'an* as the word of *Allah* SWT who has chosen Muhammad PBUH as a Prophet to convey the message of Islam to mankind (Ash-Shawkani, 2000). The communication between Allah SWT and Muhammad PBUH, which last for twenty three years, is called '*Al-wahi*' or the Revelation and it was via the angel Gabriel who was known in the *Holy Qur'an* as '*Ruoh Al-qudus*' or the Holy Spirit.

The *Holy Qur'an* contains 114 chapters of unequal length called '*Surah(s)*'. Each chapter has a number of verses '*Aya(t)*'. These *Surahs* and *Ayat* were revealed in an excellent Arabic Language that challenge the Arab society as well as all the mankind and Jinn together to bring even a single chapter similar to it. This was mentioned in the *Holy Qur'an*: *Say:*

> If the whole of mankind and Jinns were to gather together to produce the like of this Qur'an, they could not produce the like thereof, even if they backed up each other with help and support[2] (Al-Isra'17:88). Or do they say, He forged it? Say: Bring then a Sura like unto it, and call (to your aid) anyone you can besides Allah, if it be ye speak the truth! (Yunus 10:38)

In addition, the reason behind the variety of the verses in such a long period was mentioned in the *Holy Qur'an*:

---

[1] Some classify these sources as two primary and two secondary sources such as Shafi'i, others as three primaries and one secondary such as Al-Ghazali.

[2] It should be noted that all verses quoted are translated from the original text (Arabic) to English, using the translation of the Holy Quran by Ali, A. Yusuf, 2006.

> Those who reject Faith say: Why is not the Qur'an revealed to him all at once? Thus (is it revealed), that we may strengthen thy heart thereby, and we have rehearsed it to thee in slow, well-arranged stages, gradually. (Al-Furqan 25:32)

The *Holy Qur'an* is believed to be a comprehensive in the way that covers every aspect of human's religious, political and social life. For instance, some *Ayat* came to disapprove and repeal some traditions and customs that were used at that time such as drinking alcohol, taking others' properties in vanities including gambling and robbery, dealing with usury, retaliation and; others have dealt with the pillars of Islam such as monotheism (*Ash-Shahadatan*), prayer (*As-Salah*), fasting (*As-Sawm*), the religious tax (*Az-Zakah*), and pilgrimage (*Al-Hajj*). Moreover, some of them cover the family status such as marriage and divorce, *Iddah*, dower, inheritance, children custody, paternity and adoption; some *Ayat*, furthermore, deal with the rules of commercial relationships between people such as commercial and non-commercial indebtedness, loan, lease, sale, writing of financial transactions, testimony, and justice (Hannan, 1999).

The term '*Shariah'* is the principles of Islamic legislations that based on the commandments revealed in the *Holy Qur'an* and the *Sunnah*. The independent science and methodology used to abstract the regulations of Islamic law is called '*Usul al-Fiqh*' (singular: *Asl*, means 'root'). In other words, Islamic jurists use the knowledge of *Fiqh* to determine the rules of Islamic law from the commandments of *Allah* SWT and teachings of his Prophet PBUH. The total norms and commandments revealed in the *Holy Qur'an* are classified into three categories namely:

(1) *Ibadat*: Norms regulating worship and rituals.
(2) *Muamalat*: Civil and other legal obligations, which *Fiqh* deals with.
(3) *Ugubat*: punishments (Hassan, 1982).

The *Sunnah* of the Prophet Muhammad PBUH

The *Sunnah*, the second source of Islamic Law, as defined by the Islamic jurist Ibn Rajab:

> … the path that is trodden (*Al-Tariq Al-Masluk*), which entails holding fast to whatever the Prophet and his rightly-guided successors held of doctrines, deeds, and sayings. This is the perfect and complete *Sunnah*. That is why the *Salaf* of old refrained from applying the name of *Sunnah* to anything that fell short of this. (Haddad, 1999)

Therefore, the lexical meaning of *Sunnah* in Arabic Language is a followed way, path, road or track. This meaning was mentioned in the *Holy Qur'an*:

> (This was our) way with the apostles we sent before thee: thou wilt find no change in our ways. (Al-Isra' 17:77)

The literal meaning was also mentioned in the *Sunnah* '*Hadith*'

> You will certainly follow the ways of those who came before you hand span by hand span, cubit by cubit, …[3] (Al-Bukhari, 2002, p. 1808)

The *Sunnah* of the prophet Muhammad PBUH or '*Al-Sunnah Al-Nabawyya*' generally denotes the saying (*Qawl*), action (*Fi'l*) and both direct and tacit approvals (*Taqrir*) of him. However, *Fiqh* scholars refer to the term as the part of *Shariah that* is not obligatory. Moreover, in *Usul Al-Fiqh*, the *Sunnah* refers specifically to the source of *Shariah* in addition to the *Holy Qur'an* that explains it in details or creates obligations under the Qur'an's umbrella (Ash-Shawkani, 2000, p. 186).

Al-Ijma'

Although the *Holy Qur'an* and the *Sunnah* of the prophet are the only original sources of Islamic law, *Al-Ijma'* or consensus is classified as a source of Islamic Law that is in the line with the *Holy Qur'an* and the *Sunnah* of the prophet PBUH. This was emphasized by the great scholar *Shafi'i*:

> No one has any right whatsoever to say that something is permissible or prohibited except on the basis of knowledge, and the basis of knowledge is a text in the Qur'an or *Sunnah*, or *Al-Ijma'* (scholarly consensus) or Al-*Qiyas* (analogy). (Shafi'i 1940, p. 39)

Al-Ijma' comes from the Arabic verb '*Ajma'a - Ujmio*' that literally means the agreement upon something. Islamic scholars agree that *Al-Ijma'* started after the death of the prophet Muhammad PBUH as the revelation was stopped. It can be defined as the consensus agreements about various matters in Islam by the prophet's companions and Muslim scholars who came after them (Ash-Shawkani, 2000, p. 348). It should be mentioned that those matters exclude what was clearly revealed in the *Holy Qur'an* and the *Sunnah* and therefore need to be judged by Muslim scholars. Nevertheless, not everyone can do *Ijtihad* or the right of deducting the law from its original sources (Albalawi, 2006, p. 52). That is why *Al-Ijma'* among those who are '*Mujtahid*[4] (en)' is considered as a source of Islamic law and is not subject to incorrect matters (Hannan, 1999; Hassan, 1982). There are many instances form the *Holy Qur'an* and the *Sunnah* which support *Al-Ijma'*:

> If anyone contends with the Messenger even after guidance has been plainly conveyed to him, and follows a path other than that becoming to men of Faith, We shall leave him in the path he has chosen, and land him in Hell,- what an evil refuge! (An-nisa: 4:115)

In addition, the Prophet encourages Muslims to be with '*Al-jama'a*':

> the Muslim scholars and this would be an obvious evidence for the necessity of *Al-Ijma'*. (Shafi'i 1940, p. 403)

[3] Kitab Al-etisam bil kitab wa as-sunnah, hadith No. 7320.

[4] Mujtahid is a person who has an extensive knowledge in the Holy Qur'an and the *Sunnah* of the Prophet Muhammad PBUH which enables them to derive solutions to matters that are not mentioned or explained in the original sources.

Al-Qiyas

One verbal meaning of Al-Qiyas or analogy is the measurement of things in comparison to a standard such as the measurement of weight and length (Hannan, 1999, p. 20). Another is the recognition and equivalence (Abdukaliq, 2007). However, as a source of Islamic law, it means "the extension of a Shariah ruling from an original case (Asl) to a new case (Far') because the new case has the same effective cause (Illah) as the original case" (Hannan, 1999, p. 20). Therefore, four elements are required for Al-Qiyas to be applied: Al-Asl (the original case from the *Holy Qur'an* and the Sunnah of the Prophet PBUH), Al-far' (the new case), Al-Hukm (ruling on the original), and Al-Illah (the cause of ruling in the original case) (Abdukaliq, 2007; Hannan, 1999, p. 21). Table 1 is an example of Ai-Qiyas:

Table 1. An example of *Al-Qiyas*

Original case *(Asl)*	New case *(Far')*	Ruling on the original *(Illah)*	Cause of ruling on the original case *(Hukm)*
Wine drinking	Taking narcotics	Intoxicating Effects	Prohibition

Source: (Hannan, 1999, p. 21).

Some Islamic scholars regard *Al-Ijtihad* as a source of Islamic law. They define it as "the independent interpretation of law by one who is learned to solve a situation that is new or for which there is no precedent or authoritative pronouncement in other sources of *Fiqh*" (Hassan, 1982, p. 67).

2. Fundamentals of Islamic Finance

It is an undeniable fact that in the language of financial and banking institutions, "time value of money" creates a heavy relying on dealing with the interest (Djojosugito, 2004, p. 252). Although religions followed by the majority of the world such as Judaism, Christianity, Hinduism and Islam prohibit such a dealing, the interest-based system has been internationally used for more than two hundred years, which has led to the introduction of a new model of financial institutions designed for replacing the interest-based system with Islamic financial system in the Muslim world (Chapra, 2004, p. 25). Islamic financial institutions are similar to their peers in terms of they are private profit-seeking business enterprises that operate according to the market mechanism (Al-Jarhi, 2004, p. 18). Nevertheless, the philosophy of Islamic finance is completely different from those of other financial Institutions with respect to money and business matters. The following sections discuss some distinguishing features of Islamic financial system.

The True Owner of the Property (*Al-Mal*)

Under the umbrella of *Shariah*, the only absolute owner of all things that exist in the world including the wealth is *Allah* SWT who made mankind as trustees of it (Naqvi & Qadir, 1997). This was mentioned in the *Holy Qur'an*:

> … to Allah belong the dominion of the heavens and the earth, and all that is between. He createth what He pleases. For Allah hath power over all things. (Al-maidah: 5:17). … And spend (in charity) out of the (substance) whereof He has made you heirs. (Al-hadeed: 57:7)

The *Holy Qur'an*, therefore, has comprehensively embodied every aspect of human daily life including dealings with the above mentioned heritage:

> … Nothing have we omitted from the Book … (Al-an'am: 6:38)

Thus, the reward and punishment are according to people's behaviour in relation to the *Shariah* teachings:

> Then shall anyone who has done an atom's weight of good, see it, and anyone who has done an atom's weight of evil, shall see it. (Az-zalzalah: 99:7&8)

Consequently, the Islamic point of view with respect to the idea of 'property' contradicts both the encouragement of private property by the Capitalism and the opposite conception by the Socialism (Naqvi & Qadir, 1997). Instead, the right of all sources exist in the world is regarded by Islam as a collective. This can be seen in the relationship between rich and poor people defined by the *Holy Qur'an* and the *Sunnah* of the prophet (See the *Holy Qur'an* 2:177; 9:60; 17:26-27; 24:22; and 89:17-20).

Intergration between Various Systems in Islam

Economic, religious, social and political systems are inseparable in Islam (Iqbal, 1997). Thus, in order to analyse one of these systems, the other system should also be closely followed and illustrated (Abu-Guddah, 2000). For instance, the prayer '*Salah*' which is considered as a main pillar of Islam was paired with the payment of *Az-Zakah* (the religious tax) in 26 verse in the *Holy Qur'an* (See 2:43; 2:83; 4:77; 4:162; 7:156; 19:55; 22:41; 22:78; and 58:13). The economic system under *Shariah* principles, moreover, is strongly linked to social responsibilities. In this manner, every person in the society is accountable for whatever has Allah SWT entrusted them to as the Prophet PBUH mentioned:

> Each of you is a shepherd and each of you is responsible for his flock … [5] (Al-Bukhari, 2002, p. 618)

---

[5] Kitab Al-etq, Hadith number 2552.

This means that people are socially and financially responsible for their needy parents, relatives and those who are Orphans and poor in the society.

The *Shariah* term '*Muamalat'* embodies all dealings between people including the financial transactions. These dealings -after attributing Oneness to Allah- are the ideal measure of the person's faith (*Iman*). Instances from the *Holy Qur'an* vary with respect to the *Muamalat* (See 2:83; 4:36; 6:151-152; and 17:23-37) and from the teachings of the Prophet PBUH:

> There is no Iman (faith) for the one who cannot be trusted and there is no religion for the one who does not keep his promise.[6] (Bin Hanbal, 1998, P. 873)

Another important aspect is the Islamic concept of 'reward'. In order to sustain a strong relationship between rich and poor people in the society, the payment of *Az-Zakah* and charity should not be seen as a favour by the giver nor should they expect a reward from their society. Instead, *Shariah* encourages givers to deal with these payments contently, in a secret manner and for the sake of Allah SWT:

> If you disclose (acts of) charity, even so it is well, but if you conceal them, and make them rich those (really) in need, that is best for you … (Al-Baqara, 2:271). Those who spend their substance in the cause of Allah, and follow not up their gifts with reminders of their generosity or with injury,-for them their reward is with their Lord: on them shall be no fear, nor shall they grieve. (Al-Baqara, 2:262)

In addition, the intention itself determines the extent of the reward regardless the amount of money or substance (except for *Az-Zakah* which should be a fixed amount). Thus, the reward that is given to those who spend their wealth for the sake of Allah SWT can be unlimited in this life as well as in the hereafter:

> The parable of those who spend their substance in the way of Allah is that of a grain of corn: it growth seven years, and each ear Has a hundred grains. Allah gives manifold increase to whom He pleases … (Al-Baqara, 2:261)

It was also narrated in the *sunnah* that:

> … three things I swear to you and narrate to you,: no person's wealth decreases because of charity, no person is wronged and bears it with patience but Allah will increase him in honor, and no one humbles himself before Allah but Allah raises him in status[7] (Muslim, 1991)

Following the middle course, moreover, and avoiding extremism[8] is highly recommended by Islamic *Shariah*:

> Thus, have we made of you an Ummat justly balanced … (Al-Baqara, 2:143)

---

[6] Hadith number 12410.

[7] Hadith number 2588.

[8] It can be either way: by falling short and not following the commandments of AllahnSWT, or committing excessive acts in all norms and commandments of *Shariah*.

Following the middle course, in fact, can be seen in the teachings of *Shariah* with respect to human daily lives. For example, Muslims are encouraged to be moderate even in eating and drinking:

> … eat and drink: But waste not by excess, for Allah loves not the wasters. (Al-a'raf, 7:31)

Another example is the role of 'moderation' in spending money and the balance between various directions emphasized by the Islamic principles:

> But seek, with the (wealth) which Allah has bestowed on you, the Home of the Hereafter, nor forget thy portion in this world: but do thou good, as Allah has been good to you, and seek not (occasions for) mischief in the land: for Allah loves not those who do mischief. (Al-qsas, 28:77)

and

> Make not your hand tied (like a niggard's) to thy neck, nor stretch it forth to its utmost reach, so that thou become blameworthy and destitute. (Al-isra', 17:29)

Moreover, one of the characteristics of the righteous people '*Al-Muttaqoon*' is:

> Those who, when they spend, are not extravagant and not niggardly, but hold a just (balance) between those (extremes). (Al-Furqan, 25:67)

However, the ideals mentioned in the *Holy Qur'an* and the *Sunnah* sometimes differ from practice (Naqvi & Qadir, 1997).

The Prohibition of Unjustified Practices

One of the most important principles of *Shariah* is the prohibition of all sources of unethical financial activities for the purpose of establishing justice in the society (Albalawi, 2006, p. 54). Such a prohibition was mentioned in the *Holy Qur'an*:

> And do not eat up[9] your property among yourselves for vanities … (Al-Baqara 2:188)

The Arabic term '*Akl Amwal An-nas bil-batil'* is a general concept that refers to the unjust dealing with people's property including swindling, usury, monopoly, usurpation and theft (Abu-Guddah, 2000, p. 46). On the other hand, Islam encourages financial activities that bring financial and social benefits to the society. The relationship between the various parties in the financial transactions is controlled by Shariah Figh. The following section describes the principles of Islamic banking.

---

[9] The verb 'eat up' in this verse means 'to take the property' or 'to have the property'.

Treatment of Riba under Shariah

Riba is an Arabic word that, in general, has verbal and conceptual meanings. According to the Language experts, the literal meaning of the word is the 'Increase' or the 'growth' (Baej, 2006). However, the term is specifically used by *Shariah* jurists and scholars to refer to either *Riba al- Nasi'ah* which means *Riba* of delay or *Riba al-fadl*, means *Riba* of excess (Albalawi, 2006; Baej, 2006; Chapra, 2009; Jafri & Margolis, 1999). *Riba al-Nasi'ah* means the excess over capital in a loan in exchange for a delayed period of payment (Albalawi, 2006, p. 55). This type of *Riba* is known as *Riba Al-jahiliyah* (pre-Islamic period) which was mentioned in the *Holy Qur'an* (Baej, 2006) whereas *Riba al-fadl* belongs to trade and means anything that is unjustifiably received as 'extra' by one of the counterparties to a trade transaction (Chapra, 2009, p. 8). It can be best described by an example from the *Sunnah* of the Prophet PBUH:

> Gold for gold, silver for silver, wheat for wheat, barley for barley, dates for dates, salt for salt, like for like, same for same, hand to hand. If any of these types are different, then sell however you like, so long as it is hand to hand[10]. (Muslim, 1991)

Table (2) illustrates these six species that based on a comprehensive *Hadith* in '*Riba Albou'a'* or *Riba* of transactions.

Muslim scholars divide the species into two categories: the precious metals which include gold and silver and the foods which describes four main types, namely wheat, barley, dates and salt (Albalawi, 2006, p. 55). In addition, the table shows that there are three principles for all *Riba* transactions in order to be excluded. According to Almasri (1981), these principles are:

(i) If the exchange is between two species from the same category, the amount (e.g., 85.21g for 85.21g) and the type (e.g., gold for gold or barely for barely) of the species must be equal and the exchange must be made on the spot.
(ii) If the exchange is between two different types from the same category (e.g., gold for silver or wheat for barely) then the exchange has to be made on the spot.
(iii) If the exchange is between two types form different categories (e.g., gold for wheat or silver for barely) then it is free from *Riba Al-fadl.*

It is worthwhile to mention that *Riba* was prohibited in Hinduism, Judaism, Christianity and Islam which are the world's four major religions. Although few studies claim that the *Riba* (usury) mentioned in theses religions is different from the banking Interest (an example of these studies has been conducted by Hendi (1996). However, there is a consensus (*Ijma'*) among Muslim scholars that *Riba Al-Nasi'ah'* is the Interest which the current banking system deals with (Chapra, 2009, p. 3). Moreover, Baej (2006) states that the transaction of *Riba Al-Nasi'ah* has the same conditions which can be exactly applied for the banking Interest. These conditions include an increase over capital, a period of time which defines the increase, and the amount of money over capital is assured and stipulated. Consequently, being an intermediary between lenders and borrowers is the primary function that banks were sat up

[10] Hadith number 2917.

for. Further, the *Riba* that exists in the banking system nowadays is said to be worse than in the pre-Islamic era (Baej, 2006), as in the later if the borrower chooses to pay the loan back in the date of maturity, there would be no interest, and otherwise an interest would be calculated for the additional period (Albalawi, 2006, p. 71).

It is believed that *Shariah* has followed a gradual methodology to forbid some issues that were practiced in the pr-Islamic society such as drinking alcohol and dealing with *Riba* even though the stages followed in the prohibition of the two matters were different (Al-Hiti, 1998). The reason behind the gradual prohibition might be because it is not easy for people who were addicted to such practices to immediately give up. The prohibition of *Riba* has been mentioned in four revelations including nine verses in the *Holy Qur'an* (Albalawi, 2006; Almasri, 2001; Chapra, 2009). In the first verse, which was revealed in Mecca (*Makkah*), there is an explanation of the difference between the expenditure for the sake of Allah SWT and for other purposes (*Ar-room*, 30:39). Albalawi (2006) and Chapra (2009) state that the *Riba* mentioned in this verse is the Interest. However, an interpretation by Muslim scholars has shown that the *Riba* mentioned in this verse carries a literal meaning and not as they stated (Baej, 2006). According to Al-Hiti (1998), the prohibition of *Riba* has started from the second stage (*An-nisa*, 4:161), which narrates, that Allah had forbidden the Interest upon Jews. However, they had dealt with. Therefore, this rule is applied for Muslims unless the *Holy Qur'an* and the *Sunnah* contradict it, which are not. In the third revelation, (*A'l Imran*, 3:130), the prohibition of the *Riba* (interest) is obvious. The revelation of this verse was after the settlement of Muslims in the *Madina* (Albalawi, 2006). The meaning of 'doubled and multiplied' has come to describe how the pre-Islamic society was dealing with the *Riba* and it includes the simple Interest as well. The last revelation has carried some teachings with regard to the *Riba* or Interest, which mentioned in chapter 2 of the *Holy Qur'an* (*Al-Baqara*, 2:275-280). Baej (2006) and Chapra (2009) have summarized these teachings as:

(i) the verses carry commandments from Allah that strictly prohibit any amount of Interest Dealing with *Riba* was clearly prohibited in any amount.
(ii) There is a clear distinction between the prohibited Interest and the permitted trade.
(iii) The verses show a comparison between the *Az-Zakah* which increases the wealth and the *Riba* that destroys it.
(iv) Those were practicing the *Riba* are being asked to fair Allah and annul all outstanding Interest even the small amount. However, for those who turn back, they have the right to take back the principle loan.

The *Sunnah* of the Prophet PBUH has strictly condemned dealing with *Riba* as well. In addition to the previous *Hadith* that explains *Riba Al-fadl*, it is narrated that the Prophet PBUH

> … cursed the one who consumes Riba, the one who pays it, the one who writes it down and the two who witness it, and he said: They are all the same[11]. (Muslim, 1991)

Although Albalawi (2006) has brought long discussion regarding the modern banking Interest and how it differs from the *Riba* that was mentioned in the sources of Islamic law, it

[11] The Hadith number is 1598.

remains individual opinions that do not represent *Al-jma'* or consensus among Muslim scholars and jurists. However, the vast majority of them agree that conditions of *Riba Al-Nasi'ah* apply for interest which banks use nowadays. Moreover, judging between two opinions should be by fully addressing both viewpoints which has not been in Albalawi's study.

Table 2. *Riba* al-fadl

		Precious metals		Foods			
		Gold	Silver	Wheat	Barley	Dates	Salt
Precious metals	Gold	A	B	C	C	C	C
	Silver	B	A	C	C	C	C
Foods	Wheat	C	C	A	B	B	B
	Barley	C	C	B	A	B	B
	Dates	C	C	B	B	A	B
	Salt	C	C	B	B	B	A

Notes: A – amount and type are equal and exchange must be on the spot. B – exchange must be on the spot. C – free (no *Riba*). Source in Arabic: (Almasri, 2001, p. 94).

The Prohibition of *Al-Gharar*

Al-Gharar can be translated as risk or uncertainty. The concept of *Al-Gharar* has received a great attention from the early Islamic jurists as it was generally prohibited in the *Holy Qur'an* (it is classified under the previously mentioned section: the prohibition of unjustified financial practices and included in the term *Akl Amwal Annas bil-batil* (2:188 & 4:29). In addition, it was specifically forbidden in the *Sunnah* of the Prophet Muhammad PBUH as Muslim narrated from Abu Hurayrah that the Prophet PBUH forbade *Al-Gharar* (ambiguous) transactions[12] (Muslim, 1991).

There are some definitions of *Al-Gharar* adopted by scholars such as the definition of Mustafa Al-Zarqa: *Al-Gharar* is the sale of probable items whose existence or characteristics are not certain, due to the risky nature which makes the trade similar to gambling (El-Gamal, 2000, p. 7). Al-Khattaabi defines it as any transaction which is based on ambiguity or on inability to achieve something is *Al-Gharar*. There are many kinds of ambiguity, which all involve not knowing exactly what the transaction involves (Al-Munajjid, 2010). A third definition by El-Gamal (2001, p. 3) refers to *Al-Gharar* as sales in which *Al-Gharar* was the major component (*Ghalaba 'Alayhi*) until the sale unjustifiably described as *Bay'u Al-Gharar*. Therefore, not all contracts that consist of *Al-Gharar* are prohibited due to the availability of risk in any transaction. It depends on whether the risk is substantial, however.

The ambiguity that might cover the sale contracts or commercial transactions was explained in some *Hadiths* of the Prophet Muhammad PBUH. Some of these examples include the sale of a bird in the sky, a fish in the sea, an unborn animal in its mother's womb, and the sale of the milk in the animal's udder without measurement (El-Gamal, 2000).

---

[12] The number of the Hadith is 1513.

In modern financial transactions, there are two areas where *Al-Gharar* can be seen which are the use of financial derivatives and the financial insurance contracts (Albalawi, 2006). In the insurance contracts, for instance, while the premium is paid in a regular base to the company, the compensation would be for real losses which might either happen to the insured in the first month -where they claim for a huge amount of money whereas they have just paid one premium- or might never happen in the period of the contract(s).

The Prohibition of *Al-Maysir*

Al-Maysir is a general Arabic term refers to three meanings: the first meaning is *Al-Maysir* in its broad meaning when players compete for a purpose other than money such as having fun. The second meaning called *Al-Qimar* or gambling, when competitors put forth for winning some money. The last meaning is called '*Ar-Rihan*' which involves getting money without effort such as the games of lotteries and casinos (Al-Saati, 2007). Some authors argue that the game of chance which requires some skills is a speculation. In this sense, *Al-Maysir* includes the meaning of gambling which is defined as a voluntary and deliberate risk taking (Al-Saati, 2003, p. 8). The usual motivation of such action is gaining wealth in a very short period of time which carries a huge risk of losing the entire money if not.

There is no doubt that most if not all contracts include a percentage of risk. However, *Shariah* prohibits some financial activities due to their excessive exposure to risk such as *Al-Gharar* and *Al-Maysir* with its three specific meanings. The *Holy Qur'an* refers to the prohibition of such activities in chapter 5 (*Al-maida*, 5:90-91). Al-Satti (2007) claims that Christianity prohibits games of chance including gambling, which was criticised by a number of Western studies prior to the First World War, for the following reasons:

(i) gambling eliminates the useful economic functions.
(ii) It is an irrational behaviour and which leads to financial problems at the level of the individual and society.
(iii) It leads to addiction, which destroys the relationship between the addicted people and their families and friends. These results support what mentioned in the *Holy Qur'an*, chapter 5 (*Al-maida* 5:91).

The Prohibition of Forbidden Assets

One of the fundamentals of Islamic finance is the prohibition of dealing with certain products and services such as alcohol, drugs, pork products, gambling and pornography (See The *Holy Qur'an* 5:3&5:90; and from the *Sunnah,* for example *Al-Bukhari, Kitab Al-Ashriba*: 5575-5590). The reason behind forbidding investment in or financing of these commodities might be because of the five necessities in all religions including Islam which are: the preservation of religion, life, intellect, offspring, and property (Al-Khalifah, 1994). Therefore, Islamic financial institutions, including Islamic banks, are prohibited from financing activities linked to such practices.

3. Islamic Financial products and Services

Shariah prohibited financial activities, which were described in the previous sections, are an exception from the role. In other words, most types of the trade are permitted in Islamic Shariah (El-Gamal, 2000). In addition, there is a variety of financial services and markets such as banks, capital markets, insurance, asset management and advisory services covered by Islamic methods of finance that are permissible (Austrade, 2010). Az-Zakah, profit-loss-sharing, At-takaful, and A-Qard Al-Hassan are examples of permitted activites that are discussed in the following points.

Table 3. Islamic financial products and services

Method	Description
Cost-plus sales (*Al-Murabaha*)	A contract involves an agreement between the client and the bank that the latter buys a commodity at cash price and resell it to the former at a higher price but the payment would be in installments for an agreed period of time (Al-Jarhi & Iqbal, 2001).
Full partnership (*Al-Musharakah*)	A contract where both the client and the bank participate in the capital. The management can be by one or both of the partners or even by an appointed, third party. Profit may be shared in a pre-determined ratio; while losses are shared in accordance with the percentage of capital participated (Austrade, 2010, p. 8).
Silent partnership (*Al-Mudarabah*)	In *Mudarabah* contract, there are two parties: a capital owner (*Rabb Al-aml*) and the investment manager (*Mudarib)*. The first part provides capital for specific venture indicated by the second part (Gait & Worthington, 2009). Profit is distributed in a pre-agreed ratio while losses, if any, are borne by capital owner whereas the manager would lose the opportunity cost of their labour (Al-Jarhi & Iqbal, 2001).
Leasing (*Al-Ijarah*)	A contract where the bank purchases an asset and then rent it to the customer for agreed period of time and price (Austrade, 2010).
Contract of manufacture (*Al-Istesna'*)	It is a contract where the customer orders the institution to manufacture and provide a commodity to them. The details of the payment time, the delivery time, the price and any other information necessary would be described in the contract (Al-Jarhi & Iqbal, 2001). The payment and delivery depend on the agreement written in the contract (Gait & Worthington, 2009).
Sale of *Salam* (*Bai us salam*)	*Bai us salam* refers to a contract between the seller and buyer where the payment is made by the latter in advance, making a commitment for the former to deliver specified quantity and quality of goods at a future point.

Az-Zakah (Religious Tax)

Az-Zakah is one of the five pillars of Islam. In the *Holy Qur'an*, It is mentioned as *Az-Zakah* or *As-Sadaqa* (Gait & Worthington, 2009). However, *As-Sadaqa* (charity or alms) which is a voluntary payment differs from the payment of *Az-Zakah* which is obligatory. Ahmed (2004) defines *Az-Zakah* as one of the fundamentals of Islam that has direct economic implications. It requires Muslims to distribute a part of their wealth among the specified heads in order to alleviate poverty and achieve economic emancipation. There is a verse in the *Holy Qur'an* explains eight specified heads to whom the *Az-Zakah* should be distributed, namely: poor and needy; workers in *Az-Zakah* administration; those whose hearts are being reconciled; freeing slaves; those under liabilities; in the way of Allah; and wayfarers (Al Qardawi, 1986).

At-Takaful (Islamic insurance)

Insurance as viewed by conventional insurance companies is not acceptable by *Shariah*. Wahab et al. (2007, p. 374–75) explain why Islamic law objects conventional insurance:

(1) Standard insurance violates the prohibition of *Al-Gharar* (uncertainty) since the benefits to be paid depend on the outcome of future events that are not known at the time of signing the contract.
(2) Insurance is regarded as gambling (*Al-Maysir)* because policy-holders are held to be betting premiums on the condition that the insurer will make payment (indemnity) consequent to the circumstance of a specified event.
(3) Many forms of life insurance in particular are merely thinly disguised investment methods, and the insurance companies conduct their business by investing collected premiums in a mix of investments that includes interest-based or other such investments, thereby contravening the Islamic laws regarding *Riba* along with *Al-Gharar* and *Al-Maysir*.

In contrast, El-Gamal (2000) argues that the cooperative (*Takaful*) insurance is permitted by *Shariah*. It is basically a group of participants agree to contribute to a pool of funds for the purpose of facing losses based on certain risks that might be exposed to any one of them. Each of them pays a certain amount of money 'premium' to be used for legitimate claims relative to the agreement or the contract. The rest of funds can be invested in Islamic permissible way on behalf of the subscribers with a distribution of the profit among them.

Al-Qard Al-Hassan (Benevolent Loans)

It is a loan used by Islamic banks to help the society especially those poor and needy. It can be used for various purposes such as education, marriage and housing (Gait & Worthington, 2009). It should be noted, however that the benevolent loan differs from the distribution of *Az-Zakah* in the sense that the former should be paid back but without any interest while the later is an offered amount of money.

Profit-and-loss Sharing

There is no doubt that Islam prohibits dealing with Interest. However, the alternative, which has been mentioned in the *Riba* section, is the trade. Gait and Worthington (2009) claim that instead of having a fixed amount of Interest, risk as well as profit in Islamic finance should be shared between the two parts (lenders and borrowers) of financial contract which called profit and loss sharing. Therefore, the idea of Islamic methods of finance, which Islamic banks use, has been derived from such role. The following points, represented in Table 3, are definitions the key Islamic financial products and services practiced by Islamic financial institutions including banks.

4. Islamic Banking

It has been almost half a century since the first Islamic bank was established. In this period, Islamic banking and finance industry has been one of the fastest growing sectors in global finance. According to Austrade (2010), *Shariah*-compliant financial assets have been growing at over 10% annually over the last ten years with estimation of US$822 billion for the global Islamic finance industry. As a result, new institutions are adapting Islamic financial products and services with some Arabic and Muslim countries converting their financial system completely to operate according to *Shariah* (Iqbal, 2001). Such expansion has not been only in Muslim countries, but also in other countries where Muslim population represents the minority such as the USA, UK and Australia. Despite that, Islamic banking industry remains a new territory for some finance researchers and practitioners.

Al-Jarhi and Iqbal (2001, p. 23), define an Islamic bank as a company whose main business is to mobilize funds from savers and supply these funds to businessmen/ entrepreneurs. It is organized as a joint stock company with the shareholders supplying the initial capital. It is managed by shareholders through their representatives on the Board of Directors. While a conventional bank uses the rate of interest for both obtaining funds from savers and supplying these funds to businessmen, an Islamic bank performs these functions using various financial modes compatible with the *Shariah*. On the mobilization side, it uses either the contract of *Mudarabah* or *Wakalah* (agent) with the fund owners.

Similar to conventional banks and other financial institutions, Islamic banks are profit-seeking organizations. However, both banks are different in terms of the way they make the profit and the objectives beyond it. In other words, Islamic banks need to comply with *Shariah* principles (mentioned in the previous section) in all their financial transactions on one hand, and to fulfill social obligations such as collecting and distributing *Az-Zakah*, giving loans without interest and bringing welfare to the society, on the other.

The Transformation Process to Islamic Banking

Since the existence of Islamic banking industry, there have been some different approaches applied in Muslim and non-Muslim countries to move from Interest-based to *Shariah*-based banking system. One technique is establishing new Islamic bank(s) parallel to those conventional banks either to gradually move towards a complete Islamic financial system or merely combining between both systems. Another is to introduce Islamic windows and/or subsidiaries within existing Islamic banks for similar purposes. However, choosing one of these techniques depend on some factors such as which country is applying the new system and what is the percentage of Muslim population on it. Moreover, Moving from conventional to Islamic banking rely on the following principles (Baej, 2006; Hazaz, 2002):

- Enjoining what is just and forbidding what is wrong (*Al-amru Bel Maru'f Wa Annhu Ani Elmunkar*). The implementation of this principle requires finding an alternative to the Interest-based system, which is the Islamic banking system, as the interest is strictly prohibited and regarded as a wrong action in Islam.
- Response to *Allah* SWT and His Messenger PBUH. Obeying *Allah* and His messenger is obligatory when it comes to permissible and prohibited tasks: ... *give your response to Allah and His Messenger, when He calls you to that which will give you life* ... (*Al-anfal* 8:24).
- Call-to-goodness (*Ad-dawa Ela Al-khair*). Establishing Islamic financial institutions is from *Ad-dawa Ela Al-khair*, and everyone should take into consideration all the causes that Might help in so doing. *Let there arise out of you a band of people inviting to all that is good* ... (*A'l Imran* 3:104).
- *Halal* is substitute to *Haram. Shariah* prohibited financial activities which were described previously are exception from the rule. For instance, the trade is an alternative to the *Riba*: *"... but Allah has permitted trade and forbidden usury ..."* (*Al-Baqara* 2:275)
- Applying gradualism while transforming to Islamic banking. This approach was adopted by Islam in prohibiting the *Riba* and alcohol as well as obligating the prayer and fasting. Therefore, gradualism should be applied while moving from conventional to Islamic banking system.

Forms of Transformation to Islamic Banking

Although the reason behind the transformation from conventional to Islamic banking varies between some countries and even between some banks in a same country, there are some forms for introducing Islamic banking to a conventional bank including:

- *Islamic Investment Funds*: An Islamic investment fund is a combination of people's small savings to be invested according to Islamic *Shariah*. The management and supervision of the fund should be either by investment companies or Islamic banks. This approach has been adopted by some Saudi banks (Alqirri, 2000).
- *Islamic Financial Products and Services in Conventional Banks*: According to this approach, conventional banks introduce some Islamic financial products and services in order to compete with their counterparties and to satisfy their customers' needs (Martan, 2000). Nevertheless, this approach raises some questions such as whether the Islamic and conventional funds are fully segregated as well as the application of *Shariah* principles in conventional banks.
- *Islamic Windows and Subsidiaries in Conventional Banks*: Opening Islamic windows and/or subsidiaries in conventional banks seems to be a well-known way to introduce Islamic banking to conventional banking system. According to Martan (2000), this approach has been adopted by many banks in Islamic and non-Islamic countries

including the Saudi National Bank, ANZ, Citibank, and the Kuwait United Bank. However, the success of the transformation depends heavily on the purpose of the opening an Islamic window or subsidiary. In other word, there are some issues related to the relationship between the transforming bank and the new subsidiary(s) or window(s) such as the segregation of fund, the accounting and financial system and the management (Baej, 2006).

CONCLUSION

The term 'Shariah' refers to the principles of Islamic law that govern and organize Muslims' political, economic, and social live. The idea of Islamic finance in general and Islamic banking specifically is based on the teachings of the two primary sources of Islamic legislation, the *Holy Qur'an* and the Sunnah of the prophet. In addition to these two original sources and based on them, Muslim scholars derived *Al-Ijma'* (scholarly consensus) and *Al-Qiyas* (analogy). Based on these sources, financial contracts involve interest (Riba), substantial uncertainty (*Al-Gharar*), and gambling (*Al-Maysir*) are all prohibited as well as financing certain products and services such as alcohol, drugs, pork products, and pornography. On the other hand, Islam made it permissible for people and institutions to practise other types of trade and investment such as *Murabahah* (cost-plus sales); *Musharakah* (full partnership); *Mudarabah* (silent partnership); *Ijarah* (Leasing); and Istisna' (contract of manufacture); which are seen as an alternative to the interest-based system. With conventional institutions worldwide adopting Shariah principles for various purposes, there are several forms of transformation available such as Islamic windows and subsidiaries for banks willing to adopt Islamic banking products and services, and a full, gradual transformation from a conventional to an Islamic bank.

REFERENCES

Abdukaliq, A. (2007). Al-ijma, Al-Qitas and Usul Al-*Fiqh*. *Islamic Guidance* Retrieved 7th &12th of October 2010, 2010, from: http://www.hadielislam.com/arabic/.

Abu-Guddah, A. (2000). The Implementation of *Shariah* Principles in the Economy. In O. B. Ahmed (Ed.), *The contemporary Islamic Economic Applications* (pp. 647). Morocco: Islamic Research and Training Institute (IRTI).

Ahmed, H. (2004). *Role of Zakah and Awqaf in Poverty Alleviation*: Islamic Development Bank, Islamic Research and Training Institute, 8.

Al-Bukhari, M. I. I. (2002). *Sahih Al-bukhari* (1 ed.). Damascus-Beirut: Dar Ibn Kathir.

Al-Ghazali, A. H. (1993). *Almustasfa Min Ilm Alosoul* (1 ed. Vol. 1). Egypt: Dar Al-Kutub.

Al-Hiti, A. R. (1998). *Almasarif Aleslamiyyah bain Alnazariyyah Wa Altatbiq. Islamic banks between theory and practice*. Amman, Jordan: Dar Usama.

Al-Jarhi, M., & Iqbal, M. (2001). *Islamic banking: Answers to some frequently asked questions* (Vol. 4). Jeddah, Saudi Arabia: Islamic Research and Training Institute.

Al-Jarhi, M. A. (Ed.). (2004). Islamic Banking and Finance: Philosophical Underpinnings (First ed.). *Islamic banking and finance: Fundamentals and contemporary issues*. Brunei: Islamic Research and Training Institute (IRTI).

Al-Khalifah, A. (1994). Religiosity in Islam as a Protective Mechanism against Criminal Temptation. *The American Journal of Islamic Social Sciences, 11*, 12.

Al-Munajjid, M., S. (2010). *Islam QA*. Retrieved 11th of October & 27th of August 2010, 2010, from http://www.islam-qa.com/en.

Al-Saati, A. (2003). The Permissible Gharar (Risk) in Classical Islamic Jurisprudence. *Islamic Economics, 16*(2), 3-19.

Al-Saati, A. (2007). Speculation and Gambling in Financial Markets Economic and Legal Analysis. *Islamic Economics, 20*(1), 3-33.

Al-Qardawi, Y. (1986). *Fiqh az-Zakah*. 1, 345. Retrieved from http://monzer.kahf.com/books/english/fiqhalzakah_vol1.pdf.

Albalawi, S. H. (2006). *Banking system in Islamic countries: Saudi Arabia and Egypt*. Stanford University.

Almasri, R. (1981). *Islamic Development Bank* (2 ed.). Beirut, Lebanon: Alresalah 'the message' Institution.

Almasri, R. (2001). *Aljama'a Fi Usul Al-Riba* (2 ed.). Damascus: Dar Al-Qalam.

Alqirri, M. A. (2000). Islamic Investment funds. In O. B. Ahmed (Ed.), *The contemporary Islamic Economic Applications* (pp. 647). Morocco: Islamic Research and Training Institute (IRTI).

Ash-Shawkani, M. (2000). *Irshad al-Fuhul fi Tahqiq al-Haqq min 'Ilm al-Usul* (1 ed.). Ar-riyad: Dar Al- fadilah.

Austrade. (2010). *Islamic Finance - Financial Services*. Retrieved from http://www.austrade.gov.au/ArticleDocuments/2792/Islamic-Finance - Publication.pdf.aspx.

Baej, Y. M. A. (2006). *Possibility of Using the Model of Islamic banks in Libyan Banks*. University of Aljabal Algharbi, Gharian.

Bin Hanbal, A. (1998). *Musnad Ahmad*. Ar-riyad, Saudi Arabia: Bayt al-Afkar al-Dawliya.

Chapra, M. (2009). The Nature Of *Riba* In Islam. *Jurnal Millah (Jurnal Studi Agama), 8*(1).

Chapra, M. U. (2004). *The case against Interest: Is it Compelling?* Paper presented at the Islamic Banking and Finance: Fundamentals and Contemporary Issues, Brunei.

Djojosugito, R. (Ed.). (2004). Legal Aspects of Islamic Project Finance and Asset Securitization in Indonesia: A vehicle for the development of Islamic banking (1st ed. Vol. 10). *Islamic banking and finance: Fundamentals and contemporary issues*, Brunei: Islamic Research and Training Institute (IRTI).

El-Gamal, M. (2000). *A basic guide to contemporary Islamic banking and finance Available* from http://www.la Riba.com/dev/knowledge-center/islamic-banking-guide.pdf.

El-Gamal, M. (2001). An economic explication of the prohibition of gharar in classical Islamic jurisprudence. *Islamic Economic Studies, 8*(2), 29–58.

Gait, A., & Worthington, A. (2009). A primer on Islamic finance: Definitions, sources, principles and methods. [Discussion Paper]. *Islamic Finance*, 26.

Haddad, G. F. (1999). *The Meaning of Sunna*. Retrieved 26th of August, 2010, from http://www.livingislam.org/n/ms_e.html.

Hannan, S. A. (1999). USUL AL *FIQH*: Islamic Jurisprudence Available from http://www.2muslims.com/books/usul_al_Fiqh.pdf.

Hassan, F. A. (1982). The Sources of Islamic Law. *American Society of International Law,* 76, 10. Retrieved from http://www.jstor.org/stable/25658109.

Hazaz, B. H. (2002). Required, a system regulating the work of Islamic windows in conventional banks and others that want to transition to full Islamic banking. *Alwatan, 776.*

Hendi, M. I. (1996). *Suspicion of usury in transactions of conventional and Islamic banks* Eskadria, Egypt: Modern Arabic's Bureau 'Almaktab Al-arabi Alhadith'.

Iqbal, M. (2001). Islamic and conventional banking in the nineties: a comparative study. *Islamic Economic Studies, 8*(2), 1-27.

Iqbal, Z. (1997). Islamic financial systems. *Finance & development, 34*(2), 42-45.

Jafri, S. H. A., & Margolis, L. S. (1999). The treatment of usury in the holy scriptures. *Thunderbird International Business Review, 41*(4-5), 371-379.

Martan, S. S. (2000). Islamic subsidiaries and windows in conventional banks In O. B. Ahmed (Ed.), *The contemporary Islamic Economic Applications* (pp. 647). Morocco: Islamic Research and Training Institute (IRTI).

Muslim, I. A.-H. N. (1991). *Sahih Muslim.* Beirut, Lebanon: Dar al-Kutub al-Ilmiyyah.

Naqvi, S., & Qadir, A. (1997). The Dimensions of an Islamic Economic Model. *Islamic Economic Studies, 4*(2), 1-24.

Shafi'i, M. b. I. (1940). *Al-Risalah* (1 ed.). Eygpt: Alhalabi Library.

Wahab, A., Lewis, M., & Hassan, M. (2007). Islamic takaful: Business models, *Shariah* concerns, and proposed solutions. *Thunderbird International Business Review, 49*(3), 371-396.

In: Contemporary Issues in Islamic Finance
Editor: Andrew C. Worthington
ISBN: 978-1-62948-905-6

Chapter 4

DEVELOPMENT OF ISLAMIC MUTUAL FUNDS IN MALAYSIA

Ainulashikin Marzuki[1,*] *and Andrew C. Worthington*[2]
[1]Universiti Sains Islam Malaysia, Malaysia
[2]Griffith University, Australia

ABSTRACT

Islamic mutual funds (IMFs) continue to grow as an alternative investment vehicle for investors wishing to integrate Islamic values and secular financial objectives in their investments. The most distinctive feature of IMFs lies in screening strategies based on the application of *Shariah* (Islamic law). Conventionally, this mainly involves the application of exclusionary screening, whereby fund managers screen out companies involved in certain activities, including *riba* (interest), *gharar* (uncertainty), and *maysir* (gambling), and prohibited products from their portfolios as prescribed by the Quran, *Sunnah* and related Islamic texts. The central outcome is that the managers of IMFs, unlike those of conventional mutual funds (CMFs), necessarily access only a subset of the population of investments available. This has dramatic implications for many conventional dimensions of mutual fund behavior, including performance, the flow of funds, and the fund selection behavior of investors. This chapter provides a comprehensive overview of the development of Islamic managed funds in Malaysia. It discusses the historical, regulatory framework, financial reporting, benchmark indices and operational aspects of Islamic managed funds.

1. INTRODUCTION

Islamic finance is one of the fastest growing segments of the global finance industry, comprising financial institutions, products and services complying with *Shariah* (Islamic law) (Gait and Worthington, 2008). While the practice of Islamic finance in the modern world only

* Corresponding author: Faculty of Economics & Muamalat, Universiti Sains Islam Malaysia, Bandar Baru Nilai 71800 Nilai, Negeri Sembilan, Malaysia. Email. ainulashikin@usim.edu.my.

commenced with savings institutions in 1963 (in Egypt and Malaysia), it has now spread to many other types of financial products and services, including banking, funds management (including mutual funds), *takaful* (Islamic insurance) and *sukuk* (Islamic bonds). Islamic financial products have now proliferated across almost every aspect of contemporary financial services, with comparable products complimenting those found in the conventional finance sector. Consequently, the number of financial institutions offering Islamic financial products and services has also increased, from just 300 in 2005 (El Qorchi, 2005) to 628 at the end of 2009 (Lee and Menon, 2010) with operations in more than 75 countries (El Qorchi, 2005). Additionally, the value of *Shariah* compliant assets grew 25 percent from US$758 billion in 2007 to US$951 billion at the end of 2008 (International Financial Services London, 2010).

One of the fastest growing Islamic financial products is Islamic mutual funds (IMFs), growing strongly since at least the pronouncement by the Council of the Islamic Fiqh Academy in Jeddah in 1990 that equity investment was permissible as long as it complied with *Shariah* (Nathie, 2009). Since then, many asset management companies have offered IMFs alongside their existing conventional mutual funds (CMFs) and socially responsible investment (SRI) funds. For example, the number of IMFs worldwide has risen more than threefold from 200 funds in 2003 to 680 funds in 2008, representing various types of IMFs (Eurekahedge, 2008). Concomitantly, the value of assets managed under these funds has also grown, from US$20 billion in 2003 to US$44 billion in 2008 (Ernst & Young, 2009). At present, equity funds represent the largest segment of IMFs (about 40 percent), followed by fixed income (16 percent), real estate and private equity (13 percent) with the remainder in cash or commodities or other Islamic funds (Eurekahedge, 2008). For the most part, these funds are concentrated in several regions, including the Middle East and North Africa, the Asia Pacific, North America and Europe, with more than half currently invested in the Middle East and the Asia Pacific (International Financial Services London, 2010, p. 5).

In Malaysia, the development of IMFs is relatively more important for several reasons. First, IMFs have a prospective role as a policy tool in the ongoing development of the Malaysian capital market. Malaysia already has one of the most well developed conventional and Islamic capital markets in South-East Asia and among Islamic countries, respectively. In fact, the Malaysian government has highlighted the importance of IMFs in its Malaysian Capital Market 2001 blueprint. According to this, the government will "... facilitate the development of a wide range of competitive products and services related to the Islamic capital market" and "... create a viable market for the effective mobilization of Islamic funds", one of which is IMFs (Securities Commission Malaysia, 2001).

Second, the equity market, including investment funds, is an important buffer to the significant increase in household debt in the Malaysian economy (Bank Negara Malaysia, 2011). However, the size of mutual fund assets relative to the total financial assets of Malaysian household remains small compared to other developed and developing countries. In 2010, total mutual fund assets (net asset value) in Malaysia were RM226.81 billion (Securities Commission Malaysia, 2012), constituting about 16 percent of the total financial assets of Malaysian households as reported in the 2010 report (Bank Negara Malaysia, 2011). Of this, RM24.04 billion was in IMFs, and thus they account for about 1.67 percent of Malaysian household sector financial assets (Securities Commission Malaysia, 2012). This size implies that there is potential for IMFs to grow further and become the main catalyst for the growth of the overall mutual fund industry in Malaysia (Securities Commission Malaysia,

2011). This will not only help to support the growth of the Malaysian capital markets (including the Islamic capital market) but also the Malaysian economy as a whole.

Third, even though the asset size of IMF industry is small relative to that of the total mutual fund industry, Malaysia's IMF is among the largest in both asset under management and number of funds launched in the world besides Saudi Arabia and Kuwait [see, for instance, Securities Commission Malaysia (2012), Eurekahedge (2008), Hoepner et al. (2011), Abderrezak (2008), and Nainggolan (2011)]. This makes Malaysia one of the major players of the IMFs globally. Finally, IMFs potentially appeal to not only the Muslim investors but also to non-Muslim investors who may regard these funds as another variant of an ethical or SRI fund. Investors who are ethically (religiously) concerned are interested to integrate ethical (*Shariah*) values as well as financial objectives in their investment decisions. The distinctive feature of IMFs lies in their screening strategies with IMFs applying screening based on *Shariah*. However, in contrast to ethical/SRI funds, IMFs mainly apply exclusionary screening as against both positive and negative screening in SRI funds.US.

The remainder of this chapter provides an overview of the development of Malaysian IMFs industry with a focus on historical, regulatory framework, financial reporting, benchmark indices and the operational aspect of Islamic mutual funds.

2. Historical Aspects

Before the existence of IMFs, the Malaysian public invested in CMFs. Mutual funds were first introduced in the Malaysian financial system in 1959 where the first mutual fund management company was established, namely, the Malaysian Unit Trust Limited (Rahman et al., 2010). The company was later renamed the Asia Unit Trust Berhad and launched its first mutual funds in 1966. As shown in Table 1, in comparison to other neighboring countries, Malaysia is one of the pioneers in the mutual fund investment in the Southeast Asian region.

A year later, another company entered the industry, which was the MARA Unit Trust Berhad. During the 1960s and 1970s, mutual funds as an alternative investment were not very popular compared to direct investing in the stock market. This may be due to the lack of awareness among the public concerning the new investment method. The significant growth of the local mutual fund industry started in the 1980s, when the Malaysian government through the Permodalan Nasional Berhad (PNB) launched the Sekim Amanah Saham National (ASN) in 1981. The following fund from PNB was the Amanah Saham Bumiputera (ASB). These funds were to encourage *bumiputera* (indigenous Malays) to increase their equity participation in the corporate sectors and, hence, improve their socioeconomic standing. About two years after the launching of ASN, the fund surprisingly reached RM1 million and further increased to RM1.1 billion at the end of March 1984 (Rahman et al., 2010). From this point in time, the number of mutual fund management companies gradually increased together with the number of funds launched.

The peak growth was evidenced from 1991 to 1996 where the net asset value (NAV) almost quadrupled from RM15.72 to RM59.95 billion (Rahman et al., 2010; Taib and Isa, 2007). This was due to many factors, among them being the aggressive promotion adopted by PNB (to brand mutual fund as a household product in Malaysia) and the establishment of the

SCM in 1993. There were many measures taken by the SCM following its formation, which was done through an enactment of the SCM (Unit Trust Scheme) regulations 1996 (Singh and Yusof, 2002).

Table 1. Establishment of first Islamic mutual fund by country

Countries	Year
Malaysia	1959
Thailand	1995
Singapore	1959
Indonesia	1996
Philippines	1958
China	2001
Korea	1969
Pakistan	1962
UK	1934
US	1924
Australia	1965

Source: Khorana et al. (2005).

Table 2. Growth of Malaysian mutual fund industry, 1999-2010

	2000	2002	2004	2006	2008	2010
No. of companies	34	39	36	38	39	39
No. of approved funds*	127	188	291	416	579	564
Conventional	110	144	220	316	430	412
Islamic	17	44	71	100	149	152
NAV (RM bil.)	43.3	53.7	87.39	121.76	134.41	226.81
Conventional	41.62	50.5	80.62	112.59	117.22	202.77
Islamic	1.68	3.2	6.76	9.17	17.19	24.04
Bursa Malaysia market cap (RM bil.)	444.35	481.61	722.04	848.71	663.8	1,275
% of NAV to BM market cap.	9.74	11.15	12.1	14.35	20.25	17.79

Source: Securities Commission annual reports (Securities Commission Malaysia, 2012).

* Includes fund approved but not yet launched.

Not including unit holders account at IUTA that operates nominee account system.

The success of ASN and ASB then paved the way for the development of Shariah based mutual funds. As the majority of *bumiputera* are Muslim, they felt there was a need to introduce mutual funds, which fit not only their financial objectives but also their religious obligations. Fulfilling the demand for IMFs, the Arab Malaysian Unit Trust Berhad launched the first IMFs in Malaysia in 1993, named the Tabung Ittikal. This was about 30 years after the existence of the first CMFs. Subsequently, the government was very responsive to the development of IMFs. For example, in 1996, the SCM established the *Shariah* Advisory Council (SAC) to advise the SCM on all *Shariah* matters related to the comprehensive development of the Islamic capital market (ICM) activities. The Malaysian Securities Exchange Board (now known as Bursa Malaysia Securities Berhad) further catalyzed the development of the industry by launching the KLSE *Shariah* index (now Kuala Lumpur

Shariah Index or KLSI) in 1999. The index includes all Main Board shares that are on the *Shariah* approved securities list. The *Shariah* based mutual funds further grew with overwhelming demand from not only the Malaysian Muslim population but also from their non-Muslim counterparts.

As shown in Table 2, a decade after it was first introduced, the number of IMFs, as at the end of 2003, was 55 with NAV amounting to RM4.75 billion compared to RM65.33 billion for its conventional counterpart. Hence, IMFs had received modest acceptance, which represented 8 percent of the total mutual fund industry. From 1995 to 1999, the total number of accounts grew at a compounded annual growth rate of approximately 25 percent. As at 31 December 2008, 15 new *Shariah* based mutual funds were approved, which makes the total for the year to increase to 149 funds with total NAV amounting to RM17.19 billion, representing 25.7 percent of the total mutual funds industry. This comprises 68 equity funds, 21 balanced funds, 18 *sukuk* funds and the remaining figure consists of money market funds, structured products, feeding funds, fixed income funds and mixed asset funds (Rahman et al., 2010). It is interesting to note that the NAV of IMFs for the past five years grew at a compounded annual growth of 26.3 percent compared to the total industry, which recorded a growth rate of only 11.4 percent in the same period. At the international level, Malaysia is the major player for the IMFs as Malaysia dominating 25 percent of the total IMFs available globally (Eurekahedge, 2008).

Currently, the funds management industry in Malaysia comprises funds managed by provident and pension funds, mutual fund management companies, asset management companies and insurance companies. Of this, mutual funds asset represents an average of 70 percent of total sources of funds managed (Securities Commission Malaysia, 2012). Other types of assets under management include assets from charitable bodies, corporate bodies, EPF and EPF contributors, government bodies or government agencies, individuals, insurance companies and private pension funds (Securities Commission Malaysia, 2012).

The fund management market is highly concentrated. The five largest fund management companies managed an average of 70 percent of the total assets under management for the past 10 years (Securities Commission Malaysia, 2012). As at the end of 2008, total funds under management were RM215 billion compared to RM40 billion at the end of 1999, a five-fold increase. Of this amount RM134 billion were mutual funds (Securities Commission Malaysia, 2012).

Part of the mutual funds are also under the collective investment schemes available in Malaysia such as exchange-traded funds (ETF), real estate investment trusts funds (REITs) and restricted investment schemes (RIS). However, these investment schemes are relatively new and small compared to mutual funds. For example the total NAVs for ETFs, REITs and RIS were RM1.0 billion, RM4.07 billion and RM893.1 million, respectively, compared to mutual funds RM134.41 billion in 2008 (Securities Commission Malaysia, 2012). Currently, there are only two Islamic REITs listed on Bursa Malaysia, namely, KPJ *Al-'Aqar* REITs and *Al Hadharah* Bousted REITs and three ETFs, ABF Malaysia Bond Index Fund, FBM30 ETF and My ETF Dow Jones Islamic Market Malaysia Titans 25 (Securities Commission Malaysia, 2012). Locally incorporated fund management companies (39 companies) dominate the mutual fund industry (Securities Commission Malaysia, 2012). As at 31 May 2009, out of 39 companies, 11 unit trust companies belong to federal or state governments while the remainder are privately owned companies.

The mutual funds market in Malaysia is highly concentrated. Government mutual funds remain the major player in the industry with Permodalan National Berhad (PNB) leading the investment management industry. For example, in 1997, the total NAV for the industry was RM8.26 million and the net NAV before accounting for PNB mutual fund products was only RM1.43 million (Securities Commission Malaysia, 2012). In terms of units in circulation, the total industry accounted for 45.25 billion and 63 billion units in 1997 and 2000, respectively, compared to the total units for PNB alone, which were 13.27 billion and 35 billion units, respectively, in 1997 and 2000 (Permodalan National Berhad, 2001, p. 72). This trend continues. Among the privately owned mutual fund management companies, the biggest player in terms of assets under management in 2004 was Public Mutual Berhad (25.8 percent) followed by SBB Mutual Berhad (13.4 percent), Am Investment Services berhad (8.5 percent), Prudential Unit Trusts Berhad (7.5 percent) and Mayban Unit Trust Berhad (6.4 percent) (Lipper, 2005).

These companies operated a total of 557 funds, as at the end of 2008, up 12.5 percent from the end of 2007 (Securities Commission Malaysia, 2012). Out of this, 149 are IMFs, which represent 26 percent of the total industry. In terms of NAV, IMFs represent 13 percent of the total NAV compared to only 3 percent in 1999. In terms of growth, it shows more than 300 percent growth over the period of 10 years. The NAV of IMFs has grown at a compounded annual growth rate of 29 percent over the last 10 years while the total industry recorded a growth rate of 12 percent for the same period (Securities Commission Malaysia, 2012). This is a fast growing industry since its inception in 1993. It started with only two IMFs at the end of that year. The demand for IMFs comes from Muslim as well as non-Muslim investors who seek for investment diversification beyond CMFs.

From the global perspective, it is estimated that the Islamic wealth and fund management industry will grow to USD 1 trillion assets under management based on an aggressive growth rate of 15 percent per annum (Malaysia International Islamic Financial Centre, 2009). Total assets managed in a *Shariah* compliant manner contributes to 6 percent of this figure. As at June 2008, Malaysia was the second largest country after Saudi Arabia in terms of assets under management (AUM), which made up 23 percent of the world IMFs. In addition, Malaysia owns the highest number of IMFs in the world (Securities Commission Malaysia, 2012). Even though Malaysia is a dominant player in the industry globally, the average fund size in Malaysia is relatively small (i.e., US$44 million) compared with Saudi Arabia (US$170 million) and Kuwait (US$100 million) (Eurekahedge, 2008). Realizing the importance of the Islamic fund management industry to Malaysia's economic growth, the Malaysian government has taken several measures to provide the necessary infrastructure and various incentives to facilitate the growth of the industry. Among others are, promoting a continuous product innovation, producing a large and diverse pool of Islamic finance talent, providing a comprehensive financial infrastructure and supportive regulatory, legal and *Shariah* frameworks and also offering various tax incentives and privileges for fund managers, either domestic or international, who establish an Islamic fund management company (Securities Commission Malaysia, 2012). Therefore, the development of the Islamic fund management industry is then the key to maintaining Malaysia's position as a leading ICM hub (Securities Commission Malaysia, 2012).

To this end, the Prime Minister had announced in the 2008 Budget, that the government was allowing the establishment of Islamic fund management companies (IFMCs) in Malaysia with up to 100 percent foreign-owned equity (Securities Commission Malaysia, 2009). In recent years, the Malaysian government had also introduced various incentives to promote the Islamic fund management industry, including a flexible exchange control regime, tax incentives and seed funding (Securities Commission Malaysia, 2012).

3. ASSET CLASSES AND BENCHMARK INDICES

All efficiency measures assume we know the production behavior and outcomes of the fully efficient airport or airports. There are three main categories of IMFs available in Malaysia. These are Islamic equity funds, balanced funds and *sukuk* funds. Equity funds remain the largest number of funds launched every year. For example, at the end of 2000, 97 percent of the total NAV of the industry was invested in equity based funds (Permodalan National Berhad, 2001, p. 105). Currently, out of 149 funds approved in 2008, 70 or almost 50 percent are equity funds and the remaining are balanced funds, *sukuk* funds and other fund categories such as feeder funds, fixed income funds, money market funds and mixed funds. However, this is not only evident in the Malaysian Islamic fund industry, but is also prominent in the global region. For example, as reported by Eurekahedge (2008) in Table 3, the equity proportion makes up about 50 percent of the total funds of all Islamic funds across the world. This also applies in Malaysia as shown in Table 4.

Table 3. Percentage of asset class in Islamic investment funds by region, 2007

Types of funds	Asia Pacific	Europe	Global	Middle East	North America	Total
Equity	51	67	54	49	63	52
Fixed income	13	–	1	5	–	7
Balanced	15	7	8	7	–	10
Money market	10	–	27	14	8	13
Others	11	27	10	26	29	18

Source: Eurekahedge (2008).

Table 4. *Shariah-b*ased mutual funds by category, 2006-10

	2006		2007		2008		2009		2010	
Types of funds	No.	NAV	No.	NAV	No.	NAV	No.	NAV	No.	NAV
Balanced funds	19	1.25	21	1.7	21	1.24	22	1.6	22	1.6
Sukuk funds	18	1.56	19	1.8	18	1.5	20	1.4	21	1.8
Equity funds	50	5.6	62	10.4	70	9	72	4.7	78	17.2
Others*	13	0.75	32	3	40	5.45	36	4.4	34	3.4
Total	100	9.16	134	16.9	149	17.19	150	12.1	155	24

* Including feeder funds, fixed income funds, money market funds, structured products and mixed asset funds. NAV in RM billions.

Source: Securities Commission Annual Report 2006–10 (Securities Commission Malaysia, 2012).

The main types of Islamic equity funds are income funds, capital growth funds, and aggressive growth funds. An income fund comprises major investments in *Shariah* compliant shares with high dividend yield and Islamic fixed income securities. It aims to provide investors with income and some amount of capital appreciation. An income fund is mostly suitable for low risk appetite investors. Investors that aim for capital accumulation may invest in capital growth funds. This fund invests in *Shariah* compliant shares, which are able to provide maximum capital growth in the long run through capital appreciation. Investors who are risk tolerant and aim for capital accumulation may choose this fund in their portfolio. Aggressive growth funds are funds with the highest risk level in the Islamic equity group. Similarly, aggressive growth funds invest in *Shariah* compliant companies that are able to provide high returns with a higher amount of risk. Investors with a high level of risk tolerance and that seek a maximum return with maximum risk may opt for this fund type.

The objectives of balanced funds are to provide income, a moderate level of capital appreciation and capital preservation. The asset allocation includes investment in broad asset categories such as *Shariah* compliant securities, Islamic income fund securities, and cash. A balanced fund is a well-diversified portfolio with lower risk and average returns. *Sukuk* funds only invest in *Shariah* compliant fixed income securities such as *sukuk* and the short-term money market. It provides investors with high capital protection and income with a minimum amount of risk. Risk-averse investors may opt for this fund. Finally, index funds are a passively managed Islamic portfolio, which tracks the performance of a selected *Shariah* compliant index. This is suitable for investors who seek medium to long-term capital appreciation.

In order to make an informed decision about the selection and performance of the *Shariah* securities and benchmarking purposes, having a reliable *Shariah* index is important. In Malaysia there are two[1] types of benchmark indices used to benchmark for *Shariah* compliant investments. These indices are under the FTSE Bursa Malaysia. The main *Shariah* index is the FTSE Bursa Malaysia EMAS *Shariah* index, which is designed to provide Malaysian investors a broad benchmark for *Shariah* compliant investments. The second index is the FTSE Bursa Malaysia *Hijrah Shariah* index, which is designed to be used as the basis of *Shariah* compliant investment products that need screening requirements of international Islamic investors. The Malaysian SCM's SAC and the leading global *Shariah* consultancy, Yassar Ltd. screen companies to be included in the index against a clear set of guiding principles.

The screening strategies employed by these indices are similar concerning sectoral screening. As a general criteria, both indices exclude companies with activities prohibited by *Shariah*. Examples of these activities are financial services based on *riba*, gambling, manufacture or sale of non-*halal* products or related products, conventional insurance, entertainment activities that are non-permissible according to *Shariah*, manufacture, or sale of tobacco-based products or related products, stock broking or share trading in *Shariah* noncompliant securities and other activities deemed non-permissible according to *Shariah*. In addition to these criteria, the latter index employ additional screening that excludes companies that have a high level of debt ratio, ratio of debt service, liquidity, percentage of interest to total income and purification ratio. In summary, the second index employs relatively higher restrictive screening compared to the first index.

Problematically, the inability of conventional DEA modeling to take account of statistical error is also likely to cause complications in very many airport contexts. For example, most national airport industries comprise both large (national and major regional) and small

[1] A Dow Jones–RHB Islamic Malaysia Index that complemented the FTSE family index was discontinued in 2007.

(regional and local) airports, with a least some likely to be candidates for outliers (especially given the relatively small number of individual airports in any particular national context and/or the data gathering process) and hence a source of bias in the results. Further, the airports in many countries include a mix of both public and private entities, such that competing behavioral assumptions governing the determination of inputs and outputs for superficially similar entities may misjudge the actual or intended behavior of the airports included.

4. Fee Structures and Distribution Channels

The structure of Malaysian mutual fund fees includes annual management fees, annual trustee fees and other fees (fees to brokers/dealers, fees to sub custodian-trustee outsource to another trustee, tax and duties by government, auditors fees, valuation fees, and fees related to deed modification). In order to ensure greater transparency in the mutual fund investment, the SCM has introduced a single pricing system, effective 1st July 2007 (Federation of Malaysian Unit Trust Managers, 2008). With this system, the pricing of mutual funds is based on the NAV and there is only one pricing for all mutual fund transactions such as buying, selling, and switching. Unit trust management companies (UTMC) are required to disclose separately in the prospectus any charges imposed to investors such as sales charge and exit fee, which include any variations of sales charges among distribution channels. The new regulations allow investors to negotiate on the sales charges from any of the unit trust agents. To promote transparency, UTMC has to disclose the investment amount before and after the sales charge in the investment certificate and the number of units purchased is only shown after the sales charge. In addition, the new regulation does not allow UTMCs to offer any discounts or rebates to entice investors, thus, competition is merely based on the performance and good brand name.

The management fee for mutual fund investment is relatively higher compared with funds in neighboring countries. On average, equity funds are charged at 1.5 percent while bond funds are charged between 0.50 to 1.0 percent (Lipper, 2005). The management expense ratios (MER) do vary significantly within fund sectors. Sales commission charges for equity funds are higher than bond and money market funds, which range from 5 to 7 percent and 0.25 percent, respectively (Lipper, 2005).

In Malaysia, there are various distribution channels where investors can purchase mutual funds. Mutual funds are available for purchase from bank branch staff, financial planners and tied agents attached to the fund management companies. To widen further the distribution channels, the SCM approved another license to distribute multiple products, thus, one is not limited to sell only mutual funds belonging to a particular fund complex but able to sell other companies mutual fund products as well. In order to encourage greater participation among the public and institutional investors in mutual fund investment, the SCM has introduced a wider distribution channel that includes unit trust consultants (UTC), corporate unit trust advisers (CUTA) and institutional unit trust agents (IUTA). All mutual fund distributors are required to register with the Federation of Malaysian Investment Managers (FMIM) (previously the Federation of Malaysian Unit Trust Managers, FMUTM). In 2004, the SCM issued Guidelines on Online Transaction of Online Activities in relation to mutual funds to enable the use of technology such as online trading on mutual funds. This allows investors to purchase mutual funds online. Recently, the market trend in the investment fund industry in Malaysia is moving towards outsourcing the function of portfolio (investment management responsibilities) management to third party fund managers while fund sponsors concentrate on the marketing and distribution strategy.

Investors can purchase mutual fund products through four channels available. First, investors may purchase mutual funds from unit trust consultants (UTC). Since October 2007, the main mutual funds distributors, persons dealing in unit trusts (PDUT) have been rebranded as unit trust consultants (UTC). The reason being is to give a new professional look to the mutual fund agents from being merely marketing personnel to an investment advisory service provider (Federation of Malaysian Unit Trust Managers, 2007). The total number of UTC has been growing from year to year reflecting the growth of the mutual fund industry. In 2007 alone, there was an increase of about 40.5 percent from 38,709 in 2006. In 2008, the number increased approximately 18 percent to 63,205 from 53,496 in the previous year. Of this figure, 85.2 percent were tied agents and the balance were representatives of unit trust management companies (UTMC), IUTA and CUTA.

The second distribution channel is through IUTA. IUTA was introduced in 2000 to allow financial institutions such as banking and other eligible institutions to participate in selling third party funds to both institutional and retail customers. As at 31 December 2008, there were 42 IUTAs registered with the FIMM (Securities Commission Malaysia, 2012).

The third distribution channel is the CUTA. Effective 1 October 2007, the SCM issued another guideline, namely, Guidelines for the Registration of Corporate Unit Trust Advisers. Under this guideline, financial planners are allowed to register as CUTA to distribute mutual fund products of multiple mutual fund management companies just like other financial institutions such as banks and stockbrokers (Federation of Malaysian Unit Trust Managers, 2007). As at the end of 2008, there were two CUTA approved by the SCM and registered by FIMM (Securities Commission Malaysia, 2012). The introduction of financial planning as one of the regulated activities is hoped to further accelerate the growth of mutual funds in Malaysia in particular and investment in general.

Finally, potential investors may also choose to purchase mutual funds online. A few companies have set up online facilities that appeal to investors who do not need personalized services from mutual fund agents. Investors may directly invest in these funds and actively manage their own portfolio. The mutual fund industry in Malaysia is now mainly retail-based (Kadir, 2000). Realizing this, the SCM has enhanced the distribution channel to allow financial institutions to distribute third party funds to their institutional and retail customers. This distribution model is to encourage participation in the mutual funds from institutional investors.

Recently, the SCM also introduced a separate guideline for wholesale funds for fund managers while the mutual fund guidelines will remain as a guideline for retail mutual funds products. As at May 2009, there were 21 fund managers specializing in wholesale funds with the number of approved funds being 71 out of which 14 were Islamic based wholesale funds (Securities Commission Malaysia, 2012). Institutional investors include the Employees Provident Fund (EPF) and insurance companies.

5. Regulations and Reporting Requirements

There are three main regulators responsible for the orderly development of financial markets in Malaysia. These are the Central bank of Malaysia (Bank Negara Malaysia), the SCM, and the Labuan Offshore Financial Services Authority (LOFSA). However, the SCM is the main regulator for the Malaysian capital market, which includes the mutual fund industry.

The SCM was established on 1st March 1993 and is mandated by the Securities Commission Act 1993 to solely regulate, supervise and develop the Malaysian capital markets (Securities Commission Malaysia, 2001). Prior to its establishment, the regulatory frameworks for the capital market were fragmented where different regulators or agencies had different areas of authority that in some cases may have overlapped. Since its establishment, the SCM's first effort was to streamline the regulatory frameworks. In relation to the mutual fund industry, the SCM absorbed the functions of the Capital Issues Committee (CIC) and the Panel Takeover and Mergers and the agencies were dissolved. The objective of streamlining the regulatory frameworks was to improve the overall efficiency of the capital market. This is important as the capital market is expanding together with the level of investors' sophistication.

The SCM has made many changes to the mutual fund industry since its inception. Among others are the introduction of disclosure-based regulation, enhanced disclosure in the prospectus and financial statements, introduction of a code of ethics to the industry profession and mutual fund marketing guidelines. The SCM regulates the mutual fund industry based on the Capital Market Services Act 2007 (CMSA), the Guidelines on Unit Trust and other relevant laws. In addition to the government regulation, it is the aspiration of the SCM to develop a self-regulatory organization (SRO) as a co-regulator for the industry. The SCM appointed the Federation of Malaysian Unit Trust Management (FMUTM) as SRO to regulate jointly the mutual fund market in September 2009. While the SCM is responsible for overseeing the overall regulations, the FMUTM as a SRO will be responsible for regulating its own members in terms of sales conduct and business practice.

The SCM employs two tier regulations for IMFs (Mohd, 2007). The first tier of regulation applies to all mutual funds. The second tier regulation is an additional regulation for a management company, which manages *Shariah* based mutual funds. These include requirements to appoint a *Shariah* committee or advisor, the appointment of two Muslims as the investment committee member and a compliance officer with a basic knowledge of *Shariah* and its principles. Additional disclosures in the prospectus and reports are also required. In addition, the *Shariah* committee or advisors are required to prepare special reports in annual and interim reports to unit holders (Securities Commission Malaysia, 2012).

Under the Capital Markets and Services Act 2007 (CMSA), a company who invites application from the public to purchase securities, which includes mutual fund funds, is required to prepare a prospectus and disclose sufficient information for the public to make informed decisions. The SCM has issued the Prospectus Guidelines for Collective Investment Schemes, which specifies the minimum disclosure requirements in prospectus. This information includes background information on the management company or issuing entity, details of the trustee and detailed information on the fund including the name of the fund, category and type of the fund, the investment objectives, investment policies and strategies, performance benchmark, investor profile most suitable for the fund and distribution policy. In addition, information on fees, charges, and expenses; units of distribution, offering price and the expected net proceeds; information on fund performance; disclosure on risks factors and the application forms and procedures for the purchase of funds are to be enclosed.

For *Shariah* mutual funds, there is additional information requiring disclosure. This is a statement from an appointed *Shariah* advisor certifying that the funds offered in the prospectus are *Shariah* compliant. This information needs to be disclosed either on the inside cover or in the first page of the prospectus. The information the *Shariah* advisor is required to disclose includes names, relevant qualifications, and experience of each member of the *Shariah* advisor. In cases where the *Shariah* advisor is a company, the corporate information of the company, experience relevant to its appointment as an advisor and number of funds in which it acts as advisor are to be disclosed. In addition, roles and primary functions of the *Shariah* advisor, including the frequency of meetings and review by the *Shariah* advisor concerning the assets of the fund to ensure compliance with *Shariah* principles or any other relevant principle at all times.

The prospectus should also include the following information related to the funds – a clear description of the *Shariah*-approval process, including details of methodologies, rulings, screening process, and a statement to the effect that the investment portfolio of the fund comprises securities that have been classified as *Shariah* compliant by the SAC of the SCM. For securities not certified by the SAC of the SCM, a statement stating that the status of the securities has been determined in accordance with the ruling issued by the *Shariah* advisor.

In addition to the fund's prospectus, a management company is also required to prepare two types of reports, which are the annual and interim reports. The Unit Trust Guidelines 2009 clearly defines this requirement. The guidelines specify that the content of the report should include information such as fund information, report on fund performance, manager's report, and trustee's report. For IMFs, the *Shariah* advisor's report is an additional report to be included. In addition, audited financial statements for the accounting period (or interim where applicable) and auditor's report (for annual report only) are other documents to insert in the fund's prospectus.

Even though there are issues relating to the appropriate financial accounting and reporting, disclosure and transparency of Islamic or *Shariah* financial products, the SAC is of the opinion that currently the generally accepted accounting principles do not contradict *Shariah* principles (Anwar, 2009). In terms of disclosure, however, it varies between products depending on the underlying Islamic contract a fund adopts. Currently, Malaysia adopts Islamic accounting and reporting standards developed by the Malaysian Accounting Standards Board (MASB). In addition to the Guidelines on Unit Trust Funds, the SCM has also issued Guidelines on Islamic Fund Management in 2007 (Securities Commission Malaysia, 2007a).

In the recent development of fund management activities, Bank Negara Malaysia has liberalized regulations pertaining to investment abroad by the fund managers including mutual fund managers. This ruling provides additional flexibility for fund management companies in diversifying and constructing their portfolios in order to improve returns for investors. The first liberalization took place in 2005, where fund management companies for the first time can invest in foreign assets up to 30 percent of NAV per funds for funds subscribed to by Malaysian residents. The Bank Negara Malaysia announced further liberalization in April 2007, fund management companies in Malaysia can invest in foreign assets up to 50 percent of NAV per fund for funds subscribed to by Malaysian residents. For

Islamic fund management companies, there is further liberalization of these rules where effective October 2007 Islamic fund management companies can invest in foreign assets up to the full amount of NAV per funds for funds subscribed to by Malaysian residents. Additionally, in March 2008, the SCM has removed the requirement to seek its approval for foreign markets investment other than stock exchanges approved by Bursa Malaysia. It would be a useful development if future researchers were to sound out performance indicators already in place in airports as a means of better informing their specification of inputs and outputs in efficiency studies.

7. Operational Aspects of Malaysian IMFs

Unlike conventional and SRI funds, Islamic investment or specifically IMFs are guided by the *Shariah* principles. *Shariah* governs several aspects of IMFs such as in fund selection (portfolio formation, asset allocation, portfolio screening), operation of the business (investment and trading practices) and income distribution or (issues of income purification) (*zakah* and cleansing the impure elements by giving to charity) (Elfakhani and Hassan, 2005). Thus, the unique feature of IMFs lies in three main elements. These are the presence of *Shariah* advisory boards (SAB), the process of security selection through *Shariah* screening to form a *Shariah* compliant portfolio and purification activities. SAB governs the activities and transactions of the Islamic investment to ensure it complies with the *Shariah* rules and regulations. Screening is the process of portfolio construction that excludes companies from the pool of investment for *Shariah* mutual funds while purification is the product of screening to fulfill the social obligation of mutual fund companies and investors. This section reviews the roles of these features to the IMFs in the Malaysian context.

Shariah Advisory Board (SAB)

Similar to other Islamic financial institutions (for example, Islamic commercial banking and *takaful*), the requirement to establish a *Shariah* advisory (or supervisory) board (or committee) is required under the regulations specified in the Guidelines on Islamic fund management (Securities Commission Malaysia, 2007a). The main function of the board is to oversee the structures of the financial products and services as well as its operation to ensure that it complies with *Shariah*. At the end of the financial year, the board has to produce a *Shariah* compliance report as part of the IMFs annual report verifying that the funds are in accordance with *Shariah*. The *Shariah* advisory board plays an important role in the ICM. The compliance of products and services to the *Shariah* guidelines is critical in the development of the ICM infrastructure. Non-conformity with the *Shariah* rules and principles could undermine investors' confidence in the ICM. However, the legal requirement to have a *Shariah* advisory board is only present in certain jurisdictions such as in Malaysia, Sudan and Iran, while in other jurisdictions such as the UK and Singapore, the legislation is silent on the matter (Australian Trade Commission, 2010).

In Malaysia, the presence of *Shariah* advisors operates at two levels. First, at the national level, namely, the *Shariah* Advisory Council (SAC) and, second, at the fund level commonly called the *Shariah* Advisory Board (SAB). The SCM established the *Shariah* Advisory Council (SAC) in 1996, which acts as an authoritative body to advise the SCM on *Shariah* matters pertaining ICM operations. The members of the SAC comprise prominent Islamic scholars or jurists and Islamic Finance experts. The main objectives of the SAC, as mandated under the Securities Commission Act 1993, are to advise the SCM on *Shariah* related matters, to provide *Shariah* guidance on ICM transactions and activities, to endorse the list of *Shariah* approved securities and to review the *Shariah* compatibility of conventional instruments and new Islamic instruments. Having the SAC in place at the national level ensures standardization and harmonization of the application of *Shariah* principles and concepts. The SAC will further facilitate product innovation, which is significant to the development of ICM. In addition, the SAC in their respective capacity as advisory bodies can make pronouncements; respond to enquiries and proposals from the industry as well as encourage innovation through progressive guideline formulation (Securities Commission Malaysia, 2001).

One of the main responsibilities of the SAC is to conduct a screening process to determine the *Shariah* compliant companies. They carry out the process twice a year and publish the results on the SCM website in April and October every year. The SCM together with the SAC monitors the activities of all companies listed on the Bursa Malaysia to ensure the status of *Shariah* compliance. They gather information on public listed companies from various sources such as the company's annual report, the company's response to the survey and through enquiries made to the company's management. The resolutions of the SAC have been published twice, in 2002 and in 2006 (Securities Commission Malaysia, 2001). This is to ensure that clear guidance on the *Shariah* rules and principles adopted in the ICM is conveyed to the relevant and interested parties.

In addition to the SAC, any financial institutions offering Islamic financial services or products are also required by the Guidelines on the Unit Trust Fund 1997 (now the latest update is the Guidelines on Unit Trust 2009) to form an independent *Shariah* Advisory Board, which means independent from the fund management company to avoid agency conflict. In 2002, the SCM made it mandatory for the *Shariah* advisors to register with the SCM. As per the guidelines, *Shariah* advisor can be an individual or a corporate body. In either form, registration with the SCM is compulsory. In addition, if individual *Shariah* advisors are appointed, it is mandatory to appoint at least three individuals. The practice of having two levels of *Shariah* supervision has attracted other countries to emulate, such as Indonesia. This model will ensure that the products generated are strictly following the *Shariah* guidelines outlined by the SAC.

Screening Process

The availability of *Shariah* compliant securities is significant to ensure further development of ICM in general and the IMF industry in particular. Thus, there are specific frameworks used to screen companies whose activities contradict the *Shariah* principles leaving only companies or securities that are *Shariah* compliant in the asset portfolio. The screening process described in this section refers to screening adopted by the SAC at the national level to determine the list of *Shariah* compliant securities, which is updated on the SCM website twice yearly.

Table 5. Benchmarks employed by the Malaysian Securities Commission

Benchmarks	Activities	Examples
5	Activities that are prohibited clearly under the *Shariah*	Interest based companies, gambling, liquor and pork
10	Activities that involve the element of *umum balwa*	Interest income from fixed deposits in conventional banks, tobacco related activities
15	Amount of rental receivables from prohibited activities	Rental received from premises that relate to activities such as liquor, gambling and other activities
25	Activities that are generally permissible according to *Shariah* and have element of *maslahah* but there are other elements that could affect *Shariah* status	Hotel and resort operations, share trading, stock broking

Source: Securities Commission Malaysia (2007b).

In Malaysia, the SCM and the SAC do the screening process at the central level. The screening process adopted is more liberal and unique to Malaysia (Derigs and Marzban, 2008; Khatkhatay and Nisar, 2007). Accordingly, the uniqueness is in terms of the quantitative screening where it does not screen the companies in terms of the proportion of the company's liquidity and debt position. Thus the screening is mainly activity or income based (only based on the sources of income received by the company), which is prescribed as per Table 5 (Securities Commission Malaysia, 2007b, pp. 144-170).

The criteria for the qualitative screening are on the core activities of the companies. If the core activities of the companies meet any one of the four criteria set by the SAC, these companies will not be included in the SAC *Shariah* compliant list. The first three criteria are involvement in *riba*, *maysir* and *gharar*. The fourth criteria is involvement in the production and selling of goods or services that are prohibited in Islam such as process, produce, market alcoholic drinks, supply non-*halal* meat and providing immoral services like prostitution, pubs and discos as the main business of the companies.

However, in the case of a mixed company where the activities of the companies have both permissible and non-permissible elements, then the SAC will make further consideration based on two additional criteria. If the company meets these two conditions, then the SAC of SCM may certify the company as *Shariah* compliant. First, if the activities of the companies are deemed be exemplary or perceived by the public as exemplary. Second, if the core activities of the company are considered *maslahah* to the Muslim *ummah* and the country and the non-permissible elements present are minimal and involve matters such as *umum balwa* and *'uruf*.

Further, in determining the level of permissibility in the case of mixed activities between permissible and non-permissible, the SCM and SAC employ four levels as benchmarks. These benchmarks are calculated based on the level of contribution of the non-permissible activities to the revenue or profit before tax of a company. If the contribution exceeds these specified benchmarks, the company will be excluded. These benchmarks are determined based on *ijtihad* or reasoning from the source of *Shariah* by qualified *Shariah* scholars and are identified as 5, 10, 20 and 25 percent (Securities Commission Malaysia, 2009b).

Table 6. Comparison of *Shariah* screening norms

	Dow Jones	S&P	MSCI	FTSE	SCM
Qualitative screening					
Alcohol	√	√	√	√	√
Tobacco	√	√	√	√	√
Pork related activities	√	√	√	√	√
Conventional financial services	√	√	√	√	*Based on the tolerance level identified by the SAC of SCM
Weapons and defense	√	√	√	√	
Entertainment	√	√	√	√	
Quantitative screening					
Total outstanding debt	$\frac{Debt}{AMC}33\%$	$\frac{Debt}{MVE} < 33\%$	$Debt/A <$ 33.33%	$\frac{Debt}{TA} < 33\%$	N/A
Receivables and cash	$\frac{AR}{AMC} < 33\%$	$\frac{AR}{MVE} < 49\%$	$\frac{AR}{TA} <$ 33.33%	$\frac{AR}{TA} < 50\%$	N/A
Cash and interest bearing securities	$\frac{Cash + IBS}{AMC}$ < 33%	$\frac{Cash + IBS}{MVE}$ < 33%	$\frac{Cash + IBS}{TA}$ < 33.33%	$\frac{Cash + IBS}{TA} < 33\%$	N/A
Interest income					√*
Revenue share from non-compliant activities*	n/a	$\frac{NPI}{Revenue}$ < 5%	n/a	$\frac{Total\ interest\ \&\ NP}{(Total\ Revenue)}$ <5%	√*

The table presents the screening norms by Dow Jones, S&P, MSCI Barra, FTSE and the SCM. SCM is the Securities Commission of Malaysia. AMC is trailing 24-month average market capitalization. MVE is market value of equity for 36-month average. TA is total assets. AR is account receivables. IBS is interest-bearing securities. NPI is non-permissible income. * indicates other than interest income.

Source: FTSE The Index Company (2009), MSCI Barra (2009), Dow Jones (2009) and Securities Commission Malaysia (2007b).

First, the 5 percent benchmark is applicable for activities that are clearly prohibited under *Shariah* such as interest based companies, gambling, liquor, and pork. The 10 percent benchmark is used for activities that involve the element of *umum balwa,* such as interest income from fixed deposits in conventional banks and tobacco-related activities. In determining the amount of rental receivables from prohibited activities, SAC uses the 20 percent benchmark. For example, rental received from premises, and activities such as liquor, gambling, and other activities as prescribed in the *Shariah* guidelines. Finally, the 25 percent benchmark is applied to companies that are involved in activities that are generally permissible according to *Shariah* and have an element of *maslahah* (public interest) but there are other elements that could affect the *Shariah* status of these activities. These activities include hotel and resort operations, share trading, and stock broking, and, as such, may involve other related activities that are deemed non-permissible according to *Shariah* rules. Besides the screening methodology employed by the SAC of SCM in determining *Shariah* compliant securities, other index providers and fund managers may adopt other screening methodologies. Nevertheless, the qualitative method used, is mostly similar among the *Shariah* Advisors except for its quantitative screening. Hence, the main variation of Islamic screens lies in the quantitative screening methods. Even though different *Shariah* advisory boards employ different ratios, they mainly revolve around three main areas, which are debt, interest, and liquidity screening.

Debt screening means that companies are screened based on their leverage. High leveraged companies are not favored and are screened out from the Islamic portfolio. The level of leverage (or threshold level) is subjective and depends on the risk tolerance of the fund managers on the advice of the *Shariah* advisory board. There are various methods employed in the calculation of debt screening. Some employ the ratio of debt to market capitalization or total assets while others adopt the debt to equity ratio calculation.

As Islam does not allow *riba* in any business transaction, it is imperative to screen out companies that deal with giving out or receiving interest. Since the modern capital market is very complex and total avoidance of the interest element is almost impossible, the threshold for the interest element should be at the miniscule level. Another way of eliminating the interest received by companies is through purification or cleansing activities.

The objective of liquidity screening is to screen out companies that hold excessive liquid assets such as cash and receivables. The reason being that if a company has too many liquid assets it means that the company is not productive and not generating a productive income. The other reason is Islam prohibits earning interest from cash as Islam trades cash only at par value.

Table 6 presents the comparison of *Shariah* screening norms (practices/strategies) by index providers and regulators. In Malaysia, there are two Islamic equity indices, which both employ different screening methodologies. The FTSE Bursa Malaysia EMAS *Shariah* (FBMES) index adopts only the qualitative screening criteria as formulated by the SAC of SCM, while the FTSE Bursa Malaysia *Hijrah Shariah* (FBMHS) index employs both qualitative and quantitative screening strategies as formulated by its *Shariah* advisor, the Yassar Limited. The screening methodology adopted by the latter is similar with screening methodology of the FTSE in the 5th column of Table 6.

Purification Process

In addition to portfolio screening and investment trading strategies, income purification is another unique *Shariah* guideline in relation to *Shariah* compliant investment. Income purification is the process of "deducting from the returns on one's investment those earnings, the source of which is not acceptable from a *Shariah* point of view" (Elgari, 2002, p. 156). In other words, it refers to the process of taking out the portion of income derived or generated from prohibited activities such as interest, *riba* and speculation.

The need to purify income is due to the nature of economic transactions in the modern world where the avoidance of prohibited activities is almost impossible. There are elements of tainted income generated by the underlying companies where *Shariah* funds invest. Even though the *Shariah* guidelines have permitted investment in such companies, it limits the level of their involvement in these prohibited elements to a minimal level. Some jurists are of the opinion that these elements should be eliminated later in the purification process. In fact, income purification arises because of the decision to allow impermissible securities to be included in the portfolio (asset allocation). In practice, some index providers or regulators do not eliminate the total amount of prohibited element but instead use other benchmarks to compensate for the specified amount. For example, Standard & Poor's employs 5 percent of the total income as its purification benchmark. The amount of income is then channeled to charity as a donation or some may treat it as *zakah* payment. There are circumstances where the fund managers decide to reinvest it in acceptable vehicles and may use it as a buffer against future shocks (Kamal, 2008).

While income purification is widely accepted, purifying of capital gains remains debatable among Islamic scholars. Some scholars argue that capital gains purification is unnecessary because the change of the stock price does not really reflect interest, while others suggest that it is safer and more equitable to purify earnings made from selling shares as well (Khatkhatay and Nisar, 2007; Usmani, 2002). Khatkhatay and Nisar (2007) supported the argument that it is unnecessary as the movement in share prices is linked to expectations of future earnings, and that these earnings (and therefore expectations) relate to the main activities of the company, not to the marginal income being generated by interest.

There is an unresolved debate on who should be responsible to perform the process of income purification. Ideally, this process should be part of the value added services provided by the fund managers (de Lorenzo, 2000) where fund managers will take out the specific portion before distributing the income to fund holders. Instead, fund managers may leave the responsibility to individuals by reporting the percentage or ratio of impure income for investors to purify the earnings on their own from the total income in the annual report or fund prospectus. For example, the Accounting and Auditing Organization for Islamic Financial Institutions (AAOIFI) has emphasized that Islamic financial institutions should disclose this information in the financial statement if no purification is made (Accounting and Auditing Organization for Islamic Financial Institutions, 2002). The Islamic Bank of Jordan, for example, has issued a fatwa that the responsibility for income purification, which includes *zakah*, is best left to individual investors (de Lorenzo, 2000). In Malaysia, there is no specific rule relating to this. Although some may argue that this can be regarded as a value added service to Muslims investors (de Lorenzo, 2000), non-Muslim investors may find it costly.

There is another type of income purification, which is *zakat*. While the income purification discussed above is cleansing income from prohibited elements, *zakah* is an obligatory tax levied on income or capital gains that exceeds a certain limit outlined by *Shariah*. In general, 2.5 percent *zakah* is imposed on wealth possessed by Muslims.

CONCLUSION

This chapter provided the institutional background for the Malaysian funds management industry with a special emphasis on the IMF management market. It gave details on the operational aspects of Malaysian IMFs and the regulations relating to the industry. Also included important information concerning the industry and reasons why the issues of performance, screening, and fund flows were fundamentally important to a better understanding of this key financial market segment.

From the review of screening activities in Malaysia, we found that there are screening differences between two main indices in Malaysia. The main *Shariah* index, the FBMES applies mainly on qualitative screening, while the other *Shariah* index, the FBMHS applies both quantitative and qualitative screening activities. The growth of the IMF industry has been tremendous since the 1990s and this is not only happening in Malaysia but also globally. The key operational aspects of IMFs discussed were the presence of *Shariah* Advisory Board (SAB), screening and the income purification process.

REFERENCES

Abderrezak, F. (2008). *The performance of Islamic equity funds: A comparison to conventional Islamic and ethical benchmarks.* Master of International Business and Finance, University of Maastricht, Maastricht, The Netherlands.

Accounting and Auditing Organisation for Islamic Financial Institutions. (2002). Accounting, auditing and governance standards for Islamic financial institutions. Manama.

Anwar, Z. (2009). *Innovating for the future: Challenges for Islamic capital markets.* Retrieved 30 September, 2009, from http://www.sc.com.my.

Australian Trade Commission. (2010). *Islamic finance*, Retrieved 31 January, 2011, from http://www.austrade.gov.au.

Bank Negara Malaysia. (2011*). Financial stability and payment systems reports from 2009 to 2011*, Retrieved 30 June, 2012, from www.bnm.gov.my.

de Lorenzo, Y. T. (2000). *Shari'ah supervision of Islamic mutual funds.* Paper presented at the 4th Annual Harvard Forum on Islamic Finance.

Derigs, U. and Marzban, S. (2008). Review and analysis of currrent *Shariah* compliant equity screening practices. *International Journal of Islamic and Middle Eastern Finance and Management, 1*(4), 285–303.

Dow Jones. (2009). Dow Jones Islamic market indexes. *Quarterly Newsletter* Retrieved 3 March, 2010, from http://www.djindexes.com.

El Qorchi, M. (2005). Islamic finance gears up. *Finance and Development, 42,* 46-50.

Elfakhani, S. M. and Hassan, M. K. (2005). *Performance of Islamic mutual funds.* Paper presented at the 12th Economic Research Forum Conference Cairo, Egypt.

Elgari, M. A. (2002). Islamic equity Investment. In S. Archer & R. A. Abdel Karim (Eds.), *Islamic finance: Innovation and growth.* London: Euromoney Books and AAOIFI.

Ernst & Young. (2009). *The Islamic funds & investments report: Surviving and adapting in a downturn* (Vol. 3rd Edition). Dubai: Middle East Global Advisors.

Eurekahedge. (2008). *Hedge fund monthly: Key trends in Islamic funds 2008.* Retrieved from http://www.eurekahedge.com on 30 September 2009.

Federation of Malaysian Unit Trust Managers. (2007). *FMUTM annual report 2007*, Retrieved 31 January, 2010, from http://www.fimm.com.my.

Federation of Malaysian Unit Trust Managers. (2008). *FMUTM annual report 2008,* Retrieved 31 January, 2010, from http://www.fimm.com.my.

FTSE The Index Company. (2009*). FTSE Bursa Malaysia Hijrah Shariah Index*, Retrieved 31 January, 2009, from http://www.ftse.com.

Gait, A. and Worthington, A. C. (2008). An empirical survey of individual consumer, business firm and financial institution attitudes towards Islamic methods of finance. *International Journal of Social Economics, 35*(11), 783-808.

Hoepner, A. G. F., Rammal, H. G. and Rezec, M. (2011). Islamic mutual funds' financial performance and international investment style: Evidence from 20 countries. *The European Journal of Finance, 17*(9-10), 829-850.

International Financial Services London. (2010). *Islamic finance 2010.* Retrieved from http://www.ifsl.org.uk on 17 April 2010.

Kadir, A. A. (2000). *The evolution of an advanced fund management industry in the Asean region*. Paper presented at the On the Occassion of 5th Asia Oceania Regional Dinner.

Kamal, R. M. (2008). Are Islamic indices the way to go? *Islamic Finance Asia*. Retrieved from http://www.islamicfinanceasia.com on 31 January 2011.

Khatkhatay, M. H. and Nisar, S. (2007). *Shariah* compliant equity investments: An assessment of current screening norms. *Islamic Economic Studies, 15*(1), 47-76.

Khorana, A., Servaes, H. and Tufano, P. (2005). Explaining the size of the mutual fund industry around the world. *Journal of Financial Economics, 78*(2005), 145-185.

Lee, J. and Menon, A. (2010). *Islamic finance: The year that was and the outlook for 2010,* Retrieved 20 April 2010, from http://rd.kpmg.co.uk.

Lipper. (2005). *Global themes in the mutual fund industry 2004* (Single Country Edition ed.): Lipper Research Study.

Malaysia International Islamic Financial Centre. (2009). *About MIFC*, Retrieved 30 September 2009, from http://www.mifc.com.

Mohd, S. S. (2007). *Islamic unit trust. Paper presented at the The 2nd International Islamic Financial Markets Conference,* Bahrain.

MSCI Barra. (2009). *MSCI Islamic index series methodology,* 2009 Retrieved 31 January 2010, from http://uat.mscibarra.com.

Nainggolan, Y. (2011). *Taking a leap of faith: are investors left short changed.* Degree of Doctor of Philosophy, Queensland University of Technology, Brisbane, Australia.

Nathie, M. (2009). *Islamic equity investments: Determinants of investment behaviour of Malaysian Islamic equity investors under conditions of competing alternatives.* Degree of Doctor Philosophy, Griffith University, Brisbane, Australia.

Permodalan Nasional Berhad. (2001). *The Malaysian unit trust industry* (First ed.): Permodalan Nasioanal Berhad.

Rahman, A. A., Yahya, M. A. and Nasir, M. H. M. (2010). Islamic norms for stock screening: A comparison between the Kuala Lumpur Stock Exchange Islamic index and the Dow Jones Islamic Market index. *International Journal of Islamic and Middle Eastern Finance and Management, 3*(3), 228-240.

Securities Commission Malaysia. (2001). *Capital market masterplan Retrieved 31 January, 2010*, from http://www.sc.com.my.

Securities Commission Malaysia. (2007a). *Guidelines on Islamic fund management,* Retrieved 31 January, 2010, from http://www.sc.com.my.

Securities Commission Malaysia. (2007b). *Resolutions of the Securities Commission Shariah Advisory Council Second.* Retrieved 31 January, 2010, from http://www.sc.com.my.

Securities Commission Malaysia. (2009). Islamic fund management: The next phase. *Islamic Finance Asia.* Retrieved from http://www.islamicfinanceasia.com on 25 May 2010.

Securities Commission Malaysia. (2011). *Capital market masterplan 2*, Retrieved 30 September 2012, from http://www.sc.com.my.

Securities Commission Malaysia. (2012). *Securities Commission annual reports from 1998 to 2011,* Retrieved 31 June, 2012, from http://www.sc.com.my.

Singh, R. A. and Yusof, Z. A. (2002). *Development of the capital market in Malaysia.* Paper presented at the AT10 Research Conference.

Taib, F. M. and Isa, M. (2007). Malaysian unit trust aggregate performance. *Managerial Finance, 33*(2), 102-121.

Usmani, M. T. (2002). *An introduction to Islamic finance*: Kluwer Law International.

In: Contemporary Issues in Islamic Finance
Editor: Andrew C. Worthington
ISBN: 978-1-62948-905-6

Chapter 5

CREDIT RISK IN ISLAMIC FINANCIAL PRODUCTS

Md. Nurul Kabir* and Andrew C. Worthington
Griffith University, Australia

ABSTRACT

Measuring credit risk is one of the most important aspects of bank management. Whether Islamic banks have higher or lower credit risk than conventional banks depends on two important elements. First, the nature of credit risk in Islamic financial products. Second, the suitability of credit risk measurement techniques for Islamic banks. We review and critically evaluate the available literature relating to the credit risk of Islamic banks. This enables practitioners and regulators alike to gain a comprehensive awareness of the nature of credit risk in Islamic banking products from several different perspectives. We also identify the measurement techniques currently available for Islamic banks along with the pros and cons of each of the measurement techniques.

1. INTRODUCTION

Islamic finance is one of the fastest growing segments in the global financial market. Although the principles and concepts of Islamic banking are known throughout history since the founding of Islam, the application and practice of Islamic banking has only developed relatively recently. Total Islamic assets reached more than $1.3 trillion in 2011 and the number of Islamic financial institutions also has reached to more than 700 by the end 2011(The banker, 2011). The recent global financial crisis has also encouraged some to consider alternatives to the conventional financial system and Islamic financial systems have attracted at least some of this attention. To have a sustainable growth rate of Islamic banking in the future, it is vital to measure the risk properly for the bankers as well as regulators.

Of the various types of risk, credit risk is the largest risk to which banks are exposed (Bessis, 2011; Caouette, Altman, & Narayanan, 1998). Gestel and Baesens (2008) and

* Corresponding author: Department of Accounting, Finance and Economics, Griffith University, Nathan QLD 4111, Australia. Email. mdnurul.kabir@griffithuni.edu.au.

Colquitt (2007) highlighted some of the important reasons for credit risk. These are: 1) the borrower is financially distressed or in a position of bankruptcy, therefore unable to pay interest and repay the principal on direct or contingent loans; 2) a misunderstanding between the bank and borrower because of flaws in information systems and 3) a deterioration in the credit quality of the borrower. When borrowers fail to honor their commitment to the bank, banks classify this as a nonperforming loan and this and the accumulation of other nonperforming loans can lead the bank to the verge of bankruptcy (Greuning & Brajovic, 2003). Every financial product in the banking sector bears some degree of credit risk.

Measuring credit risk is one of the important parts of credit risk management in the banking system. Since, Islamic banks are different in nature in operating their business than traditional interest based banking, researcher debate on the issue that level of credit risk faced by both conventional banks and Islamic banks is also different. Whether Islamic banks have higher or lower credit risk than conventional banks depends mostly on two important elements. Firstly, one should understand the nature of credit risk in Islamic financial product, second the suitability of credit risk measurement for Islamic banks. This chapter discusses these two main important issues. Although some research is available discussing the nature of credit risk in Islamic banking, to the best knowledge of the author, there is no research discussing the different credit risk measurement techniques possible in Islamic banks. This research fills this gap by critically evaluating the available literatures related to Islamic banking.

The structure of this chapter is as follows. Section 1 briefly introduces the importance of credit risk and the problem of measuring credit risk in Islamic banks. Section 2 critically assesses the credit risk in Islamic financial products and to the extent it differs from that of conventional banks. Section 3 introduces the different risk measurement techniques available for Islamic banks with necessary adjustment to be made before applying these techniques to Islamic banks. Section 4 concludes the chapter, highlighting especially its contribution to the literature.

2. Credit Risk in Islamic Bank Products

Based on the principles described, a number of popular financial products are employed by Islamic banks. One of the aims of this chapter is to describe some of the important products found in Islamic banks and at the same time trace the credit risk associated with each product for a better understanding of credit risk in Islamic banking. It is worth noting that the Islamic banking products described here generally display the same characteristics throughout the global Islamic banking sector.

Mudarabah (Profit Sharing)

Mudarabah is one of the more popular products provided by Islamic banks. This is a type of partnership business where both parties make a contract and fix their terms and conditions. The partnership can be between a depositor (*rabb al-mal*) and a borrower (*Mudarib*) or between a lender (the bank) and a borrower. In this partnership agreement, the depositor or bank supplies the total capital required by the borrower (investor) while the borrower applies skill, knowledge and entrepreneurial ability to the task for which the funds are provided. Hence, though all of the assets purchased by the *Mudarib* are owned by the bank, even if the asset value increases in a subsequent time, the *Mudarib* is not entitled to any additional profit (Usmani, 2002). If the business incurs a loss on some transaction or makes a profit on some other transaction, then the profit will offset first the loss and the remaining profit will be distributed according to some pre-agreed ration if any profit remains. The bank can propose the profit distribution ratio based on the riskiness of project that the borrower undertakes or the ability of the bank to influence the business decisions taken by the *Mudarib*. It is noteworthy that any financial losses are borne solely by the bank, though the borrower of courses bears the opportunity cost of the venture's labor, time and skill (Ayub, 2008; Iqbal, 2002; Vogel & Hayes, 1998). The partnership contract can be terminated at any time if both parties agree.

A distinctive feature of a *Mudarabah* contract is that the bank can neither participate nor influence the decision making process in the *Mudarib*'s business nor can monitor the business activities efficiently. This creates a difficulty for Islamic banks in assessing the actual credit risk of the *Mudarib* (Hasan, 2002; Iqbal & Mirakhor, 2011). This makes this financial product riskier than many other Islamic banking products. For instance, there is a probability of a higher asymmetric information problem between the bank and the *Mudarib* in a *Mudarabah* contract. The *Mudarib* may choose a high risky project for a higher expected return, which is an adverse selection problem, or misuse the funds for purposes other than those discussed in the contract. As the bank does not have any decision making power, in principle it is likely that *Mudarib* may use any of these opportunities to transfer wealth which indeed increase the credit risk for the banks (Boumediene, 2010). Haron and Hock (2007) argued that Islamic bank are thus exposed to total capital impairment risk in the event of the default of the *Mudarib* or if the project incurs losses.

Musharakah (Profit and Loss Sharing)

Musharakah is a word of Arabic origin which literally means sharing. This is a form of partnership, but slightly different from *Mudarabah*. From the business point of view, it is a kind of joint venture partnership contract where both the lender and borrower share capital and profit and loss according to some ratio. According to many scholars, it is an ideal alternative for interest-based financing with far reaching effects on both production and distribution (Usmani, 2002). As Islam prohibits interest, Islamic finance scholars often recommend use of this instrument as an alternative. It is not allowed to fix a lump sum amount for any of the partners, or any rate of profit tied up with his capital. Profit would be distributed after the actual profit earned. However, a management fee can be paid to the manager with the permission of both partners. Another form of *Musharakah* is diminishing *Musharakah* in which one of the partners promises to progressively purchase the equity share of the other partner until the title to the equity is completely transferred to the buying partner (Ahmed & Mohamed, 2011).

Similar to *Mudarbaha, Musharakah* also bears a relatively higher credit risk which is why it is the least used among all Islamic bank products (Khan & Ahmed, 2001). Ahmed and Mohamed (2011) argued that in a *Musharakah* contract, the Islamic bank is principally exposed to two types of credit risk: capital impairment risk and credit risk with regard to the customer's payment capacity. This "capital impairment risk" is where the Islamic banks only loses that capital provided at the beginning of the contract (Haron & Hock, 2007). In addition to this, if any of the withdrawing parties owe money to the bank, bank is required to pay which is another form of credit risk in the case of *Musharakah*. However, Boumediene (2010) argued that, there is no credit risk in a *Musharakah* contract as the Islamic bank does not provide any credit to the customer, rather it should be treated as capital impairment risk as the maximum the bank is the capital provided but only in the event of liquidation. There is another type of credit risk associated with diminishing *Musharakh* contracts which is the inability and unwillingness of the partner to purchase the agreed share of an Islamic bank (Ahmed & Mohamed, 2011; Akkizidis & Khandelwal, 2008).

Murabahah (Sale on Goods with Markup)

Of all Islamic financial products, *Murabahah* is the most popular product that Islamic banks frequently use in their business operations. In an Islamic bank, 70–80% transactions are in the form of *Murabaha* contract and as a mode of finance *Murabaha* is the first choice of many Islamic bankers (Iqbal & Mirakhor, 2011). Islamic banks follow a number of steps in order to complete a *Murabaha* transaction. The contract typically involves the purchase of an asset/commodity at the request of a customer. This is a particular sale where the bank or the seller has to mention clearly the total cost needed for purchasing the designated product. The bank then adds a markup to the cost and is required to show the total cost statement to the buyer. In this contract, the bank can determine the profit margin before buying the product and the buyer of the product has to agree with this rate. The bank then buys the product and must possess the product before they "sell" it to the buyer. This is one of the most important conditions for Islamic banks to comply with *Shariah*. It will not be accepted as a *Murabaha* contract if banks only finance the purchase of the product and then add a markup. To make it a valid sale, the bank has to buy the product first, and then sell the product to the customer after adding the margin (Ayub, 2008; Usmani, 2002). *Murabaha* contracts can be both binding and nonbinding. Haron and Hock (2007) argued that Islamic banks are exposed to credit risk if the customer fails to honor the payment obligation (loss of receivables). On the other hand, in nonbinding *Murabaha*, where the customer has the right to refuse the delivery of the product purchased by the bank in a later time because of, say, subsequent price variation, then the Islamic bank is exposed to both high credit risk and high market risk (Ahmed & Mohamed, 2011; Iqbal & Mirakhor, 2011). Boumediene (2010) also mentioned these two sources of credit risk in *Murabaha* products, emphasizing the consequences of default risk in binding *Murabaha* contract. He also mentions the rulings according to *Shariah* and Accounting and Auditing Organization for Islamic Finance Institutions (AAOIFI) to undertake necessary action to reduce credit risk on the *Murabaha* contract.

Ijarah (Leasing)

Another very popular financial product of Islamic finance is *Ijarah* or leasing. This is similar to the concept of financial leasing commonly used in conventional (non-Islamic) leasing companies and banks. Like other Islamic financial contracts and products, the lease is not originally a mode of financing. More broadly, leasing is a contract whereby the owner transfers an asset to another person for an agreed period at an agreed consideration (Usmani, 2002). The subject matter asset can be divided into two types: property, including assets like buildings, machines, etc. and labor, such as a person hired by a company for a particular period at an agreed wage. An important distinction between financial leases in conventional banks and leases in Islamic bank is that the latter hold proprietorship over the object of the lease. In addition, there is no automatic transfer of proprietorship at the end of the contract. Under this contract, the lesser (bank) provides the asset on a rental basis to the lessee (creditor). The lessee then pays the rent for a specific period based on the agreement. The lessee will be liable for any damages to the asset due to negligence, but will not be liable for losses caused by factors beyond the lessee's control, for example, damage caused by a natural disaster (Ayub, 2008). The determination of rental must be done before the lease commences with the mutual consent of the bank (the lessor) and the customer (the lessee) for the whole period, but can be reviewed under mutual agreement during the lease period. In addition to this, different rents can be set up for different phases throughout the lease at the beginning of the lease period.

While this financial product also includes credit risk, it is typically lower than that for Islamic financial products. Credit risk arises here with default on the payment of rent when due. Default can be for specific instances or complete default (Ahmed & Mohamed, 2011; Boumediene, 2010; Haron & Hock, 2007). Default can also be due to variable lease rents that may distress the customer's ability to pay (loss of rental receivables). In addition to this, Boumediene (2010) mention another source of credit risk in binding *Ijarah* where the lessee may change his mind, but may then cancel the lease. In this case, bank (the lessor) will find itself with an asset purchased with expectation of no return.

Salam (Forward Sale)

Salam is a contract of sale used in Islamic banks where the delivery of goods is deferred to some future date, but the payment is at the time of making the contract. In order to make a valid sale according to Islamic *Shariah*, three conditions must be fulfilled. First, the commodity that is to be sold must exist, second, the seller must have ownership of the good before selling it to someone else, and finally, the seller must possess the commodity, either physically or constructively. However, there are some exceptions applicable for some Islamic financial products, one of which is *Salam*, under the condition of the fulfillment of some criteria at the time of making the contract.

This mode of financing is specially designed for farmers or small businessmen who do not have enough money at some initial point for running a business or conducting farming. That is why the farmer or entrepreneur has a contract with the bank specifying product details for delivery after a specific period of time and in a specific location. Banks pay the price for the products in advance to the seller. This process is similar to a conventional forward sale transaction. What distinguish this from a traditional forward contract to *Salam* are the *Shariah* rulings and procedures involved. Details of these rules and regulations are described in Ayub (2008) and Usmani (2002).

Similar to other sales-based contract like *Murabaha*, Islamic banks are exposed to credit risk in this mode of financing in a number of ways. The first source of credit risk is default in the delivery of the product or commodity or a delay in the delivery of the product or commodity (Boumediene, 2010; Haron & Hock, 2007). The seller may then face unintentional difficulty in delivering products on time or may completely default in delivering the products because of some unavoidable circumstances. In this case, the Islamic bank loses its invested capital. However, if this happens intentionally, the Islamic banks may charge a penalty to the seller. In addition to this, misspecification of the product or variation in the quality as specified in the contract is also another source of credit risk, as Islamic banks may not sell these products at a higher price (Ahmed & Mohamed, 2011). Decreasing the price of the products at the time of delivery would then result a net loss of the invested capital for the Islamic banks. For the most part, measuring the credit risk for *Salam* is similar to *Murbaha* contracts as both of these contracts are sales based.

Istisna (Order to Manufacture)

This is another sale-based mode of financing used by Islamic banks. *Istisna* means "order to manufacture". In this mode of contract, one party orders the manufacturer to produce goods according to some specification not available in the market. This is second type of sales-based contract available in the Islamic finance service. In this contract, banks behave like a manufacturer. A customer can order to manufacture the goods and can specify the types materials should be used during manufacturing. The manufacturer arranges the materials according to the buyer's specification and bears the sole responsibility to arrange the necessary materials. Unlike the *Salam* contract, the price in this case is not necessary for full advance payment and the time of delivery is not fixed. Islamic banks can use this mode of financing to manufacture aircraft, ships, or other manufacturing goods. The contract can be terminated unilaterally at any time before the manufacturer commences work; once the manufacturer starts producing the goods, it can be terminated with mutual consent. Similar to *Salam*, Islamic banks have a parallel in the *Istisna* contract. If an Islamic bank receives an order to manufacture some goods using an *Istisna* contract, Islamic banks can also order another manufacturer to produce the same goods with same specifications. There are some basic differences between *Istisna* and *Salam*, *Istisna* and *Ijarah*. Usmani (2002) and Ayub (2008) reported the details about the differences among these three financial products.

Credit risk emerges in *Istisna* in two important ways. First, it can be a failure to deliver the products, and second, if the purchaser in a parallel *Istisna* defaults on paying the due installments or the price in full. If Islamic banks take an order to manufacture the goods from a client, and the client subsequently defaults on paying for the ordered goods, the Islamic bank loses its invested capital. Ahmed and Mohamed (2011) mentioned that in non-course *Istisna* where repayment capability of the borrower mostly depends on the revenue generated by the asset, Islamic banks face revenue risk arising from the asset ability to generate the income. Completion risk may also occur in parallel *Istisna* contract, when the advance payment has been made by Islamic banks to sub-contractor and if the sub-contractor cannot finish the work on time (Haron & Hock, 2007). In relation to this, Khan and Ahmed (2001) presented the results of a comparative risk perception of the modes of financing by Islamic bank credit managers.

Table 1. Perceptions of credit risk in Islamic banking products

Product	Credit risk perception
Murabahah	2.47 (17)
Ijarah	2.64 (14)
Istisna	3.13 (8)
Salam	3.20 (5)
Mudarabah	3.38 (13)
Musharakah	3.71 (14)

Notes: Figures in parenthesis are the number of respondents. The rank has a scale of 1 to 5, with 1 indicating 'Not serious' and 5 'critically serious'.

This table details the results of a survey of the risk perceptions of risk managers for the different finds of finance used in Islamic banks. As expected, credit risk appears to be least in *Murabaha* (sale-based financing) and most in *Musharakah* (3.71). This is consistent with the argument that sales-based methods of Islamic bank finance having lower levels of credit risk than profit–loss sharing methods. As pointed out, *Musharakah* and *Mudarabah* are two Islamic financial products assumed to have high credit risk because the asymmetric information problem between the partner (borrower) and bank is high. Because of their high credit risk, most Islamic banks use these two financial products much less than sales-based financing methods. After the *Murabaha* product, which is the most frequently used product in Islamic banks, the second least credit risky product is *Ijarah* as it gives a certain amount of income periodically. *Istisna* and *Salam* also have some degree of credit risk as described earlier.

3. Credit Risk Measurement in Islamic Banks

A number of credit risk measurement techniques have developed in the last two decades. Based on the literature, credit risk measurement can be divided into three main categories: accounting based, market based credit risk measurement and ratings by external agencies. Accounting based credit risk measurement includes but is not limited to Altman's Z-score, credit risk Z-score, Non-performing loan analysis etc. External rating agencies like Standard and Poor's or Moody's provide ratings for financial companies that are relative ratings and many other local rating agencies do the same thing where the international rating agencies are absent. The more recent and more sophisticated credit risk measurement methods are based on market based indicators like Merton's probability of default, Value at Risk (VaR), credit metrics etc. This section reviews the three most common techniques used by the researchers to measure the credit risk in the banking sector. Two are based on accounting information, the financial stability Z-score and nonperforming loans, and one is a market-based indicator in the form of Merton's distance to default model.

Accounting-Based Measurement Techniques: Financial Stability Z-Score

One of the most commonly used techniques to measure the banks' soundness or stability based on accounting data is Z-score. Researchers have used Z-score extensively to measure the financial stability of the banks because it incorporates banks` buffers, both the profit and capital and standard deviation of profit to measure the riskiness of the banks based the grounded theory (Beck, Demirgüç-Kunt, & Merrouche, 2010; Boyd & Runkle, 1993; Čihák, 2007; Čihák & Hesse, 2010; McAllister & McManus, 1993). In other words, it measures how many standard deviations of profit the bank is from exhausting its capital base. The calculation of the Z-score is as follows: Z-score = (ROA + E/A) / S.D of ROA, where ROA = return on assets measured by net profit divided by total assets, E/A = total equity divided by total assets, and SD of ROA = standard deviation of ROA over the three-year time period. The three-year time window for standard deviation of ROA has been considered to allow for enough variation in the Z-score, which reduces the chances that Z-score is driven, by variation in the levels of capital and profitability.

This measure has also been used to measure the credit risk for Islamic banks by several researchers. For example, Cihak and Hesse (2008) investigated the financial stability using Z-scores across Islamic banks and conventional banks for 20 OECD countries from 1994 to 2004. In other research, Gamaginta and Rokhim (2011) also used the Z-score to measure the financial stability across Islamic and conventional banks in the Indonesian banking sector. Similarly, Abedifar, Molyneux, and Tarazi (2013) measured the credit risk of both Islamic and conventional banks using Z-score for 22 OECD countries.

The variables used to calculate credit risk are the ROA and the equity to total asset ratio. The calculation of Z-score should be similar in the theoretical point of view for both Islamic and conventional banks. However, Čihák and Hesse (2010) pointed a possible criticism of using Z-score to measure the insolvency risk for Islamic banks. According to them, the liabilities side of Islamic banks consists of investment accounts where the Islamic banks have the ability to pass their losses to the borrowers. This might inflate the financial stability of Islamic banks. Therefore, researchers should be cautious about interpreting high and low Z-scores across and between conventional and Islamic banks.

Accounting-Based Measurement Techniques: Nonperforming Loans/Finance Ratio

Another important measure of credit risk in the banking sector is the nonperforming loan (finance) ratio (NPL). Researchers use the NPL ratio for both conventional banks and Islamic banks to measure credit risk in banking systems. For example, Ahmad and Ariff (2007), Berger and DeYoung (1997), Louzis, Vouldis, and Metaxas (2011) used NPL in order to measure the credit risk of the banking sector of a particular economy. Here the NPL ratio is nonperforming loans as measured by total amount of impaired loans to the net amount of loans, where nonperforming loans are generally loans overdue for more than three months. A bank with a high NPL ratio is typically identified as a problem bank by monetary authorities.

Researchers that used NPL ratio to measure the credit risk for Islamic banks are comparatively fewer than those measured credit risk of conventional banks. Abedifar et al. (2013) used the NPL ratio and loan loss reserve ratio to measure the credit risk for both Islamic and Conventional banks. Similarly, Hayati and Ahmad (2004) also used Non performing finance (NPF) as a proxy of credit risk to investigate the determinants of credit risk of Islamic banks in Malaysia.

One of the advantages of using NPL as a measurement of credit risk is that it is a direct measurement of a bank's solvency and it is difficult to manipulate by the management. On the other hand, the criteria to classify the loan as non-performing vary slightly from country to country which makes it difficult to have a comparison between conventional and Islamic banks across the different countries of the world. Moreover, Abedifar et al. (2013) mentioned that NPL may not truly reflect the credit risk of the banks in the case where a major portion of loan repayment is yet to start. This might lower the credit risk for the banks temporarily.

Both researchers and practitioners need to have a careful investigation before using NPL/NPF as a proxy of credit risk. While conventional banking has a standard definition of loan, Islamic banks do not have the similar definition of financing among all the Islamic banks because of *Shariah* and product complexity. Islamic banks have varieties of financial products and it is difficult to classify the financing appropriately under the same definition.

Market-Based Credit Risk Measurement: Distance to Default

There are a number of credit risk measurement techniques available for measuring a bank`s default risk, based on the market information such as distance to default, bond prices and credit default swaps (Čihák, 2007). In practice, market based indicators are more sophisticated and more accurate than accounting based indicators and more useful in predicting banking failures.

The most popular market based measurement is KMV credit risk model. Moody's KMV Corporation (1995) developed an approach to estimate the default probability of a particular firm at any given point in time based on Merton's approach. This model states that a bank defaults when the market value of assets falls below the book value of liabilities. In order to calculate the probability of default, this model subtracts the face value of firm's debt from an estimated market value of the firm and then the difference is divided by the estimated volatility of the firm. This results in a Z-score often referred to as the distance to default (DD). In other worlds, the DD is defined by the number of standard deviations of market value of firms away from the default point (Harada, Ito, & Takahashi, 2010).

Merton (1974) model assumes that the equity of a firm is treated as a call option on the firm's assets, since the equity holders are the residual claimants on the firm's assets after all the liabilities have been met. In this model, the strike price of the call option is the book value of the firm's liabilities. If the value of the firm's asset is lower than the strike price, the value of equity becomes zero. The Merton model has two particularly important assumptions. First, the total market value of the firm's underlying assets follows a geometric Brownian motion,

$$dV_A = \mu V_A dt + \sigma_A V_A dW \quad (1)$$

where, V_A is the firm's assets value, μ is the expected instantaneous periodic rate of return on assets, σ_A is the instantaneous standard deviation of the rate of return on assets, or asset volatility and dW is a standard Weiner process.

The second assumption in this model is that the firm has issued one discount bond maturing in T periods. Under this assumption, the equity of the firm is a call option on the underlying value of the firm's asset with a strike price, denoted by X_t, equal to the face value of the firm's debt and a time-to-maturity of T. Based on the above information, we can calculate

$$DD_t = \frac{\ln\left(\frac{V_{A,t}}{X_t}\right)+\left(\mu-\frac{1}{2}\sigma_A^2\right)T}{\sigma_A\sqrt{T}} \quad (2)$$

$$PD= N(-DD) \quad (3)$$

where DD = distance to default, PD = probability of default, V_A= value of assets, σ_A = volatility of assets, X_t = total liabilities, μ = expected return on assets, T= time period, and N = cumulative probability distribution.

Researchers used Merton (1974) credit risk model extensively to measure the credit risk for conventional banks; however, Boumediene (2010) is the only research which investigated the credit risk for both Islamic and conventional banks using market based information such as Merton's default risk model. He measured the credit risk for nine Islamic and nine conventional banks for five years.

There are several advantages of using market prices as a base of predicting bank failure as articulated by the academic. The foremost one is availability of equity prices in high frequency. Most of the banks are listed on the stock exchange and therefore their daily prices can be extracted easily. In addition, this indicator uses equity prices, which incorporates the expectation of investor or investors' forward looking assessments. Moreover, all the relevant data are publicly available and there is no issue of confidentiality, which makes the measurement more transparent and publicly verified.

On the other hand, one of the important variables considered in this model is total liabilities. Defining this variable in the case of Islamic banks again is fairly complex. The balance sheet of Islamic banks, as stated earlier, is different to the conventional banks as some Islamic banks are engaged in profit-loss sharing (PLS) arrangements. Boumediene (2010) identified the several problems in defining and using total liabilities in Islamic banks. For example, liabilities managed through PLS arrangement are excluded from liabilities. This PLS arrangement includes investment and savings accounts of Islamic banks. Lack of standard definition of liabilities in Islamic banks, compared to conventional banks creates the complexity in comparing credit risk between conventional banks and Islamic banks based on market information. Since total liabilities is one of the most significant variables in credit risk model, identical definition of total liabilities needs to be developed in order to have a suitable comparison. Each of these three credit risk measurement techniques discussed in this paper have pros and cons in application to Islamic banks. Both researchers and practitioners need to make careful adjustments before applying this model in measuring credit risk for Islamic banks. This adjustment is necessary, since standard definition of all the variables used in these model is rarely available and more importantly it may vary from country to country.

CONCLUSION

This chapter discusses mainly the credit risk in Islamic financial products and the risk measurement techniques applicable for Islamic banks. As the operational nature of Islamic banks substantially differs from that in conventional banking, the sources of credit risk and the nature of credit risk in Islamic banking also differ. This research contributes to the literatures in two main ways. First, we gather the available literature relating to credit risk in Islamic banks and critically evaluate these from a *Shariah* point of view. From this review, a number of interested parties can obtain comprehensive information about the nature of credit risk in Islamic banking products from several different perspectives. Second, we identify the risk measurement techniques available to Islamic banks along with their pros and cons. This is useful for both researchers as well as practitioners when considering the impact of *Shariah* on credit risk. We conclude that to obtain an appropriate comparison when measuring credit risk across Islamic and conventional banks, it is necessary to have common definitions of each of the variables considered in the various models.

REFERENCES

Abedifar, P., Molyneux, P., & Tarazi, A. (2013). Risk in Islamic Banking. *Review of Finance*. doi: 10.1093/rof/rfs041. 17(6).

Ahmad, N. H., & Ariff, M. (2007). Multi-country study of bank credit risk determinants. *International Journal of Banking and Finance, 5*(1), 6.

Ahmed, E. T., & Mohamed, A. (2011). *Islamic Banking: How to Manage Risk and Improve Profitability*. New Jersey: Wiley & Sons.

Akkizidis, I. S., & Khandelwal, S. K. (2008). *Financial risk management for Islamic banking and finance*: Palgrave Macmillan.

Ayub, M. (2008). *Understanding Islamic Finance* (Vol. 458). West Sussex: Wiley.

Beck, T., Demirgüç-Kunt, A., & Merrouche, O. (2010). Islamic vs. conventional banking: business model, efficiency and stability. *World Bank Policy Research Working Paper Series.5446.*

Berger, A. N., & DeYoung, R. (1997). Problem loans and cost efficiency in commercial banks. *Journal of Banking & Finance, 21*(6), 849-870.

Bessis, J. (2011). *Risk management in banking*. West Sussex: Wiley.

Boumediene, A. (2010). Is Credit Risk Really Higher in Islamic Banks? *Available at SSRN 1689885.*

Boyd, J. H., & Runkle, D. E. (1993). Size and performance of banking firms: Testing the predictions of theory. *Journal of Monetary Economics, 31*(1), 47-67.

Caouette, J. B., Altman, E. I., & Narayanan, P. (1998). *Managing credit risk: the next great financial challenge* (Vol. 2). West Sussex: Wiley.

Čihák, M. (2007). Systemic Loss: A measure of financial stability. *Czech Journal of Economics and Finance, 57*(1-2), 5-26.

Cihak, M., & Hesse, H. (2008). Islamic banks and financial stability: An empirical analysis. *IMF Working Papers*, 1-29.

Čihák, M., & Hesse, H. (2010). Islamic banks and financial stability: An empirical analysis. *Journal of Financial Services Research, 38*(2), 95-113.

Colquitt, J. E. (2007). *Credit risk management*: McGraw-Hill Professional.

Gamaginta, & Rokhim, R. (2011). *The Stability Comparison between Islamic Banks and Conventional Banks: Evidence in Indonesia*. Paper presented at the 8th International Conference on Islamic Economics and Finance, Doha, Qatar.

Gestel, V., & Baesens, B. (2008). *Credit Risk Management: Basic Concepts: Financial Risk Components, Rating Analysis, Models, Economic and Regulatory Capital:* OUP Oxford.

Greuning, H., & Brajovic, B. S. (2003). *Analyzing and Managing Banking Risk*. Washington: World Bank.

Harada, K., Ito, T., & Takahashi, S. (2010). Is the distance to default a good measure in predicting bank failures? *case studies: National Bureau of Economic Research.*

Haron, A., & Hock, J. L. H. (2007). Inherent risk: Credit and market risks. *Islamic finance: The regulatory challenge, 2*. West Sussex: Wiley.

Hasan, Z. (2002). Mudarabah as a Mode of Finance in Islamic Banking: Theory, Practices and Problems. *Middle East Business and Economic Review*, *14*(2), 41–53.

Hayati, A. N., & Ahmad, S. N. (2004). Key factors influencing credit risk of Islamic bank: A Malaysian case. *The Journal of Muamalat and Islamic Finance Research, 1*(1), 68-80.

Iqbal, M. (2002). *Islamic banking and finance: new perspectives on profit sharing and risk.* Cheltenham: Edward Elgar Publishing.

Iqbal, & Mirakhor, A. (2011). *An introduction to Islamic finance: theory and practice* (Vol. 687). Singapore: Wiley.

Khan, T., & Ahmed, H. (2001). *Risk management: an analysis of issues in Islamic financial industry*: Islamic Development Bank, Islamic Research and Training Institute.

Louzis, D. P., Vouldis, A. T., & Metaxas, V. L. (2011). Macroeconomic and bank-specific determinants of non-performing loans in Greece: a comparative study of mortgage, business and consumer loan portfolios. *Journal of Banking & Finance*. 36(4), 1012-1027.

McAllister, P. H., & McManus, D. (1993). Resolving the scale efficiency puzzle in banking. *Journal of Banking & Finance, 17*(2), 389-405.

Merton, R. C. (1974). On the pricing of corporate debt: The risk structure of interest rates*. *The Journal of Finance, 29*(2), 449-470.

Usmani, M. T. (2002). *An introduction to Islamic finance* (Vol. 20). CN The Hague: Kluwer Law International.

Vogel, F. E., & Hayes, S. L. (1998). *Islamic law and finance: religion, risk, and return.* CN The Hague: Kluwer Law International.

In: Contemporary Issues in Islamic Finance
Editor: Andrew C. Worthington

ISBN: 978-1-62948-905-6

Chapter 6

BUSINESS FIRM ATTITUDES TOWARD ISLAMIC METHODS OF FINANCE

Alsadek Gait and Andrew C. Worthington*
Griffith University, Nathan, QLD, Australia

ABSTRACT

The analysis in this chapter establishes that while commercial Islamic finance is not yet formally practiced in Libya, most businesses have at least some knowledge about Islamic methods of finance. We can partly attribute this awareness to both knowledge of developments in other Muslim countries and to the fact that many commercial products and services offered by Islamic financial institutions bear close relation to informal financing and business arrangements already practiced among Muslims.

These include *Musharakah* (full partnerships) and *Quard Hassan* (interest-free loans), with the latter practiced personally by about one-fifth of all business respondents. We find many firms are predisposed to Islamic finance, but those that do generally have less business experience, are smaller in terms of assets and the number of employees, have lower levels of outstanding debt and fewer owners. In fact, only 5.1% of potential user firms have assets in excess of LYD500,000 compared to 73.0% of firms that are not potential users, and no potential user has liabilities exceeding LYD200,000. This would immediately suggest that while Islamic finance could potentially play a major role in business financing in Libya, it would primarily be for small and medium-sized enterprises.

1. INTRODUCTION

Islamic finance is one of the most rapidly growing segments of the global finance industry. Starting with the Dubai Islamic Bank in 1975 (and operations in the United Arab Emirates, Egypt, the Cayman Islands, Sudan, Lebanon, the Bahamas, Bosnia, Bahrain and

* Corresponding author: Department of Accounting, Finance and Economics, Griffith University, Nathan QLD 4111, Australia. Email. a.worthington@griffith.edu.au.

Pakistan), the number of Islamic financial institutions worldwide now exceeds 300, with operations in 75 countries and assets in excess of US$400 billion (El-Qorchi, 2005). Though initially concentrated in the Middle East (especially Bahrain) and South East Asia (particularly Malaysia), Islamic finance principles are now increasingly found elsewhere. This includes developing economies where the financial sector is almost entirely Islamic (Iran and Sudan) or where Islamic and 'conventional' financial systems coexist (Indonesia, Malaysia, Pakistan and the United Arab Emirates) (El-Qorchi, 2005). It also includes developed economies where a small number of Islamic financial institutions have been established and where large conventional providers have opened Islamic financing windows (as in Europe and the United States).

Importantly, while Islamic finance has been practiced for many centuries, it is only in the last thirty years that Islamic financial institutions (including banks) offering *Shariah*-compliant products and services have become more widespread and substantial. Indeed, even in Muslim countries it is only very recently that a full range of analogous Islamic finance products and services, particularly commercial products and services, have been offered in direct competition to conventional banks and other financial institutions. These products and services include, amongst others: *Mudarabah*, the provision of capital in partial equity partnerships; *Musharakah*, full equity partnerships, *Murabaha*, an instrument used for financing the purchase of goods; *Bai muajjall*, deferred payments on products; *Bai Salam*, advance sale contracts; *Istisna*, or manufacturing contracts; *Ijarah*, lease financing; and *Quard Hassan*, a system of benevolent loans.

Clearly, as Islamic products and services enter markets, an important consideration is the attitudes, perceptions, and knowledge of market participants towards these new methods of finance. For business firms, these factors determine the extent to which they choose to patronize these alternative products and services. Key concerns then include the influence of religious persuasion and the relative costs and benefits of financing, including convenience and access. Moreover, for conventional financial institutions, the presence of other financial institutions offering Islamic financial products and services may affect their competitive position and their marketing strategies. It may also influence their decision to introduce *Shariah*-compliant products and services themselves.

Libya provides an interesting context to examine these issues. First, while the majority of the population is Muslim, there are presently no Islamic financial institutions operating in Libya. Second, the Libyan government is increasingly moving towards the liberalization and reform of the country's financial system and part of this process foresees the contribution of Islamic financial institutions, products and services. Finally, there is no published work on the potential use of Islamic finance by Libyan commercial customers, and limited international work generally. This purpose of this chapter is then to provide the results of a survey of Libyan firms on their attitudes, perceptions, and motivations towards Islamic methods of finance. The chapter is structured as follows. Section 2 provides a brief review of Islamic finance, including its sources, principles, and products. Section 3 discusses the literature on the attitudes of firms towards Islamic finance. Section 4 presents the empirical methodology. Section 5 provides some descriptive statistics and Section 6 the empirical results. The final section concludes.

2. ISLAMIC FINANCE

Islamic finance is defined as a financial service or product principally implemented to comply with the main tenets of *Shariah* (or Islamic law). In turn, the main sources of *Shariah* are the *Holy Quran, Hadith, Sunna, Ijma, Qiyas* and *Ijtihad*. The *Holy Quran* is the book of revelation given to the Prophet Muhammad; *Hadith* is the narrative relating the deeds and utterances of Muhammad; *Sunna* refers to the habitual practice and behaviour of Muhammad during his lifetime; *Ijma* is the consensus among religion scholars about specific issues not envisaged in either the *Holy Quran* or the *Sunna*; *Qiyas* is the use of deduction by analogy to provide an opinion on a case not referred to in the *Quran* or the Sunna in comparison with another case referred to in the *Quran* and the *Sunna*; and *Ijtihad* represents a jurists' independent reasoning relating to the applicability of certain *Shariah* rules on cases not included in either the *Quran* or the *Sunna*.

In brief, the principles of Islamic finance are as follows: (i) the prohibition of *Riba* (usually interpreted as interest) and the removal of debt-based financing; (ii) the prohibition of *Gharar*, encompassing the full disclosure of information, removal of asymmetric information in contracts and the avoidance of risk-taking; (iii) the exclusion of financing and dealing in activities and commodities regarded as sinful or socially irresponsible (such as gambling, alcohol and pork); (iv) an emphasis on risk-sharing, where the provider of financial funds and the entrepreneur share business risk in return for a pre-determined share of profits and losses; (v) the desirability of materiality, a financial transaction needs to have 'material finality', that is a direct or indirect link to a real economic transaction; and (vi) consideration of justice, a financial transaction should not lead to the exploitation of any party to the transaction [see El-Gamal (2000), Warde (2000), Lewis and Algaoud (2001), Iqbal and Llewellyn (2002), Abdul-Gafoor (2003), Obaidullah (2005) and Iqbal and Molyneux (2005) for suitable introductions to Islamic finance].

In practical terms, these prohibitions and recommendations manifest themselves as the following commercial products and services: (i) *Mudarabah*, the provision of capital to a partial-equity partnership in return for a share of profits, but where the losses on funds lent are borne by the lender; (ii) *Musharakah*, full-equity partnerships where the provider of funds and the entrepreneur directly and wholly share in the business, (iii) *Murabaha*, an instrument used for financing the purchase of goods and services where the financial institution purchases these on behalf of the customer; (iv) *Bai muajjall*, deferred payments on products encompassed under *Murabaha*; (v) *Bai Salam*, advance or pre-paid sale contracts of goods and services; (vi) *Istisna*, or manufacturing contracts to cover work in progress and paid by the financial institution on behalf of the customer; (vii) *Ijarah*, lease financing in the form of operating leases only; (viii) *Takaful* or Islamic insurance in the form of cooperative self-help schemes, and (ix) *Quard Hassan*, benevolent loans offered interest free.

Islamic products and services also increasingly manifest themselves as mutual funds underpinned by investments in *Shariah*-compliant equity or property, *Sukuk* (Islamic bonds), *Takaful* (Islamic insurance) and *Ijarah* (Islamic leasing) constructed with Islamic principles in mind. For example, a *Shariah*-compliant equity mutual fund would, through a process of sector screening and dividend 'purification', normally exclude: banking, insurance or any other interest-related activity; alcohol, tobacco, gambling, armaments; any activity related to pork; other activities deemed offensive to Islam; and any sectors or companies significantly affected by any of the above.

3. LITERATURE REVIEW

While the attitudes of retail consumers towards Islamic financial institutions and products have been studied by researchers in Muslim and non-Muslim countries alike—including Erol and El-Bdour (1989), Erol, Kaynak and El-Bdour (1990), Omer (1992), Haron, Ahmad and Planisek (1994), Metwally (1996), Gerrard and Cunningham (1997), Al-Sultan (1999), Hamid and Nordin (2001), Zainuddin, Jahyd and Ramayah (2004), Okumkus (2005), and Dusuki and Abdullah (2007)—relatively little inquiry has been made into the attitudes of business firms. In fact, only three studies comprise the extant literature.

First, in a study of the Kuwaiti dual banking system where Islamic and conventional banks operate side-by-side, Edris (1997) focused on the bank selection criteria used by business customers. Even though Kuwait is a predominately-Muslim country, and Metwally (1996) and Al-Sultan (1999) showed the strong preference for Islamic methods of finance by Kuwaiti retail consumers, the majority of businesses were inclined to deal with conventional banks rather than Islamic banks. In addition, these business firms ranked the size of bank assets to be the primary factor in the bank selection process. On this basis, Edris (1997) suggested that business firms in Kuwait preferred to obtain financial services from banks that were large and reliable. In contrast, Islamic methods of finance ranked fifth among bank selection criteria. The study also found that most firms in Kuwait were multiple bank users because of their desire to employ the diverse services of several different banks, each with its own comparative advantage.

Second, Jalaluddin and Metwally (1999) surveyed 385 small businesses in Sydney, Australia about their opinions on the probability of applying profit/loss sharing as found in Islamic financing. Jalaluddin and Metwally (1999) concluded that factors other than religion may motivate small business firms to use Islamic-like financial services. These included the linking of financial and business risk, the lower cost of borrowing funds and a higher expected rate of return. Furthermore, the probability of applying profit/loss sharing by small firms positively depended on the level of business risk, the cost of borrowing, and the rate of return. Many firms also saw the benefits of a more active post-financing role for management.

Finally, in Malaysia, Ahamad and Haron (2002) surveyed 45 current corporate customers on their attitudes towards Islamic products and services. The major finding was that economic factors, such as profitability and the quality of service, were more significant than any religious concerns.

This could be because the majority of respondents were non-Muslims who believed that Islamic banks provided a desirable alternative to conventional finance, irrespective of any religious underpinnings. In fact, most respondents had a low level of knowledge about Islamic financial products, even though they were actively using them. They also suggest that Islamic financial institutions can provide products that are generally attractive to many (non-Muslim) business customers.

4. METHODOLOGY

A questionnaire was designed to collect data from a sample of Libyan business firms (available from the authors upon request in Arabic and English). To ensure speedy data collection, control of the sample, good flexibility, and reasonable cost, data was collected by filling the questionnaires through telephone interviews. Using $N = \pi(1-\pi)Z^2/E^2$, the optimal sample size (N) was selected using a 95 percent confidence level where Z is 1.96, the proportion (π) is 0.5 (the safest possible assumption), and the error or precision (E) is 0.05 (Waters 1994), such that $N = (0.5)(0.5)(1.96)^2/(0.05)^2 = 384.16 \approx 385$. A focus group of 20 (pre-screened) respondents representing about 5% of the sample was interviewed first to ensure the effectiveness of the questionnaire before the full survey was undertaken.

The Chambers of Commerce and Industry in each of Libya's four largest cities (Tripoli, Benghazi, Misratah and Al Murgub) were contacted for the telephone numbers of all businesses. This yielded a population of 7,011 firms. Using a systematic sampling technique, the population (7,011) was divided by the optimal sample (385) to yield a sample interval of 18. A random number (6) between 1 and 18 was selected using a table of random numbers so that the sample consisted of elements 6, 24, 42, 60 and so on. Using the list of firms as a sampling frame, the firms were alphabetically ordered and phoned using the calculated elements. When the number attempted was not successful, the next number on the same page was dialed.

The respondents were requested in the first part of the questionnaire to indicate their knowledge about the existence of Islamic banks and their methods of finance. The second part of the questionnaire was used to discern the respondents' attitudes towards Islamic methods of finance. A seven-point scale from 1 to 7 was used where 1 is not important at all and 7 is very important for 18 statements that represent perceptions of Islamic methods of finance. The questionnaire also collected information on the characteristics of the firms, including firm size, organizational structure, ownership, and industry. Unfortunately, despite best efforts only 296 complete questionnaires were obtained. In nearly all cases, the incomplete questionnaires arose from missing information on the firm's economic profile, including total assets, liabilities and share capital (if applicable) because the firm's respondent either refused or was unable to respond. The incomplete questionnaires were removed from the sample. Descriptive analysis is used to examine the degree of awareness of Libyan business firms about Islamic methods of finance; factor analysis is used to identify the main factors that motivate them to apply Islamic methods of finance and discriminant analysis is used to determine which of these factors account for the most impact on attitudes towards Islamic methods of finance.

5. DESCRIPTIVE STATISTICS

Table 1 details the main characteristics of the sample. Columns 1 and 2 contain the response frequency and percentage of responses for all firms, columns 3 and 4 the frequencies and percentage of responses for firms that are potential users of Islamic methods of finance, and columns 5 and 6 the frequencies and percentage of responses for firms that not potential users of Islamic methods of finance. In the sample, 214 firms (72.3%) indicated that they would be potential users of Islamic finance and 82 firms (27.7%) responded otherwise. Most of the sample firms are in the services and construction industries: 26.3% and 22.3% of all firms and 29.9% and 22.9% of potential users, respectively. However, the most common industries for firms that are not potentials users are importing and exporting (23.2%) and services (17.15).

Table 1. Sample characteristics

		All firms (n = 296)		Potential user (n = 214)		Not a potential user (n = 82)		Equality of variances		Equality of means	
		Freq.	%	Freq.	%	Freq.	%	F-test	p-value	t-test	p-value
Industry	Trading	12	4.1	9	4.2	3	3.7	0.18	0.67	-0.21	0.83
	Manufacturing	50	16.9	33	15.5	17	20.7	4.46	0.04	1.03	0.30
	Importing and exporting	60	20.3	41	19.1	19	23.2	2.22	0.14	0.77	0.44
	Construction	66	22.3	49	22.9	17	20.7	0.66	0.42	-0.40	0.69
	Transport and storage	20	6.7	12	5.6	8	9.7	6.32	0.01	1.14	0.26
	Services	78	26.3	64	29.9	14	17.1	26.29	<0.01	-2.46	0.02
	Other	10	3.4	6	2.8	4	4.9	3.08	0.08	0.78	0.43
Business experience	Less than 1 year	9	3.0	9	4.2	–	–	15.65	<0.01	-3.06	<0.01
	2 to 3 years	86	29.0	84	39.3	2	2.4	779.08	<0.01	-9.79	<0.01
	4 to 5 years	122	41.3	103	48.1	19	23.2	83.63	<0.01	-4.30	<0.01
	More than 5 years	79	26.7	18	8.4	61	74.4	59.36	<0.01	12.67	<0.01
Total assets	Less than LYD50,000	2	0.8	2	0.9	–	–	3.13	0.08	-1.42	0.16
	LYD50,000 to 100,000	45	15.2	44	20.6	1	1.2	122.20	<0.01	-6.39	<0.01
	LYD101,000 to 300,000	95	32.1	93	43.5	2	2.4	1288.08	<0.01	-10.78	<0.01
	LYD301,000 to 500,000	83	28.0	64	29.9	19	23.2	3.30	0.07	-0.89	0.38
	More than LYD500,000	71	23.9	11	5.1	60	73.0	127.52	<0.01	12.67	<0.01
Total liabilities	Less than LYD50,000	96	32.4	88	41.1	8	9.7	262.26	<0.01	-6.65	<0.01
	LYD50,000 to 100,000	160	54.0	112	52.4	48	58.6	4.55	0.03	0.96	0.34
	LYD101,000 to 200,000	36	12.2	14	6.5	22	26.8	95.48	<0.01	3.90	<0.01
	LYD201,000 to 300,000	4	1.4	–	–	4	4.9	48.44	<0.01	2.04	0.04
	More than LYD300,000	–	–	–	–	–	–	–	–	–	–
Equity capital	Less than LYD50,000	81	27.4	80	37.4	1	1.2	832.25	<0.01	-10.24	<0.01
	LYD50,000 to 100,000	116	39.2	105	49.1	11	13.5	243.73	<0.01	-6.98	<0.01
	LYD101,000 to 200,000	46	15.5	24	11.2	22	26.8	40.08	<0.01	2.90	<0.01
	LYD201,000 to 300,000	17	5.7	5	2.3	12	14.6	76.01	<0.01	3.03	<0.01
	More than LYD300,000	36	12.2	–	–	36	43.9	14079.58	<0.01	7.96	<0.01
Number of employees	Less than 5 employees	84	28.6	69	32.3	15	18.3	30.67	<0.01	-2.60	0.01
	5 to 10 employees	123	41.5	88	41.1	35	42.7	0.00	0.97	-0.02	0.98
	11 to 20 employees	76	25.6	52	24.3	24	29.3	2.79	0.10	0.85	0.40
	More than 20 employees	13	4.3	5	2.3	8	9.7	51.56	<0.01	2.53	0.01
Structure	Family business	10	3.4	8	3.7	2	2.4	1.24	0.27	-0.55	0.58
	Joint venture	155	52.4	87	40.7	68	83.0	91.20	<0.01	7.43	<0.01
	Partnership	131	44.2	119	55.6	12	14.6	159.92	<0.01	-7.41	<0.01
Number of owners	Less than 10 owners	90	30.4	82	38.3	8	9.7	206.17	<0.01	-6.09	<0.01
	10 to 20 owners	110	37.2	91	42.5	19	23.2	57.20	<0.01	-3.35	<0.01
	21 to 30 owners	21	7.1	16	7.5	5	6.1	0.69	0.41	-0.41	0.68
	More than 30 owners	75	25.3	25	11.7	50	61.0	91.06	<0.01	8.43	<0.01

For business experience, most potential users (87.4%) have 3 to 5 years' experience, while most nonpotential users (74.45) have experience greater than 5 years. In terms of total assets, liabilities and capital, potential users are clearly smaller than non-potential users. For instance, 65% of potential user firms have less than LYD300,000 in assets compared to just 3.6% for non-potential user firms (LYD/AUD0.94967). A similar picture emerges with business size measured by the number of employees: 73.4% of potential users have 10 or fewer employees compared to 61.0% for firms that are not potential users of Islamic finance. The structure and type of business organization also varies, with most potential users being joint ventures (40.7%) or partnerships (55.6%) with fewer than 20 owners (80.8%) while firms that are not potential users are typically joint ventures (83.0%) with more than 30 owners (61.0%).

6. Empirical Results

Table 2 provides the frequencies and percentages of the sample for the awareness and past use responses of Libyan business firms concerning Islamic methods of finance. Similar to findings by Ahamad and Haron (2002) in their study of 45 Malaysian corporate bank customers, the results indicate that the majority of Libyan business firms are aware of Islamic banking and some Islamic methods of finance, but are generally unaware of many specific financing methods. For example, 88.5% of respondents have knowledge of Islamic banking, and *Musharakah* and *Quard Hassan* are known by 71.3% of respondents. Interestingly, *Musharakah* has been practiced by 72.3% of all respondents. However, most respondents are relatively uninformed of the other principal Islamic financing methods, including *Mudarabah*, *Morabahah*, *Bai muajjall* and *Istisna*.

Table 2 also clearly suggests that the majority of respondents who are aware of Islamic methods of finance are potential users. More particularly, 78.6% of the 262 respondents knowledgeable about the existence of Islamic banks are potential users, 77.7% of the 211 respondents aware of *Musharakah* and *Quard Hassan* are potential users, and 78.9% of the 214 respondents who have practiced *Musharakah* are potential users (excludes respondents that are unaware of *Musharakah*).

Table 2. Awareness and practice of Islamic methods of finance

Variable	Knowledge and practice	All firms		Potential user		Not a potential user	
		Freq.	%	Freq.	%	Freq.	%
Knowledge of Islamic banking	Yes	262	88.5	206	78.6	56	21.4
	No	34	11.5	8	23.5	26	76.5
Knowledge of *Musharakah* and *Quard Hassan*	Yes	211	71.3	164	77.7	47	22.3
	No	25	8.4	23	92	2	8
Past practice of *Musharakah*	Yes	214	72.3	169	78.9	45	21.1
	No	33	11.1	8	24.2	25	75.6

Respondents were also asked to indicate the degree of importance placed on for 18 statements that represent perceptions of the use of Islamic methods of finance on a seven-point Likert scale. Table 3 details the means and standard deviations of the variable scores. As shown, the primary motivation for Islamic methods of finance is that an Islamic bank may encourage business expansion (3.854) and that it would share business risk with the firm (3.817). In contrast, interest-free banking (3.199) and the provision of lease financing (*Ijarah*) (3.317) provide less motivation.

Table 3. Perceptions of Islamic methods of finance and rotated component matrix

Variable			Components			
	Mean	Std. dev.	1	2	3	4
Islamic bank's methods of finance are interest-free	3.199	1.676	**.920**	.276	.054	.083
Islamic bank provides products in accordance with *Shariah*	3.550	1.726	**.895**	.285	.078	.119
Deposits with Islamic bank would realise a higher variable rate of return	3.679	1.592	.335	**.902**	-.135	.090
Religious motivation for depositing with Islamic bank	3.628	1.921	**.821**	.321	-.080	.310
Cost of borrowing from Islamic bank depends on business outcomes	3.638	1.502	.428	**.815**	-.036	.165
Religious motivation for borrowing from Islamic bank	3.746	1.729	**.822**	.379	.212	.042
Islamic bank may invest according to profit sharing (*Musharakah*)	3.435	1.714	.264	**.812**	.009	.194
Islamic bank considers repayment of debt according to business conditions	3.641	1.800	.484	**.576**	.265	.290
Islamic bank lends money according to profit sharing (*Musharakah*)	3.753	1.656	.084	-.006	.277	**.861**
Islamic bank shares the risk of business	3.817	1.929	.463	**.764**	.249	.080
Profit/loss sharing method allows you to invest or borrow on a fair basis	3.422	1.092	-.065	.096	.520	**.778**
Islamic bank may support you in your business management	3.614	1.498	.122	-.034	**.948**	.216
Islamic bank would encourage business innovation	3.422	1.257	.081	.024	**.937**	.115
Islamic bank may encourage business expansion	3.854	1.130	-.059	.501	**.624**	.132
Islamic bank would help improve business efficiency	3.750	1.517	.108	-.046	**.945**	.214
Islamic bank provides lease financing (*Ijarah*)	3.317	1.270	.255	.282	-.021	**.831**
Islamic bank provides trade financing such as (*Morabahah)*	3.466	1.416	.329	.239	-.018	**.851**
Islamic bank provides industrial financing (*Istisna*)	3.516	1.325	.007	.119	.490	**.812**

Factor analysis is performed on the explanatory variables with the goal of data reduction. The data in the correlation matrix (not shown) indicates high correlations among the explanatory variables significant at the 0.01 level. This justifies the appropriateness of factor analysis to reduce these highly correlated variables to a smaller more manageable number of factors. However, investigation indicates that the coefficients on the diagonals of the anti-image correlation matrix are greater than 0.5 for each variable. Therefore, there is no need to eliminate any of the variables. Bartlett's test of sphericity is used to test the null hypothesis that the explanatory variables are uncorrelated in the population. The test statistic (7583.466) and p-value (<0.01) reject the null. The Kaiser–Meyer–Olkin measure of sampling adequacy is also calculated. A value of 0.839 is obtained, meaning that all of the partial correlation coefficients are small compared to the ordinary correlation coefficients. This also indicates that it's reasonable to proceed with factor analysis. The 18 explanatory variables can be reduced to just four factors with eigenvalues greater than 1. These factors account for about 86.62% of the total variance.

Table 3 includes the factors and their coefficients from the rotated factor matrix obtained by the varimax procedure. Factor 1 has large coefficients (> 0.5) on four variables in bold in column 1. These are (i) Islamic bank's methods of finance are interest-free, (ii) Islamic bank provides Islamic methods of finance in accordance with *Shariah*, (iii) religious motivation for depositing with Islamic bank, and (iv) religious motivation for borrowing from Islamic bank. We refer to this factor as "Religion" as these perceptions link most closely with compliance with Islamic religious principles.

Factor 2 has large coefficients on five variables in bold in column 2. These are (i) deposits with Islamic banks realize a higher variable rate of return, (ii) Islamic bank's cost of borrowing depends on the outcomes of the business, (iii) Islamic bank may invest according to profit-sharing (*Mudarabah*), (iv) Islamic bank would consider repayment of debt according to business conditions, and (v) Islamic bank shares the risk of business. As these perceptions generally suggest the intention of firms to increase profits and reduce losses they are referred to as "Profitability". Factor 3 has large coefficients on four variables in bold in column 3. These are; (i) Islamic bank may support your business management, (ii) Islamic bank would encourage business innovation, (iii) Islamic bank may encourage business expansion, and (iv) Islamic bank would help improve business efficiency. As these motivations relate to business operations they are labeled "Business Support". Finally, factor 4 has large coefficients on five variables in bold in column 4. These motivations are, (i) Islamic bank lends money according to profit/loss sharing method (*Musharakah*), (ii) Profit/loss sharing method allows you to invest or borrow on a fair basis, (iii) Islamic bank provides lease financing (*Ijarah*), (iv) Islamic bank provides trade financing methods such as (*Morabahah)*, and (v) Islamic bank provides industrial financing (*Istisna*). As these variables indicate new methods of finance not offered by the conventional banking system they are referred to as "Unique Services".

These factor scores (Religion, Profitability, Business Support, and Unique Services) are suitable for use in subsequent multivariate analysis. Firms are divided into two groups: namely, firms that are potential users of Islamic methods of finance and firms that are not potential users of Islamic methods of finance. The mean and standard deviation of the factor scores for these firm groups and all firms (not shown) suggest that the two groups are most widely separated in terms of the value of factor scores 1 (Religion) and 2 (Profitability) while the differences are smallest for factor scores 3 (Business Support) and 4 (Unique services).

Wilks' Lambda (p-value in brackets) is the proportion of variance not explained by differences between the groups: Religion 0.596 (<0.01), Profitability 0.693 (<0.01), Business Support 0.924 (<0.01), and Unique Services 0.965 (<0.01). Because all of these values are less than 1, most of the observed variability in the factor scores can be attributed to the differences between the groups. The polled within-group correlation matrix also indicates relatively low (negative) correlations between the factor scores (Religion and Profitability, –

0.548; Religion and Business Support, –0.237; Religion and Unique Services, –0.156; Profitability and Business Support, –0.191; Profitability and Unique Services, –0.126; and Business Support and Unique Services, –0.055).

Box's *M* (F-statistic = 42.590, p-value = <0.01) rejects the null hypothesis that the covariance matrices are equal. The eigenvalue (4.643) is large and accounts for 100% of the explained variance. The canonical correlation is another measure of the degree of association between the discriminant scores and the groups. The canonical correlation of the discriminant function is about 0.91. The square of this coefficient shows that 82.8% of the variance of the dependent variable (potential use of Islamic methods of finance) is explained or accounted for by this model. Wilks' lambda associated with the discriminant function is 0.178. This is the ratio of the within-groups sum of squares to the total sum of squares. This can be transformed to a chi-square value of 504.801, which is statistically significant at the 0.01 level with degrees of freedom equal to the number of factor scores. Therefore, it is acceptable to reject the null hypothesis that respondents who are potential users have the same average discriminant function score in the population.

Table 4. Classification results

Classification		Predicted group membership		Total
	Groups	Potential users	Not potential users	Potential users
Number	Potential users	79	3	82
	Not potential users	3	211	214
Percentage of group	Potential users	96.3	3.7	100.0
	Not potential users	1.4	98.6	100.0

The absolute magnitude of the standardized canonical discriminant function coefficients clearly indicate that Religion (1.284), Profitability (1.207) and Business Support (0.695) are the most important in discriminating between the two groups of Libyan business firms: that is, potential and nonpotential users of Islamic finance. More particularly, religion is the primary motivation for the potential use of Islamic methods of finance among Libyan business firms. Accordingly, religious factors have a significant influence on Libyan business firms' attitudes towards the potential use of Islamic methods of finance. However, religion is not the only factor determining the potential user of Islamic methods of finance, and that rather more temporal concerns for profitability, business support, and unique services have a role to play. This contrasts with Jalaluddin and Metwally (1999) and Ahamad and Haron (2002) where religion was not the primary motivation for Islamic finance. The classification results in Table 4 show that attitudes held by business firms toward Islamic methods of finance are crucial in predicting potential usage, with 96.3 percent of potential users and 98.6% of not potential users being correctly classified.

CONCLUSION

This study establishes that while commercial Islamic finance is not yet formally practiced in Libya, most businesses have some knowledge about Islamic methods of finance. We can partly attribute this awareness to both knowledge of developments in other Muslim countries and to the fact that many commercial products and services offered by Islamic financial institutions bear close relation to informal financing and business arrangements already practiced among Muslims. These include *Musharakah* (full partnerships) and *Quard Hassan* (interest-free loans), with latter practiced personally by about one-fifth of all business respondents. However, many other Islamic financing methods that are difficult to practice on an individual basis, such as *Mudarabah*, *Morabahah*, *Bai muajjall* and *Istisna,* are relatively unknown. The study also suggests that most business firms in Libya are potential users of Islamic methods of finance. However, those firms most disposed towards the use of Islamic methods of finance generally have less business experience, are smaller in terms of assets and the number of employees, have lower levels of outstanding debt and fewer owners. In fact, only 5.1% of potential user firms have assets in excess of LYD500,000 compared to 73.0% of firms that are not potential users, and no potential user has liabilities exceeding LYD200,000. This would immediately suggest that Islamic finance could potentially play a major role in business financing, but primarily for small and medium-sized enterprises.

The motivations for potential business users of Islamic finance are narrowed to just four motivations: religion, profitability, business support, and unique services. Somewhat unexpectedly, religion is the principal motivation, followed by profitability, business support, and unique services. With the planned introduction of Islamic financial institutions in Libya, there is clearly little they can do about the religious persuasion of potential customers (though they can ensure that potential and current business customers are fully informed about the compliance of their products and services with *Shariah*). However, they can focus on the benefits of Islamic finance for profitability, business support and the provision of unique services. The risk-sharing services offered by Islamic financial institutions appear to be a particularly attractive feature, especially for smaller firms.

From a business perspective, a number of directions for further research are indicated. First, little is known about the opportunity cost of Islamic methods of finance. For example, while profit-sharing agreements avoid prohibitions on interest, what is the implied cost to firms choosing this source of finance relative to a conventional business loan or securitized asset? Data would need to be gathered from a range of Islamic financial institutions on their commercial arrangements to provide sound generalizations. Second, what interaction, if any, is there between Islamic financing by the firm and its own investment decisions? Once again, this would requirements examination of the agreements set in place between Islamic financial institutions and their customers to consider the business asset impact of any implied or explicit covenants or guarantees.

REFERENCES

Abdul-Gafoor, A. (2003), *Islamic Banking*. A.S. Noor Deen, Kuala Lumpur.

Ahmad, N and Haron S (2002). Perceptions of Malaysian corporate customers towards Islamic banking products & services. *International Journal of Islamic Financial Services* 3(4): 1–16.

Al-Sultan, W (1999). *Financial characteristics of interest-free banks and conventional banks.* Ph.D. Dissertation, University of Wollongong.

Dusuki, A and Abdullah N (2007). Why do Malaysian customers patronize Islamic banks? *International Journal of Bank Marketing*. 25(3): 142–160.

El-Gamal, M. (2000), *A Basic Guide to Contemporary Islamic Banking and Finance,* Available at http://www.witness-pioneer.org/.

El-Qorchi, M (2005). Islamic Finance Gears Up. *Finance and Development* 42(4): 46–50.

Erol, C and El-Bdour R (1989). Attitudes, behaviour and patronage factors of bank customers towards Islamic banks. *International Journal of Bank Marketing* 7(6): 31–37.

Erol, C, Kaynak E and El-Bdour R (1990). Conventional and Islamic banks: patronage behaviour of Jordanian customers. *International Journal of Bank Marketing* 8(4): 25–35.

Gerrard, P and Cunningham J (1997). Islamic banking: a study in Singapore. *International Journal of Bank Marketing* 15(6): 204–216.

Hamid, A and Nordin N (2001). A study on Islamic banking education and strategy for the new millennium-Malaysian experience. *International Journal of Islamic Financial Services* 2(4).

Haron, S, Ahmad N and Planisek S (1994). Bank patronage factors of Muslim and non-Muslim customers. *International Journal of Bank Marketing* 12(1): 32–40.

Iqbal, M. and Llewellyn, D. (eds.) (2002), *Islamic Banking and Finance: New Perspectives on Profit-Sharing and Risk,* Edward Elgar: Cheltenham, UK.

Iqbal, M. and Molyneux, P. (2005), *Thirty Years of Islamic Banking: History, Performance, and Prospects*, Palgrave Macmillan: New York.

Jalaluddin, A and Metwally M (1999). Profit/loss sharing: an alternative method of financing small businesses in Australia. *The Middle East Business and Economic Review* 11(1): 8–14.

Lewis, M. and Algaoud, L. (2001), *Islamic Banking,* Edward Elgar, Cheltenham UK.

Metwally, M (1996). Attitudes of Muslims towards Islamic banks in a dual-banking system. *American Journal of Islamic Finance* 6: 11–17.

Naser, K, Jamal A and Al-Khatib K (1999). Islamic banking: a study of customer satisfaction and preference in Jordan. *International Journal of Bank Marketing* 17(3): 135–150.

Obaidullah, M. (2005), *Islamic Financial Services*, Islamic Economics Research Centre, Jeddah.

Okumus, H (2005). Interest-free banking in Turkey: a study of customer satisfaction and bank selection criteria. *Journal of Economic Cooperation* 26(4): 51–86.

Omer, H (1992). *The Implication of Islamic Beliefs and Practice on Islamic Financial Institutions in the UK*. Ph.D. Dissertation, Loughborough University.

Rammal, H and Zurbruegg R (2007). Awareness of Islamic banking products among Muslims: The case of Australia. *Journal of Financial Services Marketing*. 12(1): 65–74.

Warde, I. (2000), *Islamic Finance in the Global Economy*, Edinburgh University Press, Edinburgh.

Waters, D (1994). *Quantitative Methods for Business*. Addison-Wesley Publishing Company. New York.

Zainuddin, Y, Jahyd N and Ramayah T (2004). Perception of Islamic banking: does it differ among users and non-users. *Journal of Management & Business* 6(3): 221–232.

In: Contemporary Issues in Islamic Finance
Editor: Andrew C. Worthington

ISBN: 978-1-62948-905-6

Chapter 7

DETERMINANTS OF CREDIT RISK IN BANGLADESHI AND MALAYSIAN ISLAMIC BANKS

***Md. Nurul Kabir**[*1] **and Suzuki Yasushi**[2]*
[1]Griffith University, Australia
[2]Ritsumiekan Asia Pacific University, Japan

ABSTRACT

In order to achieve sustainable long-run growth by Islamic banks, it is vital to focus on the risk management practices of Islamic banks, especially in managing credit risk. This study considers both macroeconomic and bank specific variables that affect the credit risk of Islamic banks in Bangladesh and Malaysia. Using ordinary least squares techniques, we find three significant determinants of credit risk in Islamic banks in Bangladesh, namely, the loan to deposit ratio, cost inefficiency, and size. In contrast, two additional variables significantly affect the credit risk of Islamic banks in Malaysia, namely, credit growth and the returns on assets. In addition, we find macroeconomic factors do not exert any significant impact on the nonperforming loans of Islamic banks in either of these countries.

1. INTRODUCTION

Islamic banking systems emerged in the late 1970s with claims its operations were entirely free from interest (Ayub, 2008; Iqbal and Mirakhor, 2007; Usmani, 2002). This new banking system spread rapidly among Muslim countries at the beginning, especially in Asia, and has now penetrated many other non-Muslim countries including the UK and Australia. Since its inception, the Islamic banking industry has experienced annual growth rate of 15–20% annually. Some Muslim-dominated countries, especially in the Middle East and South East Asia, including Bangladesh, Malaysia, Indonesia, and Pakistan, have further fueled this

[*] Corresponding author: Department of Accounting, Finance and Economics, Griffith University, Nathan QLD 4111, Australia. Email. mdnurul.kabir@griffithuni.edu.au.

extreme growth rate by adopting a number of initiatives promoting Islamic banking systems. At the extreme, Iran and Sudan have adopted fully-fledged Islamic banking systems.

Bangladesh, the world's third-largest Muslim country, joined these developments in 1983 with the establishment of its first Islamic bank, the Islamic Bank of Bangladesh. With little support from the government and regulatory bodies, Islamic banking has achieved moderate growth during the last three decades. At present, the Islamic banking sector in Bangladesh comprises seven fully-fledged Islamic banks of the 49 banks currently operating in Bangladesh and 20 branches offering Islamic banking services or 'Islamic windows' in conventional banks. Total deposits in Islamic banks attained $7 billion at the end of 2009, accounting for 17% of the total deposits held by all banks in Bangladesh. For this same period, total credit by Islamic banks in Bangladesh accounted for some $6.6 billion or nearly 20% of all national credit.

Although the Islamic banking sector in Bangladesh has experienced moderate growth in line with their conventional counterparts, most have reported nonperforming finance (NPF), comparable to nonperforming loans (NPL) in conventional banks, consistently lower than their equivalent in conventional banks of some 2–3% over the last few years. At first impression, this would suggest that Islamic banks in Bangladesh have managed their credit risk efficiently, helping them to maintain a steady growth rate.

Another pioneering country in the global Islamic banking industry is Malaysia. Like Bangladesh, Islamic banking in Malaysia began in 1983 with strong government supports. Since then, the industry has experienced rapid growth in the order of 18–20% annually. At present, there are 16 fully-fledged Islamic banks operating in Malaysia, with total assets of $116.14 billion at the end of 2010. Total credit extended by these same banks was some $74 billion, representing 22.7% of total bank finance in Malaysian. The level of NPF reported by Malaysian Islamic banks was only about 2% at the end of the 2010, again lower than the comparable NPL rate reported by conventional banks. Once again, there is the suggestion that Islamic banks have experienced rapid growth in Malaysia while maintaining a comparatively low level of credit risk.

The timing of the establishment of Islamic banking in both Bangladesh and Malaysia coincides. However, while Islamic banks in both countries have an extremely low level of NPF, growth has generally been higher in the latter than the former. Moreover, the total market share of Islamic banking in both countries is almost the same with Bangladesh at 17% and Malaysia at 20%, as too for the share of total deposits with Islamic banking accounting for 20% of all deposits in Bangladesh and 22.6% in Malaysia. Lastly, while the level of NPF in 2009 for both countries was quite similar at 2.3% for Bangladesh and 2.2% for Malaysia, NPL as reported by their banking systems as a whole was 9.2% in Bangladesh and just 2.3% in Malaysia.

Based on these observations, this chapter seeks to identify the key determinants contributing to the credit risk experienced by Islamic banks in Bangladesh and Malaysia. The remainder of the chapter is organized as follows. Section 2 presents the related literature review, Section 3 describes the methodology, and Section 4 discusses the results. Section 5 concludes.

2. LITERATURE REVIEW

A vast literature examines the determinants of credit risk in conventional banks, of which two strands are notable. The first focuses on market and industry-wide factors like economic growth, inflation, real interest rates, and regulation. The second considers the impact of bank-specific variables on credit risk.

A recent study by Louzis, Vouldis, and Metaxas (2010) of the Greek banking sector considers both macroeconomic and bank-specific factors. Using generalized method of moments (GMM) estimation techniques and a dynamic panel data set, the authors found that the level of NPL in Greek banks could be mainly explained by macroeconomic factors, most notably GDP, the unemployment rate, interest rates, and management quality. Management quality is measured by ROA, ROE and cost efficiency ratio of the banks. According to this study, there was not support for the moral hazard and procyclical credit growth hypotheses in the Greek banking system. In addition, market power appeared to have a significant impact on increasing NPL among business loans.

Elsewhere, Khemraj and Pasha (2009) investigated the determinants of NPL in the Guyanese banking sector using panel data and a fixed effects model. Again, they considered both macroeconomic and bank-specific factors. Of the macroeconomic determinants, they found a significant positive relationship between the real effective exchange rate and NPL and a negative relationship between NPL and the GDP growth rate as per theory. Moreover, they found that banks that charged higher interest rates and experienced higher credit growth incurred higher levels of NPL. Finally, they found that large banks were not necessarily effective in screening and monitoring than smaller banks nor was there a significant relationship between size and the level of NPL.

Das and Ghosh (2007) used panel data techniques to examine the macroeconomic and bank-specific determinants of credit risk in Indian state-owned banks over the period 1994–2005. Like many other studies, they found GDP had a significant negative impact on NPL, but that the real interest rate did not appear to exert any significant influence. Among the microeconomic variables, credit growth was strongly positively significant with a lag of one year. The composition of loan portfolio as well as risk premium had a negative impact on NPL, indicating that competitive pressure in the Indian banking sector placed banks in a more vulnerable position. While in theory larger banks have increased opportunities for diversification over smaller banks, Das and Ghosh (2007) concluded that larger banks displayed higher levels of NPL. Several other microeconomic variables, like branch expansion strategies, operating expenses, and the interest margin do not have any significant impact on problem loans.

Outside these single country studies, Ahmad and Ariff (2007) undertook a study of bank credit risk determinants across four developed and five emerging countries. In their study, they considered eight important determinants to examine which determinants most affected banks in developed countries and how these may differ from the factors influencing banks in emerging countries. Of these, Ahmad and Ariff (2007) found that in any banking system from two to four factors were significant determinants, with management quality being relatively more important for emerging countries and regulatory capital relatively more important for banking systems offering multiple products. Moreover, leverage was found to be irrelevant for credit risk in most countries, with credit risk as a whole being higher in emerging countries.

Other parts of this literature have emphasized the classical hypothesis of credit risk, including disaster myopia, herd behavior, agency problems, asymmetric information problems, and institutional regulations. Jimenez and Saurina (2007), for example, examined the credit growth and competition hypothesis along with the role of macroeconomic factors in the Spanish banking sector. They provided evidence that excessive credit growth would increase future NPL, especially during period of high economic growth when banks would lower their credit criteria (including collateral requirements) and risky borrowers would then have greater access to the formal credit sector.

In other work, Jiménez and Saurina (2004) investigated the effects of collateral, the type of loan, and the relationship between lender and borrower on credit risk. They found that collateralized loans had a higher probability of default as bank managers have perceptibly less incentive for prudent loan monitoring. Regarding the type of loan, they found that loans by savings banks were more prone to default. Finally, they argued that the closer the relationship between lender and borrower, the greater the probability of risk taking by the lender. This conflicts with established theory where banks that establish a good relationship with their borrowers have better access to information on the borrower, which will minimize the problem of asymmetric information.

Elsewhere, Salas and Saurina (2002) investigated the role of the type of institution, competition and asymmetric information problem as determinants of credit risk in banks. Using sophisticated panel data estimation techniques, Salas and Saurina (2002) examined credit risk factors in savings and commercial banks in Spain. They concluded that microeconomic factors significantly determined credit risk, with microeconomic variables displaying higher explanatory power for saving banks than for commercial banks. In addition, other variables that had a significant impact on NPL in savings banks included growth policy, managerial incentives and efficiency, loan portfolio composition, and market power. In contrast, branch growth, the capital ratio, and size were the only three significant determinants of credit risk in commercial banks. Together, these findings suggest that different factors determine credit risk in different types of institutions.

The effect of bank efficiency, more particularly cost efficiency on the credit risk is examined by Berger and DeYoung (1997). Using Granger- causality techniques, Berger and DeYoung (1997) tested four hypotheses relating to the level of credit risk, including bad luck, bad management, skimping, and the moral hazard hypothesis. They argued that bank failures primarily result from uncontrolled external events, whereas the bad management hypothesis suggests that most distressed financial institutions result from internal factors. Overall, the findings supported the moral hazard hypothesis that thinly capitalized banks tend to take riskier projects, which may account for an increase in problems loans for these same banks in the future.

In summary, we can divide the determinants of credit risk into two main categories: macroeconomic (market and industry) factors and microeconomic (bank-specific) factors. The former typically include GDP, the inflation rate, the exchange rate, the interest rate spread, interest rates, etc. and the latter include the size of the bank, the profit margin, credit growth, efficiency, market power, competition, and the regulatory capital ratio, etc.

3. METHODOLOGY

Data

We undertake a quantitative analysis of the determinants of credit risk in Islamic banks in Bangladesh and Malaysia, two emerging countries in Asia. One reason for choosing these countries is that they have quite similar banking systems, with the Islamic banking systems being quite similar in Bangladesh and Malaysia. Our sample period from 2006 to 2009 yields usable panel data on five of the seven Islamic banks in Bangladesh and eleven of the sixteen Islamic banks in Malaysia. We excluded banks that began operations after 2006.

Model and Dependent Variable

Based on the literature review, we postulate the following equation for the credit risk of bank *i* in year *t*. The equation for the full model used is $Credit\ Risk_{it} = X_{it}\beta + \varepsilon_i$ where β is a vector of regression coefficients, X_{it} is a matrix of explanatory variables, and ε_i is a disturbance or random error term assumed to be independently distributed across individuals with zero mean, but where arbitrary forms of heteroskedasticity across banks and time are possible.

In most of the literature concerning the determinants of credit risk in conventional banking, nonperforming loans (NPL) serve as the proxy for credit risk measurement (Ahmad and Ariff, 2007; Berger and DeYoung, 1997; Das and Ghosh, 2007). NPL is generally quite difficult to manipulate by bank management and for this and other reasons this is a suitable form of ex-post credit risk agreed upon by most researchers (Berger and DeYoung, 1997; Louzis et al., 2010). While the definition of NPL varies slightly by country, we employ the definition of NPL used by the Bank for International Settlement (BIS). In our model, we convert the standard measure of NPL used in conventional banking into nonperforming finance (NPF), thereby recognizing the differences in 'credit risk' found in Islamic banks.

Hypotheses and Independent Variables

In this section, we discuss the independent variables. As discussed, GDP growth rate, spread and the real interest rate are the three most important variables represent macroeconomic factors potentially affecting the credit risk of Islamic banks. First, the adverse selection problem is captured by rapid credit growth (Salas and Saurina, 2002) and has long been identified as one of the most important causes of increasing NPLs (Clair, 1992; Jiménez and Saurina, 2005; Kwan and Eisenbeis, 1997; Sinkey and Greenawalt, 1991). In order to increase the market share of a particular bank, banks need to relax its loan criteria and provide inferior credit quality borrowers with the opportunity to access loan facilities. In addition, the adverse selection problem can become worse if credit expansion occurs in a new geographical area or a sector where bank has insufficient experience (Salas and Saurina, 2002). We construct this variable using the annual percentage change in the size of the loan portfolio in each bank. We hypothesize a positive sign on the estimated coefficient for loan portfolio growth when regressed against NPF.

Second, to capture the moral hazard problem in the Greek banking sector, Louzis et al., (2010) specified the 'solvency ratio' and the 'loan to deposit ratio'. We calculate the former by dividing owned capital by total assets and the latter by dividing loans by deposits. The solvency ratio measures the bank's financial 'cushion' for absorbing loan losses as well as proving an indicator of the risk attitude of bank managers. If the banks are not sufficiently solvent, it increases the probability of default. Therefore, there is an inverse relationship between nonperforming finance and the solvency ratio, reflecting that the higher the solvency ratio, the lower the incentive to take risks. David and Sommer (1996) found an inverse relationship between these variables.

Third, we use the loan to deposit ratio to represent the problem of moral hazard in banking. With this variable, we are partly able to justify the risk behavior of bank: in other words, how much the bank is willing to advance against its deposits. Although banks need to adhere to minimum deposit ratios, they may undertake riskier project by providing more loans. Based on this argument, we expect a positive relationship between the loan to deposit ratio and the NPF ratio. However, Louzis et al. (2010) found no significant similar relationship.

Fourth, to proxy profit efficiency, Louzis et al. (2010) used the return on assets (ROA) and the return on equity (ROE), two very commonly used performance variables in banking. Maudos et al. (2002) also used ROA and ROE to indicate the profit efficiency of banks. If bank management is efficient in running its business, we expect the bank will not incur many bad loans. In contrast, if bank management is not skilled in prudent monitoring and screening, it is likely that banks will have higher levels of NPF. Thus, profit efficiency as measured by ROE and ROA will fall when NPF increases. In related work, while Louzis et al. (2010) found a negative relationship between profit efficiency and NPL in mortgage and consumer loans in conventional banks, they observed no significant relationship with business loans.

Fifth, we estimate costs efficiency using the ratio of operating expense to operating income. Operating expenses consist of wage and nonwage expenses, such as rent, taxes, directors' remuneration, advertising and public expenses (Das and Ghosh, 2007). A higher ratio of this variable indicates that managers are not efficient in taking advantage of their branch network and employees are not skilled enough in managing the loan portfolio (Das and Ghosh, 2007; Louzis et al., 2010; Salas and Saurina, 2002). Therefore, we hypothesize a positive relationship when regressing NPF on this variable.

Sixth, to capture the effects of competition in the respective banking markets, we specify market power and size. Size is the ratio of the total assets of a particular bank each year and the total assets of all Islamic banks operating in that year. According to Das and Ghosh (2007) and Salas and Saurina (2002), in a competitive environment, bigger banks have a greater opportunity to diversify credit risk, especially through the expansion of networks. Although banks entering a new geographical area may face adverse selection problems, they also have the opportunity to include new various customers by easily monitoring portfolio diversification, and this lowers credit risk (Hu, Li, and Chiu, 2004). However, Demsetz and Strahan (1997) argued that size may have a positive impact on diversification of banking activities, but it does not necessarily reduce the risk of banks. In addition, Jimenez and Saurina (2004) and Louzis et al. (2010) also used size to capture the competition in the banking markets. We hypothesize a positive sign on the estimated coefficient for bank size.

Finally, we measure market power using the ratio of loans of a particular bank each year to total loans by all banks in that year. Agoraki et al. (2009) and Jiménez et al. (2007) provided evidence that market power and risk-taking behavior have a negative relationship indicating that as bank`s market power increases, the NPL (here NPF) ratio decreases. However, Petersen and Rajan (1994) suggested theoretical evidence that banks with market power tend to increase their level of lower quality loans.

Estimation Technique

In the literature, different researchers have used different estimation techniques for the determinants of credit risk based on the purpose of their research as well as availability of data. Many of these argue that Generalized Method of Moments (GMM) technique is more useful for dynamic panel data analysis with fixed effects models and have duly reported consistent results (Louzis et al., 2010; Das and Ghosh, 2007, Jimenez and Saurina, 2005, Sales and Saurina, 2002). Other studies, such as Khemraj and Pasha (2009), have used pooled least squares with fixed effects models. We believe that given the relatively small sample in our analysis, ordinary least squares (OLS) technique will suffice.

4. Results

As shown in Table 1, there are significant differences between Islamic banks in Bangladesh and Malaysia in terms of the dependent and independent variables specified in this analysis. First, average nonperforming finance (NPF), our designated proxy for credit risk, is higher for Malaysian Islamic banks than Bangladeshi Islamic banks. The maximum also differs, with NPF of 5% in Bangladesh and 11% in Malaysia.

Elsewhere, average credit growth is the same for both countries though the loan to deposit ratio is much higher in Bangladesh than in Malaysia. This suggests that the moral hazard problem may be relatively more severe in Bangladesh. ROE, representing profit efficiency displays almost the same distributional properties in both countries. However, our average measure of cost efficiency is only 33% in Bangladesh and 170% in Malaysia.

Turning to the regression results in Table 2, the values of R^2 indicate that we can predict 88% of the variance in NPF in Bangladeshi Islamic banks using our set of independent variables but only 48% of the variance in NPF in Malaysian Islamic banks. Nonetheless, we conclude that the overall results of the regressions are generally reliable. To consider the effects of the macroeconomy on NPF in Islamic banks, we draw on the estimated for GDP growth rate and spread. The estimated coefficients do not indicate any significant relationship between NPF and the GDP growth rate nor between NPF and spread in either country's Islamic banking system. This result is consistent with the findings in Sales and Saurina (2002) that microeconomic factors significantly determine credit risk.

Table 1. Descriptive statistics

	Variable	Mean	Std. dev	Min.	Max.
Bangladesh	Nonperforming finance	0.025	0.014	0.001	0.050
	GDP	0.062	0.003	0.057	0.066
	Spread	0.065	0.002	0.062	0.068
	Credit growth rate	0.286	0.135	0.010	0.600
	Solvency ratio	0.196	0.035	0.141	0.264
	Loan to deposit ratio	0.915	0.058	0.830	1.040
	ROA	0.015	0.006	0.001	0.020
	ROE	0.198	0.073	0.060	0.380
	Cost efficiency	0.339	0.087	0.190	0.530
	Size effect	0.627	0.065	0.111	0.630
Malaysia	Nonperforming finance	0.029	0.026	0.001	0.108
	GDP	0.038	0.033	–0.017	0.064
	Spread	0.031	0.001	0.029	0.033
	Credit growth rate	0.280	0.566	–0.229	2.936
	Solvency ratio	4.165	1.207	0.985	7.049
	Loan to deposit ratio	0.611	0.215	0.057	0.941
	ROA	–0.001	0.043	–0.257	0.022
	ROE	0.183	0.700	–0.334	4.667
	Cost efficiency	1.705	1.021	–2.602	4.108
	Size effect	0.262	0.099	0.050	0.529

Table 2. Determinants of credit risk in Islamic banks

Coefficient	Bangladesh	Malaysia
Constant	–0.107 (0.066)	0.017 (0.087)
GDP	0.176 (0.672)	0.021 (0.126)
Spread	0.473 (0.724)	1.456 (2.733)
Credit growth rate	–0.003 (0.026)	-0.017^{***} (0.006)
Loan to deposit ratio	0.069^{*} (0.035)	-0.045^{**} (0.018)
Solvency ratio	–0.065 (0.072)	–0.002 (0.003)
ROE	–0.063 (0.063)	0.004 (0.007)
ROA	0.664 (0.593)	0.274^{**} (0.113)
Cost efficiency	0.109^{**} (0.041)	–0.011** (0.005)
Size effect	4.13E-06** (1.69E-06)	0.104^{**} (0.042)
R^2	0.811	0.675

Figures in brackets are standard errors. *, ** and *** indicate statistical significance at the 10%, 5% and 1% level, respectively.

However, the results do indicate a significant inverse relation between credit growth and NPF, thereby indicating that an increase in credit growth lowers the credit risk of banks in both countries. Salas and Saurina (2002) argued that if the credit growth increases in new geographical areas where bank managers have sufficient knowledge, they could minimize the negative impact of new loans. Khemraj and Pasha (2009) and Martin (2011) also found a negative relationship between these two variables in the banking sectors in Guyana and Africa more generally, respectively.

Regarding the inverse relationship between credit growth and NPF, one possible explanation could be that banks are increasing credit, but only in the most productive sectors of the economy where the rate of repayment is high. This is because both countries are emerging economies and many industries are experiencing high growth. Another possible explanation is that even though banks are increasing credit, it may not be necessarily to new customers or to new areas. Even in new areas, Islamic banks in both countries may face little trouble monitoring and screening their loans. On this basis, we conclude that the adverse selection problem, considered as one of the most important factors for increasing NPF in the banking sector, does not have any significant negative impact on the credit risk of Islamic banks.

We obtain mixed findings for the moral hazard hypothesis, as captured by the loan to deposit and solvency ratios. As shown in the table, the loan to deposit ratio has significant positive impact on credit risk in Bangladeshi Islamic banks but a negative impact on credit risk in Malaysian Islamic banks. Ahmad and Ariff (2007) also considered this contrasting finding in their cross-country study of credit risk in conventional banks. In their study, the loan to deposit ratio was a significant positive determinant of credit risk in Malaysia, the US, and France, but a significant negative determinant in whereas it was negatively significant with Mexico and India. Elsewhere, Louzis et al. (2010) did not find any significant relationship between the loan to deposit ratio and NPL in the Greek banking sector.

A positive relationship between these two variables indicates that the higher the loan to deposit ratio for a bank, the more the bank is relying on borrowing funds, which will tend to increase credit risk. A possible explanation for this finding contra to theory is that Malaysian Islamic banks rely relatively more on borrowed or shareholders' funds and relatively less on deposits. In evidence, the mean loan to deposit ratio for Islamic banks is 91% in Bangladesh but only 61% in Malaysia. Thus, it is equally clear that Islamic banks in Bangladesh are heavily reliant on deposits when increasing loans. As a deposit insurance scheme covers all deposits is in Bangladesh, Islamic banks there tend to invest in risky project, which may be a good indicator of moral hazard. Alternatively, as money borrowed from other financial institutions funds a significant portion of the loans of Islamic banks in Malaysia, bank management there is likely more cautious in choosing projects to finance and this lowers the level of credit risk at the institutional level. The second variable we specify to capture the moral hazard problem is the solvency ratio. We find no significant relationship between the solvency ratio and NPF in Islamic banks in either Bangladesh or Malaysia, a finding similar to Louzis et al. (2010). One suggestion is that Islamic banks in both countries are both able to control the problem of moral hazard in their loan portfolios.

In our analysis, management efficiency consists of profit efficiency and cost efficiency. The proxies for profit efficiency are ROA and ROE, of which ROA shows a positive significant impact on credit risk in Islamic banks in Malaysia. A possible explanation is that Islamic banks in Malaysia are still in their infancy and credit policies are short-term oriented, which while it brings about a better immediate return, implies management tends to undertake riskier projects. Another possible explanation could be that as ROA is increasing in the short term, this promotes confidence in the minds of bank management that motivates them to finance higher risk projects. We also find a significant positive relationship between ROA and NPF in Bangladesh. However, there is no significant relationship between ROE and NPF in either Bangladesh or Malaysia.

Another very important variable representing management's ability to minimize NPF is cost efficiency. In practice, we measure this with the ratio of total operating expense to total operating income. From the regression result, a positive and significant relation is evident between cost efficiency and credit risk in Islamic banks in Bangladesh. Louzis et al. (2010), Salas and Saurina (2002) and Berger and DeYoung (1997) obtained similar findings. In support, Berger and DeYoung (1997) argued that inefficient managers are unable to deal with the process of both granting loans and monitoring efficiency, which increases the credit risk of banks. Shortages and misuses of the resources needed for monitoring and screening procedures are also quite inefficient, and this may affect their solvency (Salas and Saurina, 2002). One reason for this is that Islamic banks in Bangladesh are operating on a very small scale and we assume that management is not skilled nor does it have the experience to monitor their clients.

In contrast, we identify a negative relation between cost efficiency and NPF in Malaysian Islamic banks. Kwan and Eisenbeis (1997) found a similar result. We obtain three important conclusions. First, management in Malaysian Islamic banks is more prudent, which assists in improving cost efficiency. Banks likely incur costs when investigating their clients' financial situation, and so monitor the performance of their clients regularly in order to minimize the NPF. Second, Islamic banks in Malaysia spend a considerable amount of their total expense in training their employees, which make them more efficient and skilled in prudent monitoring and screening. Finally, the remuneration of employees in Islamic banks in Malaysia could depend on the performance of bank. Therefore, employees may attempt to minimize NPF through incurring higher costs. Overall, we conclude that management quality is higher in Malaysian than Bangladeshi Islamic banks.

Finally, we specify bank size to capture the effects of competition on credit risk in Islamic banks. The results of the regressions for both countries show that size is a significant and positive determinant of credit risk in both Bangladesh and Malaysia. Ranjan and Dhal (2003) also found a positive significant relationship between size and NPL while Khemraj and Pasha (2009) found a positive but insignificant relationship between size and NPL in Guyana. However, these findings are contra to the diversification hypothesis, which states that bigger banks have greater opportunity to diversify their loan portfolio, thereby lowering their overall credit risk.

Conclusion

In this analysis, we identified three important factors affecting the credit risk of Islamic banks in Bangladesh. These are the loan to deposit ratio, cost efficiency, and size, respectively reflecting the impact of moral hazard, management efficiency, and competition on credit risk. On this basis, we first conclude that the management of Islamic banks in

Bangladesh faces a moral hazard problem. This moral hazard problem probably arises because of the presence of the deposit insurance scheme in Bangladesh, whereby bank managers rely more on deposits as a source of funds than either shareholders' equity or borrowed money from other financial institutions. Regarding management efficiency, Islamic bank management, at least in Bangladesh, does not appear to be effective in reducing the costs of banks. In addition, given many Islamic banks in Bangladesh only recently commenced operations, it appears that their existing management is not very skilled in prudent monitoring and screening. Finally, competition accounts for higher NPF in Bangladeshi Islamic banks, which suggests that although Islamic banks are increasing their assets they are also investing in risky projects as a means of obtaining higher returns.

In contrast, we find five significant determinants of credit risk in Islamic banks of Malaysia. These are credit growth, the loan to deposit ratio, ROA, cost efficiency and size. These five determinants represent all four hypotheses tested in this study. In Malaysian Islamic banks, credit growth, which represents the issue of adverse selection in loan portfolios, has a negative relation with NPF. In addition, the loan to deposit ratio negatively affects NPF as a major proportion of loans disbursed by Islamic banks are not funded by deposits. We also find that the management of Malaysian Islamic banks are more cost efficient, which tend to lowers NPF, but also short-term goal oriented. Finally, as in Bangladesh, bank size has a significant impact in increasing NPF in the Islamic banking sector in Malaysia.

REFERENCES

Agoraki, M. E. K., Delis, M. D. & Pasiouras, F. (2009). Regulations, competition and bank risk-taking in transition countries. *Journal of Financial Stability*, *7*(1), 38–48.

Ahmad, N. H. & Ariff, M. (2007). Multi-country study of bank credit risk determinants. *International Journal of Banking and Finance*, *5*(1), 135–152.

Ayub, M. (2008). *Understanding Islamic Finance*, (Vol. *458*). West Sussex: Wiley.

Berger, A. N. & DeYoung, R. (1997). Problem loans and cost efficiency in commercial banks. *Journal of Banking and Finance*, *21*(6), 849–870.

Clair, R. T. (1992). Loan growth and loan quality: some preliminary evidence from Texas banks. Economic Review, Federal Reserve Bank of Dallas, Third Quarter, 9–22.

Das, Abhiman & Ghosh, Saibal (2007): Determinants of Credit Risk in Indian State-owned Banks: An Empirical Investigation. Economic Issues, Vol. *12*, No. 2 (September 2007): 48-66.

David Cummins, J. & Sommer, D. W. (1996). Capital and risk in property-liability insurance markets. *Journal of Banking & Finance*, *20*(6), 1069–1092.

Demsetz, R. S. & Strahan, P. E. (1997). Diversification, size, and risk at bank holding companies. *Journal of Money, Credit and Banking*, *29*(3), 300–313.

Hu, J. I. N. L. I., Li, Y. & Chiu, Y. H. O. (2004). Ownership and nonperforming loans: evidence from Taiwan's banks. *The Developing Economies*, *42*(3), 405–420.

Iqbal, Z. & Mirakhor, A. (2007). An introduction to Islamic finance: theory and practice. Singapore: John Wiley & Sons.

Jimenez, G. & Saurina, J. (2004). Collateral, type of lender and relationship banking as determinants of credit risk. *Journal of Banking and Finance, 28*(9), 2191–2212.

Jiménez, G. & Saurina, J. (2005). Credit cycles, credit risk and prudential regulation. *International journal of Central Banking*, *2*(2), 65-98.

Jiménez, G., Lopez, J. A. & Saurina, J. (2007). How does competition impact bank risk taking. Federal Reserve Bank of San Francisco Working Paper Series, No. *23*.

Khemraj, T. & Pasha, S. (2009). The determinants of nonperforming loans: an econometric case study of Guyana. Caribbean Centre for Banking and Finance Biannual Conference on Banking and Finance, St. Augustine, Trinidad.

Kwan, S. & Eisenbeis, R. A. (1997). Bank risk, capitalization, and operating efficiency. *Journal of Financial Services Research*, *12*(2), 117–131.

Louzis, D. P., Vouldis, A. T. & Metaxas, V. L. (2010). Macroeconomic and bank-specific determinants of non-performing loans in Greece: a comparative study of mortgage, business and consumer loan portfolios. Working Paper 118. Bank of Greece.

Martin. L O. (2011). The level of non-performing loans in East African banks on the decline. Retrieved from http://www.mfw4a.org/news/news-details/the-level-of-non-performing-loans-in-east-african-banks-on-the-decline.html.

Maudos, J. Pastor, J. M. Perez, F. & Quesada, J. (2002). Cost and profit efficiency in European banks. *Journal of International Financial Markets, Institutions and Money*, *12*(1), 33–58.

Petersen, M. A. & Rajan, R. G. (1994). The Effect of Credit Market Competition on Lending Relationships. National Bureau of Economic Research Working Paper Series, No. 4921. Retrieved from http://www.nber.org/papers/w4921.

Ranjan, R. & Dhal, S. C. (2003). Non-performing Loans and Terms of Credit of Public Sector Banks in India: An Empirical Assessment. Reserve Bank of India, No. 81.

Salas, V. & Saurina, J. (2002). Credit risk in two institutional regimes: Spanish commercial and savings banks. *Journal of Financial Services Research*, *22*(3), 203–224.

Sinkey, J. F. & Greenawalt, M. B. (1991). Loan-loss experience and risk-taking behavior at large commercial banks. *Journal of Financial Services Research*, *5*(1), 43–59.

Usmani, M. T. (2002). An introduction to Islamic finance (Vol. *20*). CN The Hague: Kluwer Law International.

In: Contemporary Issues in Islamic Finance
Editor: Andrew C. Worthington
ISBN: 978-1-62948-905-6

Chapter 8

PROSPECTS, BARRIERS AND IMPEDIMENTS TO ISLAMIC BANKING IN LIBYA

Yahia M. Baej [*] ***and Andrew C. Worthington***
Griffith University, Australia

ABSTRACT

Islam is the state religion in Libya with about 97% of Libyans being Sunni Muslim. Since independence, the principles of *Shariah* have at least partly applied in the state, and successive Libyan governments have shown a willingness to implement a dual system comprising Islamic and conventional banking institutions in the future. Nonetheless, the country's financial and banking system remains largely conventional, unlike many other countries with a majority Muslim population, including Egypt, Saudi Arabia, the United Arab Emirates, Turkey, Bahrain, and Malaysia, which have witnessed the development of banking systems with a substantial Islamic component. The objective of this chapter is to investigate reasons hindering the introduction of *Shariah*-banking system in the state. We find that the weakness of Libyan economy due to long periods of international sanctions, isolation, and systematic corruption, the absence of an Islamic monetary market, the uncertain relationship between the Central Bank of Libya and the newly introduced banks, and the lack of suitable human resources in banking are major challenges facing Islamic banking in Libya.

1. INTRODUCTION

Islamic banking is one of the fastest growing banking segments in Islamic and non-Islamic countries alike. While similar to most non-Islamic (conventional) banks, Islamic banks are typically private profit-seeking enterprises subject to the usual regulatory controls placed on banking of all forms. However, the principles of Islamic law (*Shariah*) strongly dictate their behaviour, including the strict prohibition of their dealing in interest (*Riba*),

[*] Corresponding author: Department of Accounting, Finance and Economics, Griffith University, Nathan QLD 4111, Australia. Email. yahia.baej@griffithuni.edu.au.

uncertainty (*Gharar*), gambling (*Maysir*) and a number of other common but religiously noncompliant financial products and services. Nevertheless, despite these apparent difficulties, the number of conventional banks adopting at least some aspects of Islamic banking in their operations and the number of new banks offering Islamic banking products and services has continued to grow.

Despite the huge attention which has been given to the Islamic finance and banking by Islamic countries for more than three decades, Libya has been an exception. This chapter first considers the overall economic situation in Libya. It then discusses some recent theoretical work in this area and then discusses the role of the Central Bank of Libya and banking regulation in introducing Islamic banking in the state. Finally, it deals with barriers and impediments as well as the prospects and opportunities of implementing any new Islamic banking entities.

2. Modern Libya

Although the events of 2011 culminating with the ultimate removal of the Gaddafi regime have had a devastating influence on the overall Libyan economy, it was already vulnerable to such shocks. An evaluation of Libyan economy during the last century shows that although the state went through a dramatic transformation, mostly because of the discovery of oil in the 1950s, it is difficult to compare its experience comparison with other Arab oil-producing peers such as the United Arab Emirates and Saudi Arabia in terms of general economic development and social welfare. The Libyan case remains unique given its long history of political turmoil that over time has worsened its economic situation and held it back from development. The long-term application of socialism also hindered any opportunity for improving the private sector in Libya. Additionally, Muammar Gaddafi's so-called 'Green Book' with its political, economic, and social myths, fully opened the door for corruption. For example, under political principles such as 'the private property of none' and the 'the house belongs to those who inhabit it', hundreds of properties were seized by the Gaddafi regime.

Similarly, the political philosophy encompassed in the Green Book saw the forced nationalization of a number of private enterprises during the last decades of the twentieth century. In addition, the mismanagement of Libyan international relations led to sanctions imposed by the United Nations and the United States, which had a severe impact on Libya's economic status and led to massive compensation from the state budget. Another important issue that burdened the Libyan economy was the unsuccessful Great Man Made River project. The financing for this project came directly from the state treasury and at the expense of other important budgets such as education and health. A new type of tax was also imposed upon all types of taxable income and the issuing of licenses and passports (Arafat, 2011).

Despite serious difficulties that faced the economy in 2011, economic and financial trends show evidence of recovery as the security situation continues to improve in Libya (Chami et al., 2012). Solutions have already been found to some pressing economic issues, including the lack of liquidity in the financial system and the growing demand for fuel. To further ease the level of inflation, the Libyan Central Bank has taken a set of necessary steps including selling foreign currencies such as the euro and the US dollar to withdraw Libyan currency injected into the market during the uprising. Nevertheless, the domestic political and economic situation prevailing in Libya during the last four decades remains the main obstacle hindering the introduction and growth of Islamic banking in the country.

3. Past Research into Islamic Banking in Libya

A number of studies have evaluated the potential introduction of Islamic finance in general and Islamic banking in particular to Libya. Yet policymakers in the country have not recognized these attempts, at least for some time. An example was work undertaken by the first-named author of this chapter as a part of fulfilling the requirements of a master's degree entitled 'The possibility of applying Islamic banking model over the Libyan banking system'. The results showed that a complete and instant transformation of the whole system into Islamic banking was not possible, as it would have a severe impact on the economy. Rather, a more gradual transformation would be beneficial by taking into account three phases (Baej, 2006).

The first phase is the introduction phase, which consists of planning and establishing a timeline for a complete transformation. This phase should include a complete set of steps, such as appointing supervision committees, giving special care to human resources, and carefully choosing the branches and subsidiaries selected for conversion to Islamic banking services. The second phase is the implementation phase. This begins with gaining permission from the Central Bank of Libya to introduce Islamic banking services. The author recommended that a special department should be appointed for regulating and supervising the monetary issues for the new banking activities. A *Shariah* advisory board would also be nominated to ensure the compliance of the new banking activities with Islamic law. The third and final phase is the evaluation phase. In this stage, the economic and social performance of the Islamic banking system would be evaluated.

Another important doctoral study conducted by Gait (2009) concerned 'Libyan attitudes towards Islamic methods of finance'. The principle findings of this thesis were that religion plays a significant role in influencing the attitudes of using Islamic methods of finance in Libya. Similarly, work by Kumati (2008) also investigated the potential for Islamic banking in Libya. The empirical results showed that although the participants in the study were generally unfamiliar with Islamic banking products and services, there was a significant latent demand for Islamic banking in Libya. In addition, an important initiative by the Academy of Postgraduate Studies (Tripoli), was the organization of a conference on Islamic monetary services on a number of occasions, and this promoted greater awareness about Islamic banking in Libya.

Parallel to this work, the Libyan Central Bank and the Jomhouria Bank have also discussed how it would be possible to implement at least some Islamic financial products and services in Libya. As a result, Libyan banking law has already been modified in a way that may be useful in the implementation of *Shariah*-compliant methods of banking. The following section discusses the role of banking law in introducing Islamic banking in Libya.

4. Libyan Banking Law

Following independence, the principles of *Shariah* were at least partly applied in Libya even though some of the legislation, adapted largely from the Egyptian model, was not totally compliant with Islamic teachings. For instance, *Riba* was prohibited under Civil Law No. 74 in 1972. Moreover, contracts of uncertainty (*Al-Gharar*) were also cancelled under Civil Law No. 86 of 1972. However, banking law has since remained largely unchanged (Alzrigi, 2010).

Banking Law No. 1 in 2005 interpreted as the first noticeable chance aimed at introducing Islamic banks, branches, or at least some banking products in Libya. Although Article 77 of this legislation was strict with regard to prohibiting commercial banks from engaging in some activities, such as commercial agencies activities, which implies the prohibition of Islamic banking activities, point 9 of the Article 16 of the same law allows other banks to be established:

Grant the license for commercial, specialized, financing and investment banks and other banks, and establish the rules that regulate and governor their activities and introduce their memorandum of agreement and articles of association (Central Bank of Libya, 2005 p. 6).

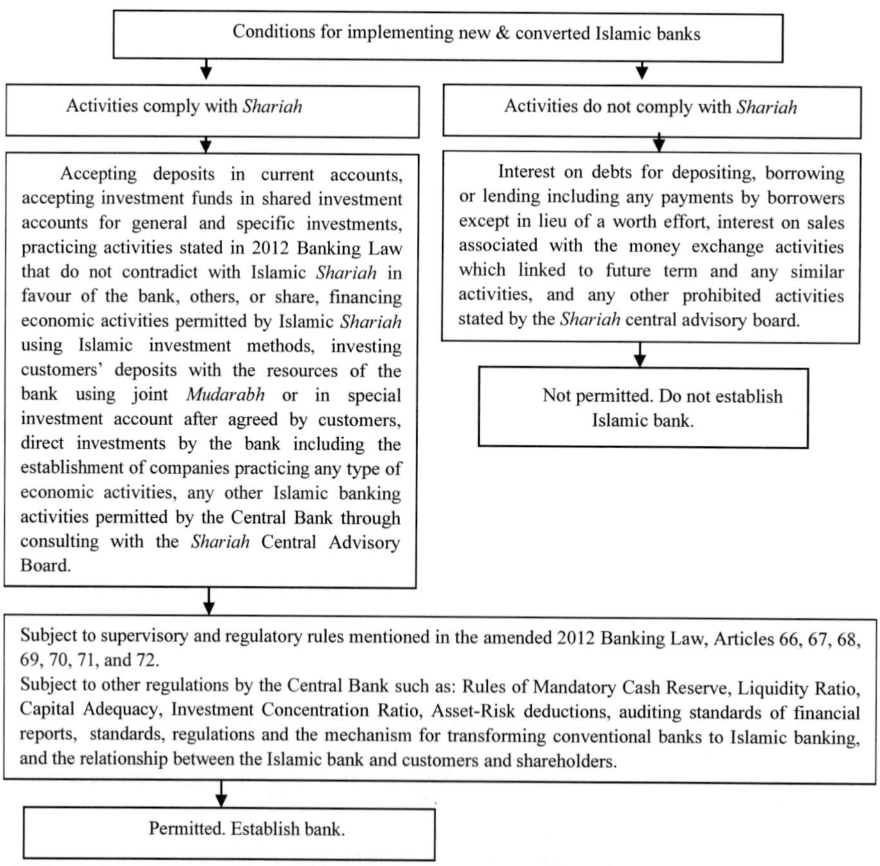

Source: Adapted from information in Central Bank of Libya, 2012(b), pp. 48–50; National Transitional Council, 2012 pp. 13–15.

Figure 1. Major conditions set by the Libyan central bank for Islamic banks.

The 2005 Banking Law, however, was amended by Law No. 1 of 2012 and followed with another important amendment by the National Transitional Council represented in Law No. 46 of 2012, which included a detailed chapter on Islamic banking. This chapter contains definitions of an Islamic bank, Islamic banking, the Central *Shariah* Advisory Board in the Libyan Central Bank, the *Shariah* Advisory Board(s) for Islamic bank(s), *Shariah* Auditing administration, Islamic banking branches, and Islamic banking windows. The law, moreover, distinguishes between permitted and prohibited activities for newly established Islamic banks or conventional banks introducing Islamic banking products and services. Figure 1 depicts the major conditions to be considered when establishing new Islamic bank or introducing Islamic banking activities into a conventional bank.

The future of Islamic banking and finance in Libya seems to be promising as it is the first direct involvement of a monetary authority in this matter since the emergence of banks in the Libyan state. Nevertheless, similar to any banking system, the new banking system in Libya requires much care to benefit from previous experience by countries who are pioneer in the field and to avoid obstacles and issues that might occur in the future. The following section outlines the challenges and opportunities for Islamic banking in Libya.

5. Barriers and Impediments

Although the long fight by academics, jurists and practitioners to settle the pillars of Islamic banking in Libya is almost at an end with the passing of the 2012 Banking Law, much more is undone with respect to the economic situation, human resources, financial and banking market, and banking regulations.

Libya's economy has long been dependent on oil revenues and the economic crisis in 2011 has proven that it remains vulnerable to economic shocks. It is also underdeveloped due to long international sanctions, isolation, and systematic corruption. The score of economic freedom of the country is 35.9, putting it as the 176th freest economy in the 2012 index. This places the country last in the Middle East and North Africa, far below the regional and world score (Index of Economic Freedom, 2012). Therefore, Islamic banking system would never survive unless the new authority in Libya takes substantial economic reforms. This could be by diversifying the economy through supporting industrial, agricultural, business and other sectors. The absence of an Islamic monetary market is another obstacle facing the entire Islamic financial industry. This gives an advantage to conventional banks over Islamic banks in Libya as the new-introduced stock market operates with conventional financial and monetary tools, which will not benefit the Islamic monetary market.

Adding to the previous barriers, the relationship between the Central Bank of Libya and the new introduced banks should be clearly determined. Seemingly, the Central Bank of Libya is adopting the lead of its peer, the Central Bank of Jordan, in terms of regulating and supervising Islamic banks. The chapter dedicated to Islamic banking in Libya published by the Central Bank states that Islamic banks are subject to the same rules as other banks with regard to mandatory cash reserves, the liquidity ratio, capital adequacy, the investment concentration ratio, asset-risk deductions, and auditing standards in financial reports. Nevertheless, this would have a negative impact on Islamic banks, as some of these rules are interest based, while others do not consider the unique nature of Islamic banks, such as the loan-to-deposit ratio (Tarrad and Huti, 2010).

Another important challenge for the Islamic banking industry in Libya is the availability of human resources (Taweel, 2010). Libya suffers a severe shortage in terms of conventional professional bankers, let alone those experienced in Islamic banking. The financial and banking education system overwhelmingly remains largely conventional. In the meantime, there is an absence of universities and colleges in Libya able to that carry out teachings of Islamic financial jurisprudence transactions together with Islamic financial and banking knowledge. Thus, the education outputs currently available in Libya are of two types: conventional accounting, economic, and finance graduates unfamiliar with Islamic banking principles or Islamic jurists unfamiliar with banking.

Therefore, the Central bank will need to rely on foreign assistance in establishing the new banking program and to supervise the conventional banking staff working in it. This may not be a problem if the situation is temporary. Immediate and appropriate actions, however, should be taken in educating and training Islamic banking staff in Libya. The establishment of *Shariah*-compatible business education is also essential.

It is not unusual for a new industry to face such challenges, as experienced in other countries with long and well-established Islamic banking systems (e.g. UAE, Bahrain, Saudi Arabia, Turkey, and Malaysia), most of which continue to experience difficulties in terms of human resources, banking regulations and market issues. It is worthwhile noting, however, that Islamic banks in Libya can benefit from the experience of these countries and avoid repeating the same mistakes. Those in authority, however, should consider the cooperation between the Islamic and conventional banking systems to insure a smooth movement to the new system without confrontation. This could be by adopting timeline and phases mentioned in the study of Baej (2006), taking into consideration the Libyan culture and other related determinants.

6. Prospects and Opportunities

Despite challenges and obstacles, some economic and banking trends reflect an improvement of the overall economic situation that helps the entire banking system in general and the establishment of the new banking system more specifically. Another factor is that Islamic banking in Libya is already attracting the attention of the new Libyan authorities, the Libyan Central Bank, other banks, academic and practitioners, and society as a whole. The unfrozen financial assets that, for long time, stayed outside the banking system could help the Central Bank dealing with the shortage of cash and properly managing the banking system. It also facilitates the movement to Islamic banking as it provides the later with the required capital for the investment.

The second factor is the attention of the Libyan authorities in implementing Islamic banking. Adding to the above mentioned law issued by the NTC in 2012 and the special chapter on Islamic banks in the 2012 amended banking law, a decision has been made by the National Congress of Libya to cancel all interest on loans to individuals granted by Libyan banks. The decision was referred to the executive committees of the national Congress for further actions and to be implemented before the end of 2012 (Quryna, 2012).

Moreover, some Libyan banks are willing to get involved to the new banking system. Since 2009, Jumhouria Bank, one of the biggest banks in Libya, has already introduced some *Shariah*-compliant products and services, including *Murabaha* for the provision of computers and motor vehicles (Jumhouria Bank, 2012). The National Commercial Bank has also introduced an Islamic banking window, also applying *Murabaha* to motor vehicles and computers, but also furniture (National Commercial Bank of Libya, 2010). More importantly, as the literature of Islamic banks in Libya discussed above suggests, the new institutions have a wide acceptance publically, although the premise of such institutions requires careful promotion, as any doubt about the validity of Islamic products and services would severely affect the Islamic banking industry in Libya in the future.

REFERENCES

Alzrigi, J. (2010). Libyan legislative position Of the Islamic financial services according to the Banking Law No. 1 of 2005. Islamic monetary services conference, Academy of Postgraduate Studies, Tripoli, Libya. (Arabic).

Arafat, M. (2011). The gear Man-Made River, North African crime carrying Gaddafi signature. *Middle East Youth.* (Arabic). Retrieved from: http://ar.mideastyouth.com/?p= 7176.

Baej, Y. M. A. (2006). Possibility of Using the Model of Islamic banks in Libyan Banks. The Master's Thesis, Department of Accounting, Economics, and Finance. Gharian, University of Aljabal Algharbi. (Arabic).

Central Bank of Libya (2005). Banking Law No. 1. of 2005. Tripoli, Central Bank of Libya: 43. Retrieved from: http://www.cbl.gov.ly/eg/.

Central Bank of Libya (2012). Law No. (1) of 2005 on the banks amended by Law No. 46 of 2012. N. T. Council. Tripoli, Libya, Central Bank of Libya. Retrieved from: http://www.cbl.gov.ly/eg/

Chami, R., Al- Darwish, A., et al. (2012) Libya beyond the Revolution: Challenges and Opportunities. 20. Retrieved from http://www.imf.org/external/pubs/ft/dp/2012/ 1201mcd.pdf.

Gait, A. H. A. (2009). Libyan attitudes towards Islamic methods of finance: An empirical analysis of retail consumers, business firms and banks. Doctoral thesis, Department of Accounting, Finance and Economics, Griffith University.

Index of Economic Freedom (2012). "2012 Index of Economic Freedom. http://www. heritage.org/index/country/libya.

Joumhoria Bank (2012). About The Bank. Retrieved August, 2012, from http://jbank.ly.

Kumati, A. (2008). Commercial banking in Libya and the potential for Islamic banking, Doctoral thesis, School of Government and International Affairs, University of Durham.

National Commercial Bank of Libya (2010). National Commercial Bank of Libya. Retrieved August, 2012, from http://ncb.ly/ar/.

National Transitional Council (2012). Law No. (46) Of 2012 by the National Transitional Council amending some provisions of Law No. (1) Of 2005 on the banks and adding special chapter on Islamic banking, National Transitional Council: 19. (Arabic)

Quryna (2012) The Libyan National Congress decided to cancel interest rate on loans. Retrieved January, 2013, from http://www.qurynanew.com.

Tarrad, I. & Huti, S. (2010). Legislations and procedures regulate the relationship between Islamic banks and central banks. A comparative study between Libya and Jordan. Islamic Monetary Services Conference, Academy of Postgraduate Studies, Tripoli, Libya. (Arabic)

Taweel, A. a. (2010). Practical tools for the introduction and implementation of financial and banking services according to Islamic Sharia rules. Islamic Monetary Services Conference, Academy of Postgraduate Studies, Tripoli, Libya. (Arabic)

In: Contemporary Issues in Islamic Finance
Editor: Andrew C. Worthington

ISBN: 978-1-62948-905-6

Chapter 9

MALAYSIAN EVIDENCE ON THE PERFORMANCE OF ISLAMIC MUTUAL FUNDS

***Ainulashikin Marzuki*[1,*] *and Andrew C. Worthington*[2]**
[1]Universiti Sains Islam Malaysia, Malaysia
[2]Griffith University, Australia

ABSTRACT

Using robust performance models, this chapter evaluates the performance of Islamic mutual funds (IMFs) in Malaysia during the period February 1996 to December 2009. We respond to the following two questions. First, how does the performance of IMFs compare with conventional mutual funds (CMFs) in Malaysia? Second, do IMFs perform better during bear markets? We find that IMFs generally outperform CMFs during the sample period. However, even though our results suggest that IMFs generally outperform CMFs during downward market trends, they do not appear to exhibit any significant investment hedging function during all crisis periods.

1. INTRODUCTION

The issue of screened fund performance has long been a source of debate. Islamic mutual funds (IMFs), which apply *Shariah* screening in their portfolio construction, face similar performance issues with other screened funds (for examples, socially responsible or ethical funds). *Shariah* screening reduces the number of stocks in the universe, which potentially reduces diversification (as unsystematic risk is not diversified away), and this screening requirement imposes additional monitoring and compliance costs. Thus, IMFs may have lower risk adjusted return than conventional mutual funds (CMFs). However, evidence from screened funds (which include socially responsible investment (SRI), ethical as well as IMFs) literature are mixed.

*Corresponding author: Faculty of Economics & Muamalat, Universiti Sains Islam Malaysia, Bandar Baru Nilai 71800 Nilai, Negeri Sembilan, Malaysia. Email. ainulashikin@usim.edu.my.

This study adds to literature by examining the performance of Malaysian IMFs in comparison to CMFs using robust performance measurement models (not limited to composite performance measures and single factor model). The sample used is recent which covers three major crises periods and free of survivorship bias. This paper addresses the following research questions. First, how is the performance of IMFs compared to CMFs? Second, do IMFs perform better during bear markets?

This study is important in at least three respects. First and the most obvious reason is the size of IMFs industry in Malaysia which valued at RM24 billion (USD$1=RM3.18 approximately) as at 31 December 2010 (Securities Commission Malaysia, 2012). Even though the net asset value (NAV) of IMFs only represents 11 percent of the total industry (Securities Commission Malaysia, 2012), Malaysia's IMFs is the second largest in asset size and is the largest in number of Islamic funds worldwide (more than 60% of the global Islamic fund market) (Abderrezak, 2008; Eurekahedge, 2008). In addition, despite the tremendous growth of IMFs, research in this area remains relatively scarce. IMFs is the fastest growing segment within the Islamic financial system with the number of Islamic funds worldwide increasing threefold from 200 funds in 2003 to 680 funds in 2008, (Eurekahedge, 2008). At the same time, the value of assets managed through IMFs has grown from US$20 billion in 2003 to US$44 billion in 2008 (Ernst & Young, 2009). Of this, equity funds represent the largest (about 40 percent) segment of IMFs, followed by fixed income (16 percent), real estate and private equity (13 percent), with the remaining funds in cash, commodities and other asset classes. IMFs are found across the globe, including North America and Europe, more than half are based in the Middle East and the Asia-Pacific (International Financial Services London, 2010, p. 5).

Secondly, there is lack of empirical investigation in Malaysia concerning the performance of mutual funds, especially the comparison between the performance of IMFs and CMFs. Specifically, Malaysian research is limited to Abdullah et al. (2007), Nassir et al. (1997), Hoepner et al. (2011), Lai and Lau (2010), Hayat and Kraeussl (2011), Low (2007) and Low (2008), Low and Ghazali (2007). Even though there are other studies that compare the performance of IMFs and CMFs, these studies use only composite portfolio performance measures. Bauer et al. (2007) argued, "not using a multifactor model to evaluate ethical funds can lead to an erroneous assessment of mutual fund performance". Furthermore, previous studies, for example Abdullah et al. (2007) is silent about survivorship bias and only have 14 IMFs. Other studies may be overcrowded by other type of mutual funds which is inappropriate to benchmark against market index (example Mansor and Bhatti (2011)). While the literature in the developed market such as the U.S, the U.K, Europe and Australia is quite extensive and well developed, evaluation of mutual funds in emerging markets especially Malaysia is significantly under researched. Thus, we enhance previous studies with robust performance measures across economic cycles using recent dataset, which is free of survivorship bias.

Finally, Malaysia is an interesting context for further investigating the performance of IMFs in comparison to CMFs. This is because of several reasons. First, the development of Islamic finance in Malaysia is one of the earliest and fastest in the Southeast Asian region. For example, in Malaysia, Islamic banking assets are currently about 18 percent of those of conventional banking while *takaful* assets account for about seven percent of the insurance industry. Likewise, IMFs form one of the more important components of the Malaysian Islamic financial system in general and Islamic capital markets in particular. Nevertheless, even though the market remains relatively small, Malaysia is one of the key players in the world of Islamic fund management. Second, ts unique capital market structure (where an Islamic financial system works in parallel with a conventional financial system) provides a unique setting to study the performance of IMFs in comparison to its counterpart, CMFs.

The remainder of the chapter is organized as follows. Section 2 reviews the past literature on the performance of screened funds. Section 3 describes the data and methodology employed while Section 4 discusses the results. Section 5 concludes.

2. BACKGROUND

The most important factor contributing to the introduction of IMFs in Malaysia was the launch of the Skim Amanah Saham Nasional (ASN) [National Unit Trust[1] Scheme] and the Amanah Saham Bumiputera (ASB) [*Bumiputera* Unit Trust] in the 1980s. The main objectives of these funds was to encourage *bumiputra* (native Malays as distinct from Chinese, Indian or other Malaysians) to participate in the corporate sector and to improve their socioeconomic standing.

The success of these funds led to strong demand for IMFs as most *bumiputra* are also Muslims, with the first Islamic equity fund introduced in 1993 by the Arab–Malaysian Unit Trust Berhad, the Tabung Ittikal (the Ittikal Fund).

The Malaysian Islamic fund management industry has since grown from just two IMFs in 1993 to 136, representing 25 percent of all 539 Malaysian mutual funds, with a combined NAV of RM16.41 billion (US$5.03 billion) as at March 2008 (Securities Commission Malaysia, 2012).

Table 1. Growth of the Malaysian mutual fund industry, 2000–10

	2000	2002	2004	2006	2008	2010
No. of companies	34	39	36	38	39	39
No. of funds*	127	188	291	416	579	564
Conventional	110	144	220	316	430	412
Islamic	17	44	71	100	149	152
NAV (RM billion)	43.3	53.7	87.39	121.76	134.41	226.81
Conv.	41.62	50.5	80.62	112.59	117.22	202.77
Islamic	1.68	3.2	6.76	9.17	17.19	24.04
Bursa Malaysia market cap (RM billion)	444.35	481.61	722.04	848.71	663.8	1,275
% of NAV to Bursa Malaysia market cap.	9.74	11.15	12.1	14.35	20.25	17.79

Source: Securities Commission annual reports (Securities Commission Malaysia, 2012). *Includes fund approved but not yet launched. #Not including unit holders account at the institutional unit trust agents (IUTA) that operate a nominee account system.

Referring to Table 1, between 2003 and 2007, assets under management (AUM) in these Islamic funds increased by 44 percent, with exponential growth expected to continue with the increase in the number of *Shariah* (Islamic law) compliant stocks listed on the Malaysian and international stock markets. As at May 2008, 85 percent of all listed companies on the Bursa

[1] In Malaysia, mutual funds are also known as unit trust funds.

Malaysia were *Shariah* compliant, accounting for 64 percent of total market capitalization (Securities Commission Malaysia, 2012). IMFs are therefore one of the most important components of the Malaysian Islamic financial system in general and the Islamic capital market in particular. Currently, Malaysia also has the largest number of IMFs in the world comprising 152 funds managed by 39 fund families. Even though the contribution of NAV of mutual funds to the overall stock market capitalization only 17.79 percent as at December 2010, the NAV of IMFs is the second largest in the world, next after Saudi Arabia.

Malaysia's success in Islamic finance lies in the integration of key structural components, namely the Islamic banking sector, Islamic debt capital and equity markets, Islamic money market, the *takaful* industry, and a number of other peripheral Islamic institutions, and its regulatory infrastructure, including financial liberalization and government incentives to promote the Islamic fund management industry. Recent incentives include allowing foreign investors to own up to 70 percent of stockbroking companies (up from 49 percent) and foreign fund managers to establish 100 percent foreign-owned fund management companies in Malaysia.

We can attribute the proliferation of *Shariah* compliant products and services, including IMFs, to the strong support of the Malaysian government as well as concerted efforts by key market players, regulators, including the Securities Commission of Malaysia (SCM) and the Federation of Investment Managers Malaysia (FIMM), and several other financial intermediaries. This has led to a significant increase in the depth and breadth of the industry.

3. Prior Research

Research in the performance of mutual funds are extensive but mostly centred in the developed markets such as the US, UK and Australia. In addition, the performance issues are always dealt with the performance of the mainstream mutual funds. Only recently, the performance of ethical or SRI funds have been getting serious interest from the academics, investors and regulators. Another type of funds, which have been experiencing tremendous growth, is IMFs. Although there has been a significant growth in the number and asset in IMFs, the volume of research in this area is still scarce.

Literature in Islamic investments particularly IMFs can be categorized into three main groups. The first group where the bulk of literature focuses on is on the performance of Islamic index [see Atta (2000), Hakim and Rashidian (2002), Girard and Hassan (2005), Hussein and Omran (2005) and Hassan et al. (2005)]. Second group is centred on the performance of Islamic funds compared to relevant benchmarks which are Islamic, conventional as well as ethical indices [see Elfakhani and Hassan (2005), Elfakhani et al. (2007), Hayat (2006), Kraeussl and Hayat (2008), Hayat and Kraeussl (2011), Abderrezak (2008), Alkassim (2008) and Hoepner et al. (2011)]. Final group which is just recently in the literature is to compare the performance of IMFs with CMFs and other types of mutual funds [see Abdullah et al. (2007), Nainggolan (2011), Mansor and Bhatti (2011), Nathie (2009) and Lai and Lau (2010)].

The first group of literature which centered on the performance of Islamic index is pioneered by among others Atta (2000), Hakim and Rashidian (2002), Girard and Hassan (2005), Hussein and Omran (2005) and Hassan et al. (2005). These studies compare the performance of Islamic index with conventional as well as ethical indices and find no difference in performance. For example, Hakim and Rashidian (2002) compared the performance between Islamic screened and unscreened indexes from 1999 to 2002 using maximum likelihood techniques with time series analysis. They found that the Dow Jones Islamic (DJI) is less risky than the Wilshire 5000 (unscreened) index. Using the Sharpe ratio, the Islamic index outperformed the conventional index. They also find that there is no difference in diversification potential between Islamic and conventional index. They suggested that the Shariah screened index presents unique risk-return characteristics that are not affected by the broaqd equity market.

Instead of comparing the index, the second group of literature compares the performance of IMFs with the Islamic, conventional as well as ethical market benchmarks. Elfakhani and Hassan (2005) compared the performance of 46 IMFs all over the world to both conventional and Islamic benchmarks. The IMFs were categorised into eight sector-based categories that included Malaysia. Their sample period was from 1997 to 2002 and employing CAPM models, they found no significant difference in performance to either Islamic or conventional benchmarks.

Abderrezak (2008) investigated whether IMFs outperform or underperform three types of market benchmarks mainly Islamic, conventional and ethical benchmarks. Using CAPM and three factor models, he found that IMFs underperform conventional and Islamic indexes. When he used matched-pair analysis, there was no significant difference between Islamic and ethical funds. However, both studies used old data sets with Abderrezak, using a data set from 1997 to 2002.

The final group of literature focuses on comparison of performance between IMFs with CMFs. Abdullah et al. (2007) investigated the performance of IMFs and compared it to conventional counterparts. Using a data set from 14 IMFs and 51 CMFs between 1995 and 2001, they found that both IMFs and CMFs suffer from lower diversification. Even though IMFs exhibit lower diversification, the difference is not significant. Relating to performance, and using seven performance models that include CAPM, Modligiani and Modigliani (MM) and Information ratio (IR), they found that IMFs performed better than CMFs when the market was down, and performed worse, when the market was in uptrend. This unique feature of IMFs is good news to investors as it may act as a hedging mechanism. According to Blake and Timmermann (2003, p. 6) mutual funds add value if they "underperform on average but nevertheless outperform during recession or during periods when the rest of the market is down". The findings above are commonly shared by the research done by Abderrezak (2008), Elfakhani and Hassan (2005) and Kraeussl and Hayat (2008) from different aspects of performance evaluation.

There is recent study that extensively compares IMFs with conventional, ethical and religious funds (Nainggolan, 2011). She finds that IMFs underperform CMFs but their performance is comparable to both ethical and other religious funds. In contrast with previous studies, she finds that IMFs do not exhibit hedging function during crises periods except for the recent Global Financial Crises. In summary, there are inconsistencies in the findings. This calls for more empirical research, using new and longer data in addition to comprehensive performance measures to understand to what extent *Shariah* screening affects mutual fund performance. This study improves on prior studies by analyzing investment return performance of 147 Malaysian funds, which consists of 46 IMFs. Examining returns performance of the IMFs sample over an extended and more recent interval of time provides a more complete and accurate depiction of the performance of IMFs in Malaysia.

4. DATA AND METHOD

4.1. Data on Mutual Funds and Benchmarks

In this study, we examine the monthly performance of 46 IMFs and 101 CMFs from February 1996 to December 2009 in Malaysia. Our primary data source is Morningstar database. To ensure that we include all available mutual funds in Malaysia with as many observations as possible, we check our data with other sources which are Bloomberg, Eurekahedge, list of funds published from time to time by the Securities Commission and funds prospectuses and annual reports available at the library of the Securities Commissions. This process also helps us to minimize the effect of survivorship bias.

The sample limits to Malaysian domestic equity funds where the classification of equity funds follows Morningstar classification. From the 605 funds available in the Morningstar database, we exclude all non-equity funds such as allocation, alternative, fixed income and money market funds. We also exclude equity funds with focus on certain sectors, funds that have international exposure, funds with less than 12 months observation and with substantial missing values.

Table 2. Population and sample distribution of conventional and Islamic mutual funds, 1996 to 2009

Year	Total		% included	CMF		% included	IMF		% included
	Total	Sample		Total	Sample		Total	Sample	
1996	77	42	55	–	35	–	–	7	–
1997	84	46	55	–	38	–	–	8	–
1998	95	52	55	–	41	–	–	11	–
1999	107	59	55	94	48	51	13	11	85
2000	127	67	53	110	56	51	17	11	65
2001	163	76	47	132	61	46	32	15	47
2002	188	86	46	144	65	45	44	21	48
2003	226	95	42	171	69	40	55	26	47
2004	291	120	41	220	87	40	71	33	46
2005	340	129	38	257	92	36	83	37	45
2006	387	131	34	295	94	32	92	37	40
2007	484	134	28	360	94	26	124	40	32
2008	532	134	25	392	91	23	140	43	31
2009	541	128	24	397	85	21	144	43	30

The samples comprise only equity funds. The classification of equity funds follows Morningstar. From 1999 to 2005, the population of funds includes a number of funds approved but not launched. From 2006 to December 2009, the population is the number of funds launched at the end of December every year.

Table 3. Sample of CMF and IMF as at December 2009

Year	No. of funds launched at 31 December 2009	Total equity funds approved at 31 December 2009	Sample of equity funds	% included
IMF	144	72	46	64
CMF	397	*198	101	51
All funds	541	*270	147	54

*As we do not have the number of conventional equity funds launched, we estimate that 50 percent of the total mutual funds are equity funds.

The final number of funds in the sample is 147 consisting both CMFs (101) and IMFs (46) funds. This number represents 52.69 percent of the total equity funds available in the Morningstar database. The main reason to limit to equity funds is that it is only appropriate to use market index as a benchmark for equity funds. The selection of benchmark is important in measuring the performance of mutual funds. As index is the only established market benchmark available.

Table 2 presents the population and sample distribution of IMFs and CMFs year by year from 1996 to 2009 and Table 3 reports the cross sectional distribution as at December 2009. Figures for total population are derived from the Malaysian Security Commission annual reports while samples are collected from the Morningstar database. From Table 2, the highest percentage of sample collected is in 1999 for both IMFs and CMFs, which are 85 and 51 percent respectively. The lowest percentage of sample collected is in 2009 for IMFs and CMFs, which are 30 and 21 percent respectively. The reduction in the sample coverage throughout the periods may be because of funds termination or merger. From Table 3, as at the end of December 2009, the annual report from the Malaysian Security Commission reports that there are 541 numbers of Malaysian mutual funds, of which 144 are IMFs. Out of 144 IMFs, 72 are equity funds. In average, the sample of equity funds represents 64 percent of the total population of IMFs.

One of the limitations of performance study is the issue of survivorship bias. Malkiel (1995) and Carhart (1997) argued that survivorship bias data might affect the result of fund performance where performance might be bias upward. This is due to having only performing funds in the sample while underperforming funds that are non-survivors are not in the sample. The effect of survivorship bias is minimized by incorporating all available funds within the period under observation. Both Morningstar and Eurekahedge maintain both dead and alive funds in their database.

We obtained monthly data for FTBM KLCI and FTBM 100 from Datastream and calculated the total return for these indices using the following formula.

$$R_{i,t} = ln\frac{P_{i,t} - P_{i,t-1}}{P_{i,t-1}} \qquad (1)$$

where $R_{i,t}$ is the monthly raw return of an index in period t, $P_{i,t}$ is the price of an index *i* in period t and $P_{i,t-1}$ is the price of an index *i* in period t-1.

We use continuously compounded monthly returns for both funds and indices. For funds, based on the monthly return from the Morningstar, we form equally weighted portfolio for each fund type and subsequently calculate continuously compounded monthly return. This study uses the three-month Malaysian Treasury bill rate as a proxy for risk free rate. This data is available from the Monthly Statistical Bulletin published by the Bank Negara Malaysia (Central Bank of Malaysia). This is an annualized holding period yield on a three-month Treasury bill and therefore is converted to a monthly equivalent consistent with the monthly returns of the mutual funds and the market's return. The monthly equivalent of the annualized yield is estimated as a geometric mean which is equivalent continuously compounded monthly rate. We also employ Carhart (1997) four factor model which the benchmark factors include market, size, style or book-to-market and the 12-months return momentum factor. We use the on-line research tool provided by Style Research Ltd. To construct monthly returns of benchmark factor portfolios. This is similar to the earlier research done by Bauer et al. (2005), Renneboog et al. (2008) and Hoepner et al. (2011). We use all Malaysian stocks in the Worldscope database to construct factor portfolios to estimate multifactor models. As according to Bauer et al. (2007), the main benefit of the Worldscope stock universe is that it covers over 98% of total market capitalization. We calculate excess market return by deducting risk free rate from the value-weighted market proxy extracted from Worldscope database.

The small-minus-big (SMB) is the difference in return between small capitalization portfolio and big capitalization portfolio. Following Fama and French (1993), the small cap portfolio covers the bottom 50% of total market capitalization after ranking all stocks according to size. The remaining top 50% is assigned to the large capitalization portfolio. The high-minus-low (HML) is the return difference between a value stock portfolio and a growth stock portfolio. Following Fama and French (1993), we first rank all stocks according to their book-to-market ratio and then assign the top 30% of market capitalization to the high book-to-market (i.e value) ratio and then assign the bottom 30% to the low book-to-market (i.e growth) portfolio.

Finally, we consider a momentum (MOM) factor which is defined as the monthly return spread between a past 12-month winner portfolio and a past 12-month loser portfolio. After having ranked all stocks on their prior 12-month return, we classify the top 30% as "winners" and the bottom 30% as "losers". Consistent with Fama and French (1993) and Carhart (1997), the SMB and HML factors are rebalanced at the end of June of each year, while the momentum factor is rebalanced at the end of each month. Since we use Worldscope market benchmark in our Carhart (1997) performance model, we also include this market benchmark in other selectivity and market timing measures for comparison purposes.

4.2. Portfolio Performance Models

4.2.1. Security Selection Models

Raw Return, Excess Return, the Sharpe (1966) and the Treynor (1965) Ratios

IMF employ screenings in their portfolio construction, thus limit the potential number of assets in their portfolio (diversification) which increase unsystematic risk. Based on this, our first hypothesis is we expect that IMFs underperform CMFs. We use various performance models to examine the performance of IMFs and CMFs in Malaysia. We use raw return, excess return, Treynor (1965), Sharpe (1966), Jensen (1968), and Carhart (1997) four factor models. There are two main reasons we include raw return and excess return in our performance measures. First, many of the previous studies of performance have included these measures. Second, these two measures are regarded as the performance measures that are not subjected to performance misspecification as argued by Kothari and Warner (1997). The inclusion of these measures will ensure that at least two measures that are not subject to their critique. While average raw return is simply the average of the time series return for each funds in the sample, average excess return measure is as follows.

$$Excessreturn_{i,t} = R_{i,t} - R_{f,t} \tag{2}$$

where $R_{i,t}$ is the mean return of fund i over the measurement period, $R_{f,t}$ is the risk-free rate of return during the corresponding period.

Sharpe (1966) ratio is average monthly excess return (over risk free rate) divided by standard deviation of fund excess return. The Sharpe ratio ranks equity fund performance relative to other mutual funds. The Sharpe (1966) ratio is defined as follows.

$$SR_i = \frac{R_{i,t} - R_{f,t}}{\sigma_{i,t}} \tag{3}$$

where SR_i is the Sharpe ratio, $R_i$is the mean return of fund i over the measurement period t, $R_f$is the risk-free rate of return during the corresponding period and $\sigma_i$is the standard deviation of a fund's mean excess returns. The Sharpe ratio ranks mutual fund performance relative to other mutual funds.

Treynor (1965) index is a measure of average monthly excess return (over risk free rate) divided by beta. The Treynor (1965) index is as follows.

$$TR_i = \frac{R_{i,t} - R_{f,t}}{\beta_{i,t}} \tag{4}$$

where TR_i is Treynor ratio, $R_i$is the mean return of fund i over the measurement period t, $R_f$is the risk-free rate of return during the corresponding period and β_i is the beta coefficient for the fund, estimated using a regression of fund returns, R_i against the market excess returns, R_m as follows.

Beta can be estimated by regression of the equity fund returns, R_i with the market return, R_m as follows.

$$\beta_i = \frac{Covariance\ (R_i, R_m)}{\sigma_m^2} \tag{5}$$

It is a measure of sensitivity between the market and the fund usually near one. A higher beta indicates that a fund is highly associated in the market and is playing a dominating role either with positive or negative returns.

One- Factor Model (Jensen, 1968)

The study also adopts risk adjusted single index measure, which is Jensen's traditional model. This measure is the most and commonly employed in the literature in addition to

Sharpe (1966). This model is based mainly on the theoretical Capital Asset Pricing Model (CAPM). In his seminal work, Jensen (1968) clearly explained how to measure risk-adjusted abnormal performance in markets, which use Jensen's alpha to capture the abnormal excess return of active funds. The alpha is estimated using ordinary least squares (OLS) regression, where an active fund return in excess of the risk-free rate is regressed on the excess return of the market proxy portfolio. The standard excess returns market model regression is as follows.

$$R_{i,t} - R_{f,t} = \alpha_i + \beta_i(R_{m,t} - R_{f,t}) + \varepsilon_{i,t} \quad (6)$$

where $R_{i,t}$is the mean excess return on fund or portfolio I at time t; ; α_p is Jensen alpha which captures any excess return above market benchmark, R_{mt}; R_{mt} is the mean return on market representing the mean-variant efficient benchmark; $R_{f,t}$ is risk-free rate at time t; $\beta_{p,i}$represents systematic risk of the fund or portfolio relative to the market return and ε_{it} is the random error of equity fund portfolio.

Four-Factor (Carhart, 1997) Model

Besides single factor model, we further examine IMF performance by using Carhart four-factor model (1997) from February 1996 to December 2009. These multifactor models give a much better sense of how IMF risk exposures differ from one another. At the same time, many studies find that the single index model is not adequate in explaining mutual fund performance [see Bauer et al. (2007)]. Carhart four-factor model (1997) is estimated using OLS as follows.

$$R_{i,t} - R_{f,t} = \alpha_i + \beta_i(R_{m,t} - R_{f,t}) + \beta_{S,i}SMB_t + \beta_{V,i}HML_t + \beta_{M,i}MOM_t + \varepsilon_{i,t} \quad (7)$$

where $R_{i,t}$ is the mean excess return on fund or portfolio *i* in time *t* ; R_{mt} is the return on a market portfolio in time *t*, $R_{f,t}$ is the risk free rate in time t; R_{mt} is the market returns; SMB_t is the return on the portfolios of small minus big stocks in time *t*; HML is the return on the portfolios of high minus low book-to-market stocks in time *t*; MOM is the return on the portfolios of high minus low momentum (prior 1-year return) stocks in time *t*; β_i measure the sensitivity between the market and the fund or portfolio, if positive and significant then fund is highly associate with the market movement; $\beta_{Si}$is a coefficient that measure the fund exposure to either size of securities where if positive and significant then the fund is associated with small-capitalisation stocks; β_{Vi} also a coefficient that measures fund exposure to either value or growth securities where if positive and significant then the fund is exposed to high book-to-market securities i.e value stock; $\beta_{M,i}$ is a coefficient that measures fund exposure to either contrarian or momentum strategies where if positive and significant then the fund is exposed to momentum strategy; α_i measures stock selection ability, if positive and significant, then the fund has superior stock selection ability and ε_{it} is the random error of a mutual fund portfolio. The SMB, HML and MOM factors are constructed using the online research tool by Style Research Ltd.

4.2.2. Market Timing Models

Our second hypothesis is to test if IMFs exhibit lower market timing abilities. This study uses two traditional market timing models, which are Treynor and Mazuy (1966) and Henriksson and Merton (1981) models.

Stock selection and market timing performances for each fund is calculated using Treynor and Mazuy (1966) model and this model is estimated as follows using Ordinary Least Square (OLS) regression technique.

$$R_{i,t} - R_{f,t} = \alpha_i + \beta_i(R_{m,t} - R_{f,t}) + \gamma_{i,t}(R_{m,t} - R_{f,t})^2 + \varepsilon_{i,t} \qquad (8)$$

where $R_{i,t}$ is the return on fund; α_i identify stock selection ability; R_{mt} is the return on market benchmark and $(R_{mt})^2$ is the squared market return. The term gamma, $\gamma_{i,t}$, indicates market timing. If $\gamma_{i,t}$ is positive and significant then fund are successful and exposure to the market is increased when markets are doing well.

For robustness, this study also uses an alternative test for market timing ability using the Henriksson and Merton (1981) model. This model is estimated as follows using OLS regression technique.

$$R_{i,t} - R_{f,t} = \alpha_i + \beta_i(R_{m,t} - R_{f,t}) + \delta_i(R_{m,t} - R_{f,t})D_t + \varepsilon_{i,t} \qquad (9)$$

where $R_{i,t}$ is the return of fund, α_i identify stock selection ability, R_{mt} is the return on market benchmark and γ identify market timing, if positive and significant then fund manager is successful market timer and know when to enter and exit the market. The D_t is the dummy variable that is equal to one if market return is positive and 0 otherwise.

4.2.3. Diversification and Net Selectivity Models

The third hypothesis is to test whether IMFs suffer severe diversification cost and thus net selectivity, the study follows Fama (1972) decomposition model. The cost of inadequate diversification is as follows.

$$DIV_{1,t} = (\sigma_i - \beta_i\sigma_m)\frac{R_{m.t}-R_{f,t}}{\sigma_m} \qquad (10)$$

where σ is the standard deviation of the portfolio excess returns, β_i is the portfolio's market beta estimated with Equation (5), $(R_{m,t} - R_{f,t})$ is the market excess return, and σ_m is the standard deviation of the market excess returns. Thus $DIV_{1,t}$ equals the idiosyncratic part of portfolio return volatility $(\sigma_i - \beta_i\sigma_m)$ multiplied by the Sharpe ratio of the market portfolio, such that the cost of inadequate diversification is the additional expected return that would just compensate the investor for the diversifiable portfolio dispersion taken by the manager.

Following Zhang (2006) and Lee et al. (2010), we use the extended Fama (1972) diversification specification (based on the four-factor model) as a performance benchmark.

$$DIV_{4,t} = \sigma_p - \sigma_b\frac{R_{b,t}}{\sigma_b} \qquad (11)$$

where σ is the standard deviation of the portfolio of excess returns, $R_{b,t}$is the return of a zero investment portfolio consisting of the four benchmark assets with the factor loadings resulting from regressing excess fund returns on factor returns in Equation (7), and σ_b is the standard deviation of returns $R_{b,t}$ Similar to the first specification, the cost of inadequate diversification $DIV_{4,t}$ equals the idiosyncratic part of portfolio return volatility $\sigma_p - \sigma_b$ times the Sharpe ratio of the four-factor benchmark portfolio. A completely diversified portfolio contains no unsystematic risk. This means that diversification measure would be zero. A completely diversified portfolio contains no idiosyncratic risk. This means that diversification measure would be zero. A positive value will signal a lack of diversification, which measures the extra return required for IMFs to compensate the loss of diversification for bearing more idiosyncratic risk.

Next, following Zhang (2006) and Lee et al. (2010),we calculate the Fama (1972) measure of fund performance, net selectivity (NS) by subtracting the diversification term from fund's risk adjusted return. Specifically, the net fund performance, termed as net selectivity is the difference between a fund's risk adjusted return (selectivity measures) and the diversification cost. The NS has the following two specifications.

$$NS_{1,t} = (\alpha_1 + \varepsilon_i) - Div_{1,t} = (R_{i,t} - R_{f,t}) - \sigma_i \frac{R_{m,t} - R_{f,t}}{\sigma_{m,t}} \quad (12)$$

$$NS_{4,t} = (\alpha_4 + \varepsilon_i) - Div_{4,t} = (R_{i,t} - R_{f,t}) - \sigma_i \frac{R_{b,t}}{\sigma_b} \quad (13)$$

If the value of net selectivity is positive, the fund manager successfully earned a fair return for diversifying away unsystematic risk. If it is negative, the manager deteriorated the overall portfolio's return correspondingly to its risk profile.

4.2.4. Fund Performance in Losing Markets and Financial Crises

The paper also tests the difference (if any) in the performance of IMFs in the losing market trend and the uptrend market trend and compares their performance to the conventional counterpart. Following Hoepner et al. (2011), the study tests the performance of IMFs in the three main crisis periods. These crises periods are the Asian financial crisis (AFC) from July 1997 to August 1998, the burst of the global internet bubble (GIB) from April 2000 to September 2002 and the global credit crisis (GCC) from July 2007 to February 2009. The first dummy variable D_0 is define as 1, if the contemporaneous observation of the domestic equity market benchmark is negative and defined as zero otherwise. If its coefficient is significantly positive, the financial performance differential between a portfolio of IMFs and the domestic equity market benchmark is significantly better for the Islamic asset during a losing market. In this case, IMFs could be understood to have a hedging function.

The remaining three dummies represent equity market crises. Recent history saw three crises, the AFC, the burst of the GIB and the GCC, which more than halved the equity markets. The diversity of these crises allowsdistinguishing the effect of a financial industry caused crisis from a crisis caused by another industry (i.e. Information Technology) on the relative performance of IMFs. Similarly, the study separates the effect of a global crisis and an Asia-Pacific crisis on IMFs from the Asia-Pacific region. Technically, the study defines our second, third and fourth dummy variables as one during the period of the respective crises and as zero otherwise. Hence, D1, D2 and D3 have the value of one from July 1997 to August 1998, April 2000 to September 2002 and July 2007 to February 2009 respectively. We use the following specifications to test the above hypothesis.

We estimate the following time-series regressions.

$$R_{i,t} = \alpha_0 + \beta_1 R_i + \beta_2 DR_{m,t} + \beta_3 DAFC_t + \beta_4 DGIB_t + \beta_5 DGCC_t + \varepsilon_{i,t} \quad (14)$$

$$R_{i,t} = \alpha_0 + \beta_1 R_i + \beta_2 SMB_{i,t} + \beta_3 HML_{i,t} + \beta_4 MOM_{i,t} + \beta_5 DR_{m,t} + \beta_6 DAFC_t + \beta_7 DGIB_t + \beta_8 DGCC_t + \varepsilon_{i,t} \quad (15)$$

where R_{mt} is the market returns which either Worldscope market, FBM100 or FBMKLCI index; while other variables are as defined in Equation (6) and (7)$DR_{m,t}$ is defined as 1, if the contemporaneous observation of the domestic equity market benchmark is negative and defined as zero otherwise. If its coefficient is significantly positive, the financial performance differential between a portfolio of Islamic funds and the domestic equity market benchmark is significantly better for the Islamic asset during a losing market. $DAFC_t$ is dummy for the AFC, $DGIB_t$ is dummy for the burst of the GIB and $DGCC_t$ is dummy for the GCC where these dummy variables take value as one during the period of the respective crises and as zero otherwise. Hence, $DAFC_t, DGIB_t$, and $DGCC_t$ have the value of one from July 1997 to August 1998, April 2000 to September 2002 and July 2007 to February 2009 respectively.

5. Analyses and Discussion

Table 4 provides a summary of the main fund characteristics of the 46 IMFs and 101 CMFs sampled for the analysis, namely, the number of fund families, NAV, age, the management expense ratio (MER) and management fees. As shown, in the sample, 24 management companies managed IMFs and 27 management companies managed CMFs. On average, each of these management companies offers two IMFs and four CMFs. Further investigation shows that three companies focus exclusively on IMFs and five companies on CMFs. This suggests that despite incentives recently introduced by financial regulators in Malaysia for fund management companies to offer IMFs, not all management companies have taken advantage of these opportunities. Interestingly, the mean NAV in IMFs greatly exceeds that of CMFs. This could be because of the smaller number of IMFs available relative to CMFs, which then causes subscriptions to center on these funds. Importantly, compared with IMFs, investors have more choices available to invest in different CMFs. The sample of IMFs is also relatively younger than CMFs by about four years. This is because IMFs are relatively new to the Malaysian market with the first IMF only introduced in 1993. As shown in the last four columns of Table 4, only NAV and age are significantly different across the two types of funds. The mean and standard deviation of NAV of IMFs are significantly larger and more dispersed than that of CMFs, at the 10 and 5 percent respectively.

Table 4. Characteristics of IMF and CMF as at December 2009

	IMF			CMF			Equality of variance		Equality of means	
Variable	N	Mean	Std. dev.	N	Mean	Std. dev	F-statistic	p-value	t- statistic	p-value
No. of funds	46	–	–	101	–	–	–	–	–	–
No. of families	24	–	–	27	–	–	–	–	–	–
NAV	43	252.27	454.84	83	122.20	221.30	13.028	0.000	1.770	0.083
AGE	46	8.92	8.96	101	12.60	9.90	2.137	0.146	–2.147	0.034
MER	42	1.59	0.49	86	1.90	2.29	0.758	0.386	–0.857	0.393
FEE	46	1.52	0.26	101	1.50	0.14	2.841	0.094	0.411	0.682

This table reports the fund characteristics of Malaysian Islamic mutual funds (IMF) and conventional mutual funds (CMF). NAV is net asset value in millions of Malaysian Ringgit. AGE is in years since inception. MER is the management expense ratio as a percentage. FEE is the management fees as a percentage. N and Std. dev. are the number of funds in the sample and the standard deviation, respectively. The null hypothesis for the two-sided variance test is equal variances for IMFs and CMFs. The null hypothesis of the one-sided test is that the mean for IMFs is less than the mean for CMFs. The variance test determines whether the means test assumes equal or unequal variances.

The age of IMFs shows no difference in dispersion, but they are significantly younger than CMFs at the 5 percent level. The differences in means for MER and management fees are very small and are not statistically significant between these types of funds. However, fees charged by IMFs are much more dispersed (the test for equality of variance is significant at 10 percent) than those of CMFs. Table 5presents the descriptive statistics and correlation coefficients of monthly excess returns of mutual fund portfolios, the three-month Malaysian Treasury bill rate, market benchmarks and other risk factors from 1996 to 2009. As shown in Panel A in Table 5, the empirical characteristics of negative skewness, excess kurtosis and non-normality in most portfolio returns are the dominant features of the data.

Panel B in Table 5 displays the Pearson correlation coefficients of each mutual fund portfolio and the risk factors. Mutual fund returns indicate high correlations with the returns of the FTSE Bursa Malaysia 100 (FBM100) and Worldscope broad market indices. Similarly, the market indices closely correlate with each other, with significantly high positive correlation coefficients. However, the correlations between the risk factors are relatively low and unlikely to lead to multicollinearity problems in the OLS regressions.

5.1. Security Selection Models

This section provides the results of the empirical analysis of six performance measures used to gauge the performance of IMFs relative to CMFs. The performance measures used are: (i) raw returns, (ii) excess returns, (iii) the Sharpe ratio, (iv) the Treynor ratio, (v) the one-factor model (CAPM), (also known as Jensen's alpha) and (vi) the Carhart's four-factor model. We estimate the models at both the portfolio and individual fund levels. At the portfolio level, we measure the difference between IMF and CMF portfolios by estimating those performance measures on a 'difference' portfolio, which is a portfolio constructed by deducting the time-series returns between IMF and CMF portfolios.

Table 5. Descriptive statistics and correlation matrix

	IMF	CMF	FBM100	World-scope	SMB	HML	MOM	TB
Panel A: Descriptive statistics								
Mean	0.0015	–0.0004	0.0006	–0.0002	–0.0023	0.0092	–0.0061	0.0030
Median	0.0063	0.0037	0.0068	0.0066	–0.0048	0.0027	0.0069	0.0024
Maximum	0.1614	0.1996	0.2930	0.2866	0.1521	0.3163	0.1681	0.0080
Minimum	–0.2157	–0.2521	–0.2776	–0.2853	–0.3434	–0.1198	–0.9084	0.0015
Std. Dev.	0.0533	0.0601	0.0804	0.0804	0.0511	0.0437	0.1043	0.0013
Skewness	–0.4040	–0.2896	–0.1265	–0.1082	–2.1145	2.7407	–5.1834	1.3706
Kurtosis	5.2796	5.6765	5.6072	5.9643	18.6567	19.6216	41.1253	3.9474
Jarque–Bera (JB)	40.7013	52.1829	47.7431	61.4696	1830.144	2131.5	10862.03	58.533
JB p-value	<0.0001	<0.0001	<0.0001	<0.0001	<0.0001	<0.0001	<0.0001	<0.0001
Panel B: Correlation matrix								
IMF	1.000	–	–	–	–	–	–	–
CMF	0.974	1.000	–	–	–	–	–	–
	<0.001							
FBM100	0.896	0.944	1.000	–	–	–	–	–
	<0.001	<0.001						
Worldscope	0.932	0.967	0.982	1.000	–	–	–	–
	<0.001	<0.001	<0.001					
SMB	0.373	0.338	0.113	0.272	1.000	–	–	–
	<0.001	<0.001	0.145	<0.001				
HML	0.347	0.388	0.422	0.450	0.273	1.000	–	–
	<0.001	<0.001	<0.001	<0.001	<0.000			
MOM	–0.387	–0.425	–0.445	–0.469	–0.308	–0.602	1.000	–
	<0.001	<0.001	<0.001	<0.001	<0.001	<0.001		
TB	–0.190	–0.235	–0.243	–0.240	–0.057	0.042	–0.070	1.000
	0.013	0.002	<0.001	<0.001	0.459	0.585	0.363	

This table reports the mean, median, maximum, minimum, and standard deviation for excess market returns. Fund returns are from equally-weighted portfolio of funds in each fund category, Islamic mutual funds (IMFs) and conventional mutual funds (CMFs). Returns are monthly excess returns in decimals, i.e. 0.068 not 6.8%. IMFs and CMFs refer to Islamic mutual funds and conventional mutual funds, respectively. N and Std. dev. denote number of funds and standard deviation, respectively. SMB is small-minus-big; HML is high-minus-low; MOM is momentum, and TB is the three-month Malaysian Treasury bill rate. In Panel B, figures below the correlation coefficients are p–values for tests of significance of coefficients.

Raw Return, Excess Return, the *Sharpe (1966) and* the *Treynor (1965)* Ratios

Table 6 presents monthly means for raw returns and excess returns, the Sharpe ratio and the Treynor ratio for IMFs and CMFs as well as the difference between IMFs and CMFs. Panel A in Table 6 presents the results for the portfolio level while Panel B presents the results for the fund level. We compare the performance of mutual fund portfolio returns using two indices, the FBM100 and the Worldscope indices.

The mean returns for both IMFs and CMFs are 0.45 and 0.26 percents per month, respectively. However, after taking into account the risk-free rate, the mean excess returns of

IMFs remain positive at 0.15 percent per month, but the mean excess returns for CMFs are negative at –0.04 percent per month. Both the mean returns and mean excess returns for IMF portfolio are higher than the market benchmarks (the FBM100 and Worldscope indices). In contrast, the means returns and excess returns for CMFs are lower than these market benchmarks as well as those of IMFs. Although the IMF returns exceed the returns of the markets, the returns are less volatile. In addition, the beta of the IMFs is lower than that of the CMFs. This gives an initial indicator of the attractiveness of IMFs compared to CMFs in that IMFs have higher returns but lower risk, both total and systematic. The Sharpe ratio shows the measurement of mean excess returns compared to the total risk represented by standard deviation. This measure gives the unit of reward received when taking an extra unit of total risk. The results suggest that investment in IMFs earn a Sharpe ratio of 2.85 percent per month, which is the higher than a comparable investment in CMFs (–0.59 percent) or investments in the Malaysian market as a whole. The Treynor ratio indicates the measurement of mean excess returns compared to the systematic risk represented by beta (β). Similar to the Sharpe ratio, the Treynor ratio shows that IMFs outperform CMFs regardless of the benchmarks used. The findings of these basic performance models lead us to conclude that IMFs outperform both the market benchmarks and CMFs when relative performance measures are used. Although the relative performance measures (raw returns, excess returns, Sharpe ratio and Treynor ratio) are commonly used in practice, and the results show that IMFs (CMFs) outperform (underperform) the market benchmarks and CMFs, these measures can only be used in ranking funds in relation to their peers in that they provide no fundamental statistical or economic meaning. Therefore, we provide the results of the single- and multi-factor models in the followings sections. These performance models, based on the CAPM, give an estimate of the intercept (alpha), which refers to fund performance in relation to the benchmark return. Using these measures allows us to explore mutual fund performance without comparing other funds.

Table 6. Mean raw return, mean excess return, Sharpe and Treynor ratios

	IMF	CMF	FBM100	Worldscope
Panel A: Mean raw return, mean excess returns and Sharpe ratio				
Mean raw return	0.0045	0.0026	0.0036	0.0028
Mean excess return	0.0015	–0.0004	0.0006	–0.0002
Std. dev.	0.0533	0.0601	0.0804	0.0804
Sharpe ratio	0.0285	–0.0059	0.0072	–0.0026
Panel B: Beta and Treynor ratio using FBM100 as equity benchmark				
Beta	0.5944	0.7068	1.000	–
Treynor	0.0026	–0.0000	–	–
Panel C: Beta and Treynor ratio using Worldscope index as equity benchmark				
Beta	0.6177	0.7234	–	1.0000
Treynor	0.0025	–0.0005	–	–

This table reports the descriptive statistics of mutual funds returns in the sample between February 1996 and December 2009. Funds grouped by Islamic mutual fund (IMF) and conventional mutual fund (CMF). All performance measures are in monthly terms.

One-Factor Model (Jensen, 1968)

Table 7 provides the results for the analysis of performance employing the using one-factor model (Jensen, 1968) using the Worldscope and FBM100 indices as market benchmarks. Panel A in Table 7 presents the results for the one-factor model at the portfolio level while Panel B estimates the individual mutual fund performance results. As shown, the alpha estimate for IMFs is 0.16 percent per month, which is higher than that of CMF portfolio (–0.02 percent). Even though the alphas of both portfolios are not significantly different from zero, the alphas of the 'difference' portfolio (IMFs–CMFs) are significant at 5 percent level for both markets benchmarks. This signifies that even though IMF portfolio underperforms both market benchmarks, it significantly outperforms CMF portfolio.

The adjusted R^2 for both portfolios ranges from 80 to 94 percent with both market benchmarks. In general, the adjusted R^2 for IMFs are lower than that of CMFs for both market benchmarks. This indicates a conventional benchmark bias toward CMFs. The high adjusted R^2 is also an indicator that fund managers employ a passive strategy by following the market closely, but are unable to perform well. Given the data used in this study is net of annual management fees, the underperformance may results from expenses and fees, as pointed in Jensen (1968) and Malkiel (1995). Nevertheless, because the available data are limited, this study is unable to investigate the performance of mutual funds before deducting fees and expenses.

Table 7. One-factor model (Jensen, 1968)

Panel A: Equally-weighted portfolios									
		IMF			CMF			IMF–CMF	
	Coef.	Std. err.	p-value	Coef.	Std. err.	p-value	Coef.	Std. err.	p-value
Worldscope as market index									
Alpha	0.0016	0.0018	0.3697	–0.0002	0.0014	0.8853	0.0019	0.0009	0.0484
Beta	0.6177	0.0480	<0.0001	0.7234	0.0470	<0.0001	–0.1057	0.0124	<0.0001
Adj. R^2	–	0.87	–	–	0.94	–	–	–	–
FBM100 as market index									
Alpha	0.0012	0.0022	0.5912	–0.0008	0.0019	0.6803	0.0019	0.0009	0.0348
Beta	0.5944	0.0479	<0.0001	0.7068	0.0473	<0.0001	–0.1124	0.0114	<0.0001
Adj. R^2	–	0.80	–	–	0.89	–	–	–	–
Panel B: Individual fund level (number of positive and negative [ ] funds)									
	Coef.#		p-value*	Coef.#		p-value*			
Worldscope as market index									
Alpha	18 [28]	–	4 [9]	44 [57]	–	6 [18]	–	–	–
FBM100 as market index									
Alpha	20 [26]	–	3 [5]	41 [60]	–	6 [16]	–	–	–

This table reports the results of the estimations of Jensen's one-factor model at the portfolio and individual levels in Panels A and B, respectively. The funds estimates are for the period February 1996 to December 2009, using ordinary least square. All t-statistics are adjusted for heteroskedasticity and autocorrelation following Newey and West (1987). The portfolio analysis in Panel A is calculated using the equally-weighted method. Alpha indicates the monthly abnormal returns of the portfolio. R2 is the adjusted R2. In Panel B, # indicates total number of funds with positive or negative [ ] coefficients in the sample. * indicates total number of funds with positive or negative coefficients [ ] that are significant at least at the10% level.

Panel B provides the results for the estimates of individual mutual fund performance. We provide figures for the number of positive and negative funds. The results suggest that only a few funds were statistically significant. In total, 13 out of 46 IMFs have significantly outperformed (4) or underperformed (9) the Worldscope index. In contrast, 24 out of 101 CMFs have significantly outperformed (6) or underperformed (18) the Worldscope index. Relative to the number of sample of each fund types, IMFs are able to generate slightly higher number of funds with positive alpha compared to CMFs (9 percent of positive alpha compared to only 6 percent in CMFs).

Using alternative index (FBM100), 8 out of 46 IMFs have significantly outperformed (3) or underperformed (5) the market index. In contrast, 22 out of 101 CMFs have significantly outperformed (6) or underperformed (16) the same index. Relative to the number of sample of each fund types, similarly, IMFs are able to generate slightly higher number of funds with positive alpha compared to CMFs (7 percent of positive alpha compared to only 6 percent in CMFs).

Four-Factor (Carhart, 1997) Model

For the four-factor model, we use benchmarks data provided by the Style Research Ltd., which in turn employs the Worldscope database to construct the benchmarks. As discussed in section 5.2.2, the factor returns for four-factor models for other countries are not easily available, so we use the on-line research tool provided by Style Research Ltd. to construct monthly returns for the four-factor return portfolios.

Table 8 summarizes the results using the four-factor model for IMFs, CMFs and the 'difference' (IMFs–CMFs) portfolios using a broad market benchmark provided by Worldscope. Panel A and Panel B in Table 8 present the results at the portfolio and individual fund levels, respectively. As shown in Panel A of Table 8, the four-factor alpha for CMFs is 0.10 percent and not statistically significant. This means that CMFs are unable to outperform the Worldscope market, size, style, and momentum benchmarks. Surprisingly, the four-factor alpha for the IMF portfolio is 0.33 percent and significant at the 5 percent level. This indicates that on average, the IMF portfolio is able to outperform these four factor benchmarks during the sample period. When we examine the difference in the four-factor alpha across IMFs and CMFs, the result indicates there is a significant difference between the four-factor alphas, as the p-value is significant at the 5 percent level. Similar to the results using the one-factor model, the IMFs market beta is 0.63 compared with 0.74 for the CMF market beta which suggests that the IMFs exhibit lower risk than CMFs, and the difference is statistically significant at the 1 percent level.

In terms of investment styles, it appears that both IMFs and CMFs have similar investment styles. In relation to size preference, both types of portfolios prefer small stocks than big stocks, given the SMB factor loading is 0.16 for IMFs and 0.11 for CMFs. However, the factor loading for SMB for IMFs is lower and the difference is statistically significant at the 1 percent level. The HML factor loading for IMFs is –0.12 and for CMFs is –0.09, suggesting that both types of portfolios display a preference for growth-to-value stocks. The 'difference' portfolio shows no significance difference between the HML factor loadings for IMFs and CMFs. Finally, considering the loadings for MOM, both portfolios exhibit no preference for a momentum investment style, as the factor loadings are not significant for both portfolios. Similarly, the 'difference' portfolio shows that the difference between these styles for both portfolios is not significant.

Table 8. Carhart's four-factor performance measure

Panel A: Equally-weighted portfolios									
	IMF			CMF			IMF–CMF		
	Coef.	Std. err.	p value	Coef.	Std. err.	p-value	Coef.	Std. err.	p-value
Alpha	0.0033	0.0015	0.0351	0.0010	0.0011	0.3676	0.0023	0.0010	0.0189
Market	0.6344	0.0493	<0.0001	0.7351	0.0526	<0.0001	–0.1007	0.0143	<0.0001
SMB	0.1615	0.0490	0.0012	0.1137	0.0506	0.0260	0.0479	0.0164	0.0039
HML	–0.1156	0.0437	0.0090	–0.0878	0.0311	0.0054	–0.0278	0.0283	0.3270
MOM	0.0269	0.0196	0.1726	0.0162	0.0164	0.3236	0.0107	0.0094	0.2598
Adj. R^2		0.89			0.94				
Panel B: Individual fund level (Number of positive and negative [ ] funds)									
	Coef.#		p-value*	Coef.#		p-value*			
Alpha	15 [31]	–	3 [4]	45 [56]	–	17 [25]	–	–	–
SMB	33 [13]	–	16 [3]	78 [23]	–	53 [8]	–	–	–
HML	21 [25]	–	6 [4]	33 [68]	–	5 [23]	–	–	–
MOM	34 [12]	–	18 [1]	67 [34]	–	34 [10]	–	–	–

This table reports the results for the estimation of Carhart's four-factor model at the portfolio and individual levels in Panels A and B, respectively. The sample period is February 1996 to December 2009 estimated using ordinary least squares. All t-statistics adjusted for heteroskedasticity and autocorrelation following Newey and West (1987). The portfolio in Panel A is equally-weighted. Alpha indicates the monthly abnormal returns of the portfolio. R2 is the adjusted R2. In Panel B, # indicates total number of funds with positive or negative [ ] coefficients in the sample. * indicates total number of funds with positive or negative coefficients [ ] that are significant at least at the10% level.

In sum, it would appear that the IMF portfolio displays a relative preference for small cap and growth oriented stocks, which is with Girard and Hassan (2005), Renneboog et al. (2008) and Hoepner et al. (2011). The strong preference of IMFs to lower beta stocks and smaller cap stock may result to the significant outperformance of IMFs over the four-factor benchmarks as well as to CMFs.

Panel B in Table 8 provides comparable estimates for the analysis of individual mutual fund performance. Similar to the results for the one-factor model, there are more funds with negative as against positive performance. In total, 7 out of 46 IMFs have significantly outperformed (3 IMFs) or underperformed (4 IMFs) the four-factor benchmarks. In contrast, 42 out of 101 CMFs have significantly outperformed (17 CMFs) or underperformed (25 CMFs) the same benchmarks. Relative to the number of sample of each fund types, CMFs are able to generate higher number of funds with positive alpha compared to CMFs (17 percent of positive alpha compared to only 7 percent in IMFs). This is in contrast to the analysis at the portfolio level.

We suggest that the differences in results are because the portfolio removes unsystematic or fund-specific risk through diversification. This makes the funds of a particular type form a portfolio only comprising systematic or market risk (even when the sample is only relatively small). This should make for a stronger relationship if there is one in any subsequent time-series regression, especially if there is time-series autocorrelation.

The constant or error term in the subsequent regression helps to remove any remaining unsystematic (non-factor) risk. However, in fund level regression, all this unsystematic risk must be captured in a single constant and the error term. In a model with a few factors, this means a lot of systematic risk remains and the market relationship as indicated by the regression coefficients will not be strong.

5.2. Market Timing Models

Table 9 and Table 10 respectively, present the results for the analysis of security selection and market timing ability following Treynor–Mazuy and Henriksson–Merton models. Table 9 (Treynor–Mazuy approach) reveals that both portfolios of managed funds exhibit security selection and market timing coefficients insignificantly different from zero irrespective of the benchmarks used.

However, there is evidence that IMFs have better security selection (when benchmarking against Worldscope and FBM100) and poorer market timing ability (when benchmarking against the FBM100) than CMFs as the 'difference portfolio' (IMF–CMF) displays significant differences in means, at the 5 percent level.

Table 9. Market timing performance measure, Treynor–Mazuy model

		IMF			CMF			IMF–CMF	
	Coef.	Std. err.	p-value	Coef.	Std. err.	p-value	Coef.	Std. err.	p-value
Panel A: Equally-weighted portfolios									
Worldscope as market index									
Alpha	0.0023	0.0017	0.1825	<0.0001	0.0011	0.9799	0.0023	0.0010	0.0257
Gamma	–0.0979	0.199	0.6233	–0.0277	0.1996	0.8898	–0.0702	0.0625	0.2628
Adj. R^2	–	0.87	–	–	–	–	–	–	–
FBM100 as market index									
Alpha	0.0018	0.0020	0.3705	–0.0007	0.0016	0.6461	0.0025	0.0010	0.0124
Gamma	–0.0998	0.2703	0.7126	–0.0072	0.2680	0.9786	–0.0926	0.0445	0.0389
Adj. R^2	–	0.80	–	–	0.89	–	–	–	–
Panel B: Individual fund level (Number of positive and negative [ ] funds)									
	Coef.#		p-value*	Coef.#		p-value*			
Worldscope as market index									
Alpha	14 [32]	–	2 [6]	45 [56]	–	8 [14]	–	–	–
Gamma	26 [20]	–	4 [5]	53 [48]	–	2 [8]	–	–	–
FBM100 as market index									
Alpha	17 [29]	–	3 [5]	23 [23]	–	3 [6]	–	–	–
$Beta^2$	42 [59]	–	7[12]	49 [52]	–	5 [10]	–	–	–

This table reports the results for the estimation of timing ability using the Treynor–Mazuy model at the portfolio and individual levels in Panels A and B, respectively. The sample period is February 1996 to December 2009 using ordinary least square. All t-statistics are adjusted for heteroskedasticity and autocorrelation following Newey and West (1987). The portfolios are constructed using equal weights. Alpha indicates the monthly abnormal returns of the portfolio. Gamma is the coefficient of the quadratic variable representing market timing ability. R2 represents the adjusted correlation coefficient. In Panel B, # indicates total number of funds with positive or negative [ ] coefficients in the sample. * indicates total number of funds with positive or negative coefficients [ ] that are significant at least at 10% level. The table omits estimates for market beta. The qualitative results are similar with the estimates using one-factor model.

Panel B inTable 9 presents the respective result of the analysis of security selection and timing ability at the individual fund level. Of 147 funds, 30 (27) funds have selectivity estimates significantly different from zero, while 10 (10) funds are significantly positive when performance is compared to the Worldscope broad (FBM100) index. More than half of the funds record negative security selection estimates.

The market timing performance of individual funds provides even greater evidence of the inability of Malaysian fund managers to outperform. Of 46 IMFs, only nine funds have timing ability significantly different from zero, where three funds are significantly positive. Six funds record negative timing estimates, which implies they time the market in the wrong direction. In contrast, five of the 101 CMF managers demonstrate positive timing ability while 10 fund managers time the market in the wrong direction.

Table 10 reports the security selection and market timing estimates using the Henriksson–Merton approach. As shown, the results are largely consistent with those in Table 9. Consistent with the security selection estimates using the Treynor–Mazuy approach, the security selection coefficients for the 'difference' portfolio (IMF–CMF) is significant at the 5 percent level. In contrast, the market timing coefficients for the 'difference' portfolios (IMF–CMF) are insignificant irrespective of the of market benchmark used.

Table 10. Market timing performance measure, Henriksson–Merton model

		IMF			CMF			IMF–CMF	
	Coef.	Std. err.	p-value	Coef.	Std. err.	p-value	Coef.	Std. err.	p-value
Panel A: Equally-weighted portfolios									
Worldscope as market index									
Alpha	0.0021	0.0021	0.3262	–0.0006	0.0016	0.7267	0.0026	0.0012	0.0333
Delta	–0.0152	0.0880	0.8630	0.0125	0.0827	0.8803	–0.0277	0.0308	0.3696
Adj. R^2	–	0.87	–	–	0.94	–	–	–	–
FBM100 as market index									
Alpha	0.0024	0.0027	0.3723	–0.0005	0.0023	0.8364	0.0029	0.0011	0.0121
Delta	–0.0451	0.1193	0.7059	–0.0107	0.1125	0.9247	–0.0344	0.0248	0.1663
Adj. R^2	–	0.80	–	–	0.89	–	–	–	–
Panel B: Individual fund level (Number of positive and negative [ ] funds)									
	Coef.#		p-value*	Coef.#		p-value*			
Worldscope as market index									
Alpha	17 [29]	–	9 [3]	42 [59]	–	15 [5]	–	–	–
Delta	27 [19]	–	4 [5]	52 [49]	–	3 [8]	–	–	–
FBM100 as market index									
Alpha	23 [23]	–	4 [4]	50 [51]	–	5[7]	–	–	–
Gamma	19 [27]	–	3 [9]	43 [58]	–	1 [10]	–	–	–

This table reports the results for the estimation of timing ability using the Henriksson–Merton model at the portfolio and individual levels in Panels A and B, respectively. The sample period is February 1996 to December 2009 using ordinary least square. All t-statistics are adjusted for heteroskedasticity and autocorrelation following Newey and West (1987). The portfolios are constructed using equal weights. Alpha indicates the monthly abnormal returns of the portfolio. Delta is the coefficient of the quadratic variable representing market timing ability. R2 represents the adjusted correlation coefficient. In Panel B, # indicates total number of funds with positive or negative [ ] coefficients in the sample. * indicates total number of funds with positive or negative coefficients [ ] that are significant at least at 10% level. The table omits estimates for market beta. The qualitative results are similar with the estimates using one-factor model.

Overall, the insignificant selectivity and timing coefficients (irrespective of the benchmark employed) suggest that Malaysian fund managers as a whole do not possess significant security selection or market timing abilities which is consistent with the most studies [see, for example, Abdullah et al. (2007), Sawicki and Ong (2000) and Sinclair (1990)].

Interestingly, supporting results of the one-factor and four-factor models, there is strong evidence that IMFs have better security selection ability compared with CMFs. In contrast, we find weak evidence that IMF managers are worse market timer compared with CMF managers. These findings support our first and second hypothesis that IMF managers exhibit different selectivity and possess lower market timing ability compared to CMF managers. The possible reason is that *Shariah* prohibits fund managers from engaging in excessive speculative activity. Thus, this prohibition affects the ability of IMF managers to undertake market timing of any form.

5.3. Diversification and Net Selectivity Models

Panel A and Panel B in Table 11 respectively provide the results of the estimation for diversification and net selectivity using the Fama's original specification and extended specification using the four-factor benchmark. Using the Worldscope index as the market benchmark, the costs of inadequate diversification for IMFs and CMFs are insignificantly negative for the one-factor (–0.01 and –0.02) and four-factor (–0.96 and –0.36) models The negative diversification is because the benchmark returns is lower than the risk free rate and this indicates a loss of performance due to portfolio allocation choice (Fama, 1972).

Table 11. Diversification and net selectivity

	IMF			CMF			IMF–CMF		
	Coef.	Std. err.	p-value	Coef.	Std. err.	p-value	Coef.	Std. err.	p-value
Panel A: One-factor model									
Worldscope as market index									
DIV_1.	–1.14E–05	2.78E–04	0.9674	–1.80E–06	2.78E–04	0.9905	–9.58E–06	1.28E–04	0.9403
NS_1	1.66E–03	1.51E–03	0.2757	–2.04E–04	1.18E–03	0.8636	1.86E–03	9.22E–04	0.0454
FBM100 as market index									
DIV_1.	4.37E–05	4.25E–04	0.9182	2.34E–05	2.56E–04	0.9276	2.04E–05	1.68E–04	0.9040
NS_1	1.13E–03	1.87E–03	0.5454	–7.84E–04	1.54E–03	0.6122	1.92E–03	8.98E–04	0.0340
Panel B: Four-factor model (Worldscope as market index)									
DIV_4.	–9.62E–05	2.16E–04	0.6570	–3.61E–05	1.24E–04	0.7710	–6.01E–05	9.31E–05	0.5194
NS_4	3.36E–03	1.34E–03	0.0129	1.01E–03	1.07E–03	0.3500	2.35E–03	8.95E–04	0.0095

This table presents the cost of inadequate diversification (DIV1 and DIV4) and net selectivity (NS1 and NS4) which were introduced by Fama (1972) [see Equations (10) – (13)], for equally-weighted IMF and CMF portfolio in Malaysia. The table also reports the differences in estimates for IMFs and CMFs. The t-statistics are one sample t-test for individual portfolios and paired samples t tests for the difference in estimates between the IMF and CMF portfolios.

Our result of negative diversification is similar with Hassan et al. (2010) in their sample of Malaysian IMFs. The differences in diversification costs between IMFs and CMFs are also not statistically significant. Using F100, the cost of inadequate diversification is economically small and there is no significant difference between IMFs and CMFs. This is an interesting finding in that even though IMFs impose *Shariah* screening on portfolios, it has little apparent influence on the diversification of unsystematic risk.

Furthermore, the performance measures of net selectivity, that is the net performance after taking into account the diversifiable risk are close to the previous results of the one-factor and the four-factor alphas. Interestingly, the difference in net selectivity between IMFs and CMFs are significant at least at the 5 percent level for both market benchmarks as well as for both one-factor and four-factor models.

The results suggest that the *Shariah* screening activities do not impose significant diversification costs on investors in that IMF investors enjoy well-diversified portfolios seemingly despite rigorous screening activity. This is consistent with the view that a portfolio does not require a large number of stocks to be well diversified, which implies that *Shariah* constraints have little influence on the diversification of idiosyncratic risk. In fact, screening activities yield additional risk-adjusted returns to IMFs as the net selectivity estimates for the IMF–CMF portfolio is significantly positive. Thus, the results do not support our hypothesis that IMFs suffer higher diversification costs in comparison to CMFs, and thus earn lower net risk adjusted returns (net selectivity).

5.4. Fund Performance In Losing Markets and Financial Crises

Table 12 presents the performance of IMFs and CMFs in losing markets and in the three crises periods, namely the AFC (July 1997 to August 1998), GIB (April 2000 to September 2002) and GCC (July 2007 to February 2009). The study uses one-factor and four-factor models to test if IMF performance is significantly better in losing markets and during financial crises.

For robustness, we use three indices to represent the losing markets, which are the Worldscope broad market index, the FBMKLCI and the FBM100.

As shown, none of the dummy variables (for both IMFs and CMFs) that represent losing markets exhibit significant coefficients. This implies that IMFs do not perform better than the market when market returns are negative. However, the estimate for this dummy in the 'difference' portfolio (IMF–CMF) is significantly different from zero at the 5 percent level. This implies that even though the IMF portfolio does not outperform the market during losing periods, it significantly outperformed the CMF portfolio by 5 percent per month during bearish markets.

Surprisingly, of three crises periods examined, IMF portfolios performed significantly worse during the GCC while the dummy coefficients representing the other two crises periods (*DGIB* and *DAFC*) were not significantly different from zero in all models. The results are also consistent for the CMF portfolio. In addition, these dummy variables were also insignificant for the 'difference' portfolio (IMF–CMF) for all models. This suggests the reactions of IMF and CMF investor towards the three major crises periods are similar. That is, both types of funds behave in the same way, and neither are immune to the financial crises.

Table 12. Financial performance in losing markets and financial crises

	One-factor model									Four-factor model		
	Model 1 (Worldscope index)			Model 2 (FBM100)			Model 3 (FBMKLCI)			Model 4 (Worldscope index)		
	IMF	CMF	IMF–CMF	IMF	CMF	IMF–CMF	IMF	CMF	IMF–CMF	IMF	CMF	IMF–CMF
Alpha	0.003	0.003	0.000	0.005	0.003	0.001	0.005	0.003	0.001	0.003	0.003	0.000
Std. err.	0.002	0.002	0.001	0.003	0.002	0.001	0.003	0.003	0.001	0.002	0.002	0.001
p-value	0.184	0.179	0.691	0.146	0.278	0.166	0.133	0.253	0.225	0.190	0.188	0.895
DCM	–0.002	–0.006	0.003	–0.004	–0.005	0.001	–0.005	–0.006	0.001	0.001	–0.005	0.005
Std. err.	0.005	0.004	0.002	0.005	0.004	0.002	0.005	0.005	0.002	0.005	0.005	0.002
p-value	0.644	0.196	0.144	0.393	0.264	0.627	0.347	0.243	0.537	0.999	0.352	0.043
DGCC	–0.008	–0.005	–0.002	–0.008	–0.005	–0.003	–0.008	–0.005	–0.003	–0.006	0.004	–0.002
Std. err.	0.003	0.002	0.002	0.004	0.002	0.002	0.004	0.002	0.002	0.003	0.001	0.002
p-value	0.034	0.011	0.288	0.047	0.083	0.240	0.042	0.049	0.253	0.022	0.014	0.336
DGIB	–0.003	–0.001	–0.002	–0.005	–0.003	–0.002	–0.005	–0.003	–0.002	–0.002	–0.000	–0.002
Std. err.	0.003	0.003	0.002	0.005	0.004	0.002	0.005	0.005	0.002	0.002	0.002	0.002
p-value	0.358	0.791	0.290	0.261	0.447	0.375	0.302	0.518	0.391	0.312	0.825	0.406
DAFC	0.006	0.001	0.004	0.001	–0.002	0.003	0.002	–0.001	0.004	0.011	0.004	0.007
Std. err.	0.015	0.011	0.007	0.017	0.015	0.006	0.017	0.014	0.006	0.011	0.009	0.007
p-value	0.688	0.914	0.533	0.935	0.875	0.557	0.890	0.908	0.551	0.300	0.629	0.296
Adj. R^2	0.87	0.94	0.35	0.80	0.89	0.38	0.80	0.88	0.37	0.90	0.95	0.41

This table presents the coefficients of five dummy variables added to the one-factor and four-factor models in estimating the performance of IMF, CMF and the 'difference' (IMF–CMF) portfolios in losing markets and financial crises as per Equations (14) and (15). DCMarket is a dummy variable for losing markets for the respective market indices and the remaining three dummy variables are for the global credit crisis (DGCC), global internet bubble (DGIB) and Asian financial crisis (AFC).

This may be because about 88 percent (as at 2010) of the total Malaysian listed securities is *Shariah* compliant. Thus, the investment universe for IMFs is close to that of CMFs. Further, this investment universe is screened only using sectoral screening where the levels of debt and liquidity ratios are not taken into account. Our results are consistent with Abdullah et al. (2007) who find that IMFs outperform CMFs during bearish economic condition. However, our findings contradict to Hoepner et al. (2011) who find that IMFs significantly performs worse than equity market during AFC and GIB but not affected at all in GCC.

5.5. Robustness Tests

For the robustness of the results, we repeat our analysis using matched-pair samples[1] of IMFs and CMFs following Mallin et al. (1995) and Kreander et al. (2005). We closely match each IMF with a comparable CMF based on the formation date, age (measured in years and taking into account if the fund ceased operation or merged with another funds) and size (in millions of RM). Owing to the small sample size of Malaysian equity funds, the matched-pair method results in a total sample of only 35 IMFs and 35 CMFs. However, the advantage of this procedure is it limits any possible effects of age and size bias, and therefore implicitly attributes any difference in risk-adjusted average performance between IMFs and CMFs to *Shariah* screens (Bauer et al., 2005). Overall, we found that formation date, age, and size-matching procedures do not alter our conclusions with respect to the differences in performance. The alphas for the 'difference' portfolios remain significantly different from zero, which indicates that IMFs outperform CMFs. In addition, both IMFs and CMFs were unable to outperform their respective market benchmarks. Further, IMFs significantly outperformed CMFs in most of the performance models used.

CONCLUSION

This chapter offers new evidence on the performance of IMFs by studying the robustness of IMF performance in two ways. First, we calculate several different measures of performance, including multifactor models to determine whether the return and risk characteristics of IMFs and CMFs differ. Second, we take into account changes in market conditions over the entire period as well as during recent crises period.

Our overall finding indicates that both IMFs and CMFs in Malaysia are generally unable to outperform various market benchmarks during the sample period, except for that IMFs appear to outperform the four-factor benchmarks. However, when we compare the performance between IMFs and CMFs (the 'difference' portfolios), it is interesting to find that IMFs are generally able to outperform CMFs at the aggregate level. This implies that *Shariah* screening does not impose a significant cost on IMF investors. In addition, the previous reported underperformance of IMFs may be due to learning phase as argued by Bauer et al. (2006). In relation to the risk factor, we find that the market index or beta is the most significant risk factor along with small cap companies. This implies that IMFs typically

[1] Results are available upon request.

invest in stocks with lower betas and smaller companies compared with CMFs. The low market beta also implies that IMFs are generally less risky than comparable CMFs.

In terms of the ability of fund managers to time the market, both IMF and CMF managers in Malaysia are poor at market timing. This is consistent with the previous literature in the mainstream managed funds [see, for example, Sawicki and Ong (2000) and Sinclair (1990)] as well as the previous literature on IMFs [see Abdullah et al. (2007)]. As expected, the timing ability of IMF managers appears slightly worse than in CMFs. This may be due to several reasons. First, the trading of securities in IMF portfolio is at least sometimes for nonfinancial reasons. Second, IMFs may have a longer time-horizon for investment. Finally, the limitation of IMF managers to involve in excessive speculative activities may impede them from market timing activities at any form.

In terms of diversification cost, both types of funds suffer the costs of diversification. However the good news is, there is no significant difference between these two types of funds. These findings further support previous findings in the fund selectivity where *Shariah* screening does not impose any differential costs on IMF investors. The results also indicate that there is no significant difference between the performance of IMFs and CMFs across the three main crises arising during the sample period. In addition, as in Abdullah et al. (2007), IMFs underperform market benchmarks but outperform CMFs in bearish markets.

REFERENCES

Abderrezak, F. (2008). The performance of Islamic equity funds: A comparison to conventional Islamic and ethical benchmarks. Master of International Business and Finance, University of Maastricht, Maastricht, The Netherlands.

Abdullah, F., Hassan, T. and Mohamad, S. (2007). Investigation of performance of Malaysian Islamic unit trust funds: Comparison with conventional unit trust funds. Managerial Finance, 33(2), 142–153.

Alkassim, F. A. (2008). Mutual fund performance: Evidence of stock selection and market timing ability from Islamic mutual funds. Doctor of Philosphy PhD thesis, Bangor University, Bangor.

Atta, H. (2000). Ethical rewards: An exmination of the effect of Islamic ethical screens on financial performance and of conditioning information on performance measures. Msc Corporate & International Finance Master, Durham University, United Kingdom.

Bauer, R., Derwall, J. and Otten, R. (2007). The ethical mutual fund performance debate: New evidence from Canada. *Journal of Business Ethics,* 70, 111–124.

Bauer, R., Koedijk, K. and Otten, R. (2005). International evidence on ethical mutual fund performance and investment style. *Journal of Banking & Finance,* 29(7), 1751–1767.

Bauer, R., Otten, R. and Rad, A. T. (2006). Ethical investing in Australia: Is there a financial penalty? *Pacific-Basin Finance Journal,* 14(1), 33–48.

Blake, D. and Timmermann, A. (2003). Performance persistence in mutual funds An independent assessment of the studies prepared by Charles River Associates for the Investment Management Association: Financial Services Authority.

Carhart, M. M. (1997). On persistence in mutual fund performance. *The Journal of Finance,* 52(1), 57–82.

Elfakhani, S. M. and Hassan, M. K. (2005). Performance of Islamic mutual funds. Paper presented at the 12th Economic Research Forum Conference Cairo, Egypt.

Elfakhani, S. M., Hassan, M. K. and Sidani, Y. M. (2007). Islamic mutual funds. In M. K. Hassan & M. K. Lewis (Eds.), Handbook of Islamic banking (pp. 253-273). Massachusetts, USA: Edward Elgar Publishing Limited.

Ernst & Young. (2009). The Islamic funds & investments report: Surviving and adapting in a downturn (Vol. 3rd Edition). Dubai: Middle East Global Advisors.

Eurekahedge. (2008). Hedge fund monthly: Key trends in Islamic funds 2008. Retrieved from http://www.eurekahedge.com on 30 September 2009.

Fama, E. F. (1972). Components of investment performance. *The Journal of Finance,* 27(3), 551–567.

Fama, E. F. and French, K. R. (1993). Common risk factors in the returns on stocks and bonds. *Journal of Financial Economics,* 33(1), 3–56.

Girard, E. and Hassan, M. K. (2005). Faith-based ethical investing: The case of Dow Jones Islamic indexes FMA Papers. Retrieved from http://www.fma.org on 22 July 2009.

Hakim, S. and Rashidian, M. (2002). Risk and return of Islamic stock market indexes. Paper presented at the Economic Research Forum Annual Meetings, Sharjah, UAE.

Hassan, A., Antoniou, A. and Paudyal, D. K. (2005). Impact of ethical screening on investment performance the case of the Dow Jones Islamic index. *Islamic Economic Studies,* 12 & 13(2 & 1).

Hassan, M. K., Khan, A. N. F. and Ngow, T. (2010). Is faith-based investing rewarding? The case for Malaysian Islamic unit trust funds. *Journal of Islamic Accounting and Business Research,* 1(2), 148–171.

Hayat, R. (2006). An empirical assessment of Islamic equity fund returns. Master thesis, Free University, Amsterdam, Netherlands.

Hayat, R. and Kraeussl, R. (2011). Risk and return characteristics of Islamic equity funds. *Emerging Markets Review,* 12(2), 189–203.

Henriksson, R. D. and Merton, R. C. (1981). On market timing and investment performance II: Statistical procedures for evaluating forecasting skills. *The Journal of Business,* 54(4), 513–533.

Hoepner, A. G. F., Rammal, H. G. and Rezec, M. (2011). Islamic mutual funds' financial performance and international investment style: Evidence from 20 countries. *The European Journal of Finance,* 17(9-10), 829–850.

Hussein, K. A. and Omran, M. (2005). Ethical investment revisited: Evidence from Dow Jones Islamic indexes. *The Journal of Investing,* 14(3), 105–126.

International Financial Services London. (2010). Islamic finance 2010. Retrieved from http://www.ifsl.org.uk on 17 April 2010.

Jensen, M. C. (1968). The performance of mutual funds in the period 1945-1964. *The Journal of Finance,* 23(2), 389–416.

Kothari, S. P. and Warner, J. B. (1997). Measuring long-horizon security price performance. *Journal of Financial Economics,* 43(3), 301–339.

Kraeussl, R. and Hayat, R. (2008). The performance of Islamic equity funds. Retrieved from http://ssrn.com/abstract=1320712 on 20 July 2009.

Kreander, N., Gray, R. H., Power, D. M. and Sinclair, C. D. (2005). Evaluating the performance of ethical and non-ethical funds: A matched pair analysis. *Journal of Business Finance & Accounting,* 32(7 & 8), 1465–1493.

Lai, M.-M. and Lau, S.-H. (2010). Evaluating mutual fund performance in an emerging Asian economy: The Malaysian experience. *Journal of Asian Economics,* 21(4), 378–390.

Lee, D. D., Humphrey, J. E., Benson, K. L. and Ahn, J. Y. K. (2010). Socially responsible investment fund performance: The impact of screening intensity. *Accounting & Finance,* 50(2), 351–370.

Low, S.-W. (2007). Malaysian unit trust funds' performance during up and down market conditions: A comparison of market benchmark. *Managerial Finance,* 33(2), 154–166.

Low, S.-W. (2008). A cross-sectional analysis of Malaysian unit trust fund expense ratios. *Journal of Asset Management,* 9(4), 270-277.

Low, S.-W. and Ghazali, N. A. (2007). The price linkages between Malaysian unit trust funds and the stock market: Short run and long run interrelationships. *Managerial Finance,* 33(2), 89-101.

Malkiel, B. G. (1995). Returns from investing in equity mutual funds 1971 to 1991. *The Journal of Finance,* 50(2), 549–572.

Mallin, C. A., Saadouni, B. and Briston, R. J. (1995). The financial performance of ethical investment funds. *Journal of Business Finance & Accounting,* 22(4), 483–496.

Mansor, F. and Bhatti, M. I. (2011). The Islamic mutual fund performance: New evidence on market timing and stock selectivity Paper presented at the 2011 International Conference on Economics and Finance Research Singapore.

Nainggolan, Y. (2011). Taking a leap of faith: are investors left short changed. Degree of Doctor of Philosophy, Queensland University of Technology, Brisbane, Australia.

Nassir, A. M., Mohamad, S. and Hua, N. M. (1997). Selectivity and timing: evidence from the performance of Malaysian unit trusts. *Pertanika Journal of Social Science & Humanity,* 5(1), 45–57.

Nathie, M. (2009). Islamic equity investments: Determinants of investment behaviour of Malaysian Islamic equity investors under conditions of competing alternatives. Degree of Doctor Philosophy, Griffith University, Brisbane, Australia.

Newey, M. and West, K. D. (1987). A simple, positive semi-definite heteroskedasticity and autocorrelation consistent variance covariance matrix. *Econometrica,* 55(3), 703–708.

Renneboog, L., Ter Horst, J. R. and Zhang, C. (2008). The price of ethics and stakeholder governance: The performance of socially responsible mutual funds. *Journal of Corporate Finance,* 14(3), 302–322.

Sawicki, J. and Ong, F. (2000). Evaluating managed fund performance using conditional measures: Australian evidence. *Pacific-Basin Finance Journal,* 8(3-4), 505–528.

Securities Commission Malaysia. (2012). Securities Commission annual reports from 1998 to 2011 Retrieved 31 June, 2012, from http://www.sc.com.my.

Sharpe, W. F. (1966). Mutual fund performance. *The Journal of Business,* 39(1), 119–138.

Sinclair, N. (1990). Market timing ability of pooled superannuation funds January 1981 to December 1987. *Accounting & Finance,* 30, 51–65.

Treynor, J. L. (1965). How to rate management of investment funds. *Harvard Business Review,* 43(1), 63–75.

Treynor, J. L. and Mazuy, K. K. (1966). Can mutual funds outguess the market? *Harvard Business Review,* 44(4), 131–136.

Zhang, C. (2006). Ethics, investments and investor behaviour. Degree of Doctor of Philosophy, Tilburg University, Tilburg, The Netherlands.

In: Contemporary Issues in Islamic Finance
Editor: Andrew C. Worthington
ISBN: 978-1-62948-905-6

Chapter 10

SHARIAH AUDIT OF FINANCIAL STATEMENTS IN ISLAMIC FINANCIAL INSTITUTIONS

Zurina Shafii*[*], *Supiah Salleh and Nurazalia Zakaria
Universiti Sains Islam Malaysia, Malaysia

ABSTRACT

Shariah audit is important as the third line of defence in ensuring the operations of Islamic Financial Institutions (IFIs) are in line with Shariah principles. The operations refer not only to day to day operations, process and procedures and management records but also the financial statements of the IFIs. Shariah audit gives an indication to the market that the IFIs are complying with the Shariah guidelines. This is especially important as the market is keener on knowing and seeing that IFIs perform its bidding. The resurgence of Islamic finance over the past 30 years plus the sub-prime crisis has caused greater emphasis for the IFIs to be ever more Shariah-compliant. The purpose of this chapter is to provide an overview on the importance of Shariah audit as one of the lines of defence in terms of internal control for IFIs. Secondly, the chapter also provides suggested auditable areas for the audit scope of Shariah audit in the financial statements of IFIs. Accordingly, the chapter provides guidance for future empirical and policy impact research on audit scope for Shariah audit in financial statements of IFIs.

1. INTRODUCTION

Islamic financial institutions (IFIs) are required to operate under the strict requirements of *Shariah*. The section of *Shariah* law that governs economic dealings are referred to as fiqh muamalat or the understanding of law of economics transactions. *Fiqh muamalat's* guidance forms the bases for *Shariah* requirements that IFIs have to adhere to. The same principles could be used as the parameters for *Shariah* Compliance Audit. This assurance is vital to ensure that *Shariah* principles are observed. *Shariah* governance mechanisms were

[*] Corresponding author: Faculty of Economics & Muamalat, Universiti Sains Islam Malaysia, Bandar Baru Nilai 71800 Nilai, Negeri Sembilan, Malaysia. Email. shafii@usim.edu.my.

introduced in the early establishments of Islamic banking and finance revolves around the role of *Shariah* advisory when the IFIs management are introducing new products and services. Progressively over the years, *Shariah* governance includes assurance measures, in addition to the fundamental *Shariah* advisory and *Shariah* review process.

In Malaysia, Bank Negara Malaysia issued the new *Shariah* Governance Framework (SGF) made effective from 1st January 2011. The framework introduces the parties that are responsible for the *Shariah* governance in IFIs; Board of Directors (BOD), the management and *Shariah* Committee (SC). The new SGF identified BOD as the main organ that has to take the responsibility for *Shariah* governance. The management shall be responsible to observe the *Shariah*-related initiatives coming from the SC. SGF 2011 also introduced the functions that have to be performed as part of the governance mechanisms. The functions encompass the pre-product approval stage to the post-product stage. The functions are *Shariah* research, *Shariah* review, *Shariah* audit and *Shariah* risk management. While the SGF identified the necessary functions, it did not provide detailed specifications and operationalisation of the functions. This leaves the implementation of the functions to the decisions from the interactions between the organs of the *Shariah* governance.

The focus of this chapter is to discuss *Shariah* audit function, specifically on audit scope for *Shariah* audit in financial statements.

2. *SHARIAH* ASSURANCE AND REVIEW

SGF refers *Shariah* audit as 'the periodical assessment conducted from time to time, to provide an independent assessment and objective assurance designed to add value and improve the degree of compliance in relation to the IFI's business operations, with the main objective of ensuring a sound and effective internal control system for *Shariah* compliance.' *Shariah* audit may be conducted as part of the IFI's thematic audit on specialised areas such as management audit and Anti-Money Laundering (AML) audit. *Shariah* audit on critical areas shall be conducted at least once a year depending on the risk profile of the IFI.

Shariah compliance checking on the operations in IFIs is carried out through *Shariah* review function. The new requirements strengthen the *Shariah* governance by requiring *Shariah* audit to be performed by internal auditors, i.e. objective assurance of *Shariah* compliance by personnel not related to policy making and day to day operations of *Shariah* matters. Internal auditors must have adequate *Shariah*-related knowledge and training. In addition, the internal auditors may engage the expertise of the IFI's *Shariah* officers in performing the audit, as long as the objectivity of the audit is not compromised.

According to SGF, the Board Audit Committee, upon consultation with the *Shariah* Committee will determine the deliverables of the *Shariah* audit function. The deliverables shall be consistent with accepted auditing standards. The scopes of *Shariah* audit stated in the BNM's SGF are as follows:

I. Audit of financial statements of the IFI;
II. Compliance audit on organisational structure, people, process and information technology application systems; and
III. Review of adequacy of the *Shariah* governance process.

For *Shariah* audit on financial statements, internal auditors could audit the accounting transactions that relates to *Shariah* matters. These include profit distribution policy, penalty charges, basis of income recognition, *zakat* policies and computations and so on (Mustafa et al, 2012). In addition, compliance audit should be performed which includes audit on organisational structure, people, process and information technology application systems.

Shariah audit in IFIs could be regarded as a form of operational risk management in IFIs. Islamic Financial Services Board (IFSB) "Guiding Principles of Risk Management for Institutions (other than Insurance institutions) offering only Islamic Financial Services" [1], in its principle 14 states that 'IFI should have in place adequate systems and controls, including *Shariah* Board or Advisor, to ensure compliance with *Shariah* rules and principles'.

Shariah audit function is the last line of defence to ensure *Shariah* compliance in IFIs. The three lines of defence principle is a long and well established concept that has been deployed in a variety of industries and situations. Typical examples of the activities of the three lines of defence are as follows:

I. The business: the day-to-day running of the operation and the front-office
II. Risk and compliance: the continual monitoring of the business
III. Audit: the periodic checking of risk and compliance.

The 'three lines of defence model' is one approach to safeguard the internal control framework. In the US, it is the preferred approach by the Financial Services Authority (FSA).

2.1. First Line of Defence

This describes the controls an organisation has in place to deal with the day-to-day business activities and operations. Controls are designed into systems and processes and assuming that the design is sound to appropriately mitigate risk, compliance with process should ensure an adequate control environment (Shafii and Salleh, 2010). There should be adequate managerial and supervisory controls in place to ensure compliance and to highlight control breakdown, inadequacy of process and unexpected events.

In IFIs' environment, the product design is championed by the Product Department, with assistance or in consultation from the *Shariah* Department which also provides *Shariah* research function in relation to *Shariah* concept to be applied. Product Department will thoroughly conduct research on development of products and the proposed *Shariah* concept/s to be used as well as identifying potential risk related to the proposed product. Product proposal will be tabled in the *Shariah* Committee meeting for concurrence / approval. The process in developing the product by the Product Department is considered as a 1st line of defense, while the *Shariah* Department is as a 2nd line of defense i.e. ensuring the *Shariah* concept is applied correctly and the product features are in *Shariah* compliance before tabling to the *Shariah* Committee for approval.

[1] Available online at: www.ifsb.org/standard/ifsb1.pdf. Retrieved on 13th July 2009

2.2. Second Line of Defence

The second line is re-enforced by the advisory and monitoring functions of risk management, legal and compliance. Risk management defines and prescribes the financial and operational risk assessment processes for the business; maintains the risk registers and undertakes regular reviews of these risks in conjunction with line management. Legal and Compliance advises on all areas of regulatory principles, rules and guidance, including leading on any changes, and undertakes monitoring activity on key areas of regulatory risk.

One would expect these functions to report upon their work undertaken and significant findings to the appropriate executive risk oversight committees in the second line. These functions may also report to the board's audit committee or a board risk committee. In relation to IFIs' operation, the second line of defence is provided by the *Shariah* review function which ensures the IFI business activities and operation are in *Shariah* compliance. This includes pre product approval and post product approval, i.e. during product offering process.

2.3. Third Line of Defence

Internal / *Shariah* audit undertakes a program of risk based audits provides 3rd line of defence. Clearly the level of assurance taken will depend on the effectiveness of the second line, including the oversight committees, and internal audit will need to coordinate its work with compliance and risk management as well as assessing the work of these functions. The findings from these audits are reported to all three lines, i.e. accountable line management, the executive and oversight committees and the board audit committee.

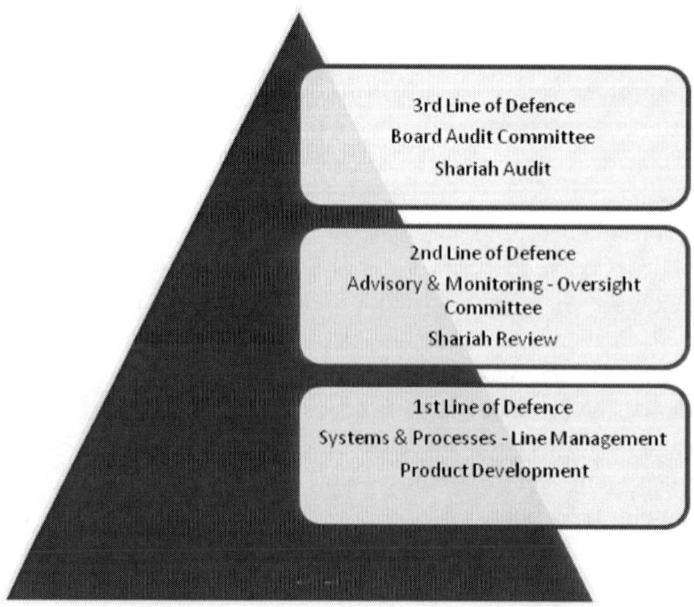

Figure 1. Three Lines of Defence (Hanefah et. *al* 2012).

This third line role likens internal audit to that of a goalkeeper in a football match. When the ball is lost in midfield (first line) and the defence (second line) fails to pick up the opposition's attack, it is left to the goalkeeper (third line) to save the day. There is a reasonable expectation that internal audit will identify the weaknesses in both first and second lines and failure to do so may lead to significant loss to the organisation.

The third line of defence applied in the IFIs' operation is the exercise of *Shariah* audit by the internal audit department, required by BNM. *Shariah* auditor will provide the independent assessment of the state of *Shariah* compliance in IFIs. *Shariah* audit reports will be tabled in the Board Audit Committee to notify the *Shariah* compliance issues and rectification measures taken to address the issues.

Figure 1 best summarises the above discussion on the three line of defence in a form of a pyramid.

3. *SHARIAH* AUDIT SCOPE IN FINANCIAL STATEMENTS

Internal *Shariah* auditors shall perform audit of financial statements in order to verify that the management of IFIs perform its fiduciary duties to the stakeholders. The scope of audit in financial statements is extracted from a focus group interviews held on *Shariah* audit functions, facilitated by International *Shariah* Research Academy (ISRA).

This study uses a qualitative method that reviews and gathers inputs and feedbacks from a session of focus group interviews. One of the advantages of focus group interview is that it highlights the uniqueness and human experience which is not being addressed and measured by using the quantitative method approach. In addition, focus group interview is useful to explore and generate ideas and issues through group interactions. Another advantage relates to the position of participants in the interview. Interviewing provides researchers with an insight into the participants' thoughts, ideas and memories in their own words rather than those of the researchers' (Houghton et. al, 2011).

A sample of knowledgeable and expert in *Shariah* audit comprised of regulators, internal auditors of Islamic banks, external auditors, *Shariah* Committee members and *Shariah* officers of the Islamic banks. An expert should not only possess Islamic jurispudence knowledge but must also possess some comparative knowledge on conventional banking law (Yaakub et. al, 2012). The initial number of the targeted sample was twenty. Although there may be a relatively limited number of experts with knowledge on *Shariah* audit, the panel size requirements are modest, and it would be practical to solicit up to 10 to 18 members in size (Krueger and Casey, 2000). However, due to their tight schedule of the respondents, only five experts agreed to participate in the study. The five repondents consist of a representative regulator, an internal auditor of an Islamic bank, an external auditor, a *Shariah* Committee and a *Shariah* officer. Although the numbers of interviewees are relatively small, the researchers are in the opinion that the sample is representative.

During the focus group interview the participants are guided by a series of questions developed based on the previous literatures. The questions are developed based on the objective of the research and validated by the subject matter expert in *Shariah* audit. All interviews were audio recorded and then transcribed. Content analysis was performed and inputs were compiled and reviewed into thematic findings. From the industry practitioners' input, the following are the areas of *Shariah* compliance in financial statements that should be audited consists of the following:

3.1. Financing

Financing of a *Shariah* compliant business must be originated from halal source, either it is inform of debt of equity financing. The maximum percentage of debt financing, in many jurisdictions is capped at 33.3% (1/3) of the total capital of the company.

Islamic banks are exposed to business risks such as market liquidity, currency and operational risk. Risk generates unexpected losses and hedging restricts the impact of the loss. Islamic hedging instrument is based on real economic activity and real balance sheet items. Hedging is permissible if derivatives involve the actual transaction and do not cause injustice. Instruments used by IFIs must be *Shariah*-compliant as indicated by the *Shariah* authorities. IFIs must be able to demonstrate and disclose that hedging is used for the purpose of hedging actual risks of the relevant party. Transaction should not be for the purpose of speculation and must be real transactions involving the actual transfer of ownership of real assets i.e. actual risk and real settlement.

Additionally, an entity engaged in Islamic financial transactions ought to disclose how it manages *Shariah* compliance risk, which would be an operational risk to the entity. Although such disclosure is not specifically mentioned in IFRS, the general principle as stated in paragraph 31 of IFRS 7 (IFRS Foundation, 2010) is that:

> "An entity shall disclose information that enables users of its financial statements to evaluate the nature and extent of risks arising from financial instruments to which the entity is exposed at the reporting date."

However, it is important to note that IFRS does not prohibit entities from making additional voluntary disclosures in their financial statements, provided they are not misleading or do not conflict with the information required by IFRS. Indeed IFRS requires an entity to provide additional disclosures if compliance with IFRS alone is insufficient to enable users to understand the impact of transactions and events on the company's financial performance and position.

IFIs must identify and disclose the amount of non-*Shariah* compliant investment previously acquired. It is the responsibility of the IFI to dispose the investment according to the guidelines by the *Shariah* authorities. Conversely, there are items which are required to be excluded from the computation of *zakat* – mainly, assets which are deemed prohibited (*haram*) such as investments in alcohol, tobacco or gaming concerns. Disclosure of assets which are deemed *haram* as well as income derived from *haram* sources are often lacking in traditional financial statements.

The additional disclosures may also include the reporting of the results of activities which are permitted *(halal)* or forbidden *(haram)* under *Shariah*. Such disclosure may well be different from a segmental analysis of business activities performed for IFRS purposes.

3.2. Profit Equalisation Reserve

Profit Equalisation Reserve (PER) and Investment Risk Reserve (IRR) is a mechanism used by IFIs to reduce the fluctuations in the profit rates payable to the Investment Account Holders (IAH). IFIs must disclose the policy on PER and state the ownership of the PER balance as at the accounting period in the notes to account. Another issue in relation to the *Mudarabah* investment accounts or deposit account is that many depositors in Islamic banks will expect rates of return to be in line with conventional market rates. Islamic banks may therefore introduce a mechanism to make this possible. Many banks endeavour to provide consistent returns to account-holders or maintain parity between *Mudarabah* profit sharing accounts and conventional fixed deposit accounts. The need to provide consistent returns on a profit-sharing arrangement is known as 'displaced commercial risk'.

In order to achieve consistent returns, when profits are low, the bank may feel obliged to forgo its own share of profit to ensure that the depositor receives a comparable market return, even if there is no legal compulsion to do so (PricewaterhouseCoopers, 2010; ACCA and KPMG, 2010). In some countries, Islamic banks address the issue described above by using a Profit Equalisation Reserve (PER) to hold back some of the excess market profits and pay them out in leaner times.

However, the operation of such PERs raises contentious issues from an accounting perspective. Contractual obligations to pay depositors will clearly be liabilities of the institution. Even where there is no formalized agreement, it may be construed that there is a constructive obligation such that the PER would also be deemed to be a liability. However, if no accounting (contractual/constructive) liability is justified, then any surplus will be the profit of the institution. If the bank's share of any PER balance is included in the liability amount, then it could constitute a hidden reserve, which would not be acceptable under IFRS.

Bank Negara Malaysia (2010) in its *Concept Paper on Accounting and Regulatory Treatment for Profit Equalisation Reserve* proposed an accounting treatment where there would be a debit to the statement of comprehensive income, instead of income statement. In this recognition, the bank's portion is recognised in reserves and the account-holders' portion is recognised as a sub-classification of customers' deposits.

The AOSSG (2010) noted that the MASB, when commenting on the proposed accounting treatment by BNM, had urged BNM to consider other alternatives instead of setting aside PER to meet the expected payments to investment account-holders. One possible solution suggested was to transfer, or 'ring-fence', the necessary amount from retained earnings to a reserve for this purpose. The AOSSG Research Report (2010) suggested that in order to enhance governance, the transfers and the computation of amounts may be regulated and monitored by the BNM. AOSSG (2010) opined that such mechanism would be more in line with generally accepted accounting principles (GAAP), while still achieving the objective of stabilizing returns to account holders.

3.3. Discount of Early Settlement

Ibra' is the discount for early settlement of financing amount, previosly agreed in the sale agreement. IFIs may incorporate the clause on undertaking to provide ***I*bra'** to customers who make early settlement in the Islamic financing agreement. This clause shall be stipulated under the method of payment. With the inclusion of the **Ibra'** clause in the financing agreement, the bank is bound to honour that promise. However, the act of granting a rebate in case of prepayment should entirely be voluntary and at the discretion of the seller. The rate of discount cannot be pre-specified in the contract. The contract per se, cannot contain a stipulation for subsequent increase or decrease in price. IFIs must clearly state the method of calculation of *Ibra'* (Declining Profit Method, or other methods) to enhance transparency of information to the customers.

3.4. *Zakat*

IFIs must have stipulated policies of *zakat* computation and the manner it is distributed as agreed by the *Shariah* Committee in the notes to the account. PricewaterhouseCoopers (2010) and the AOSSG Research Report (2010) similarly asserted that certain aspects of the financial statements will be particularly relevant to users who want to assess the performance and direction of the company from an Islamic perspective. Thus, it would be enhancing users' decision making by disclosing information that is important to Muslim users or stakeholders. For example, *zakat* (poor due) is not a concept dealt with by accounting standards for conventional firms. Muslim users would however want to have information on *zakat* calculations. According to Islamic texts, *zakat* ought to be computed based on the current (or fair) value of the assets. Although IFRS either require or permit fair valuation for many types of assets, this information may sometimes not be available. For example, International Accounting Standards (IAS) 2 on Inventories requires inventories to be carried out at the lower of cost or net realisable value. Hence, an entity may or may not disclose the fair value of the inventories, which is an asset subject to *zakat*. Figure 2 summarizes the scope of *Shariah* audit in financial statements.

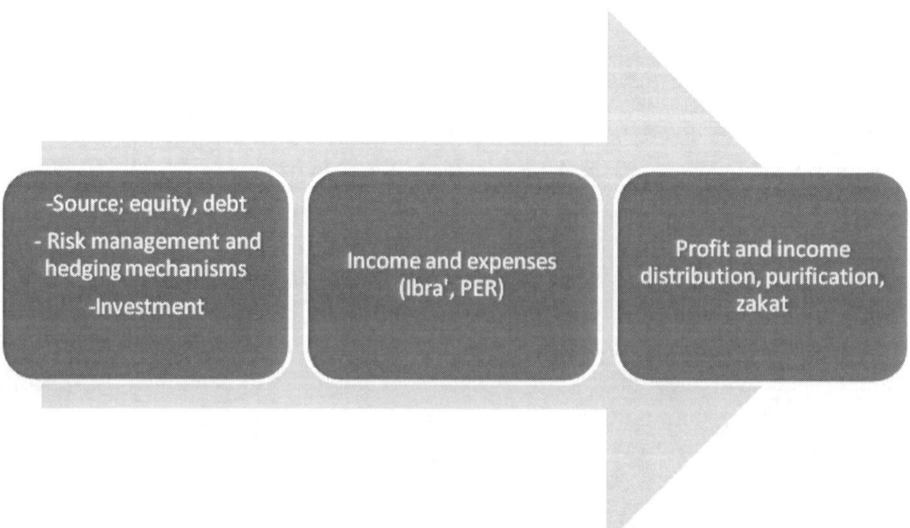

Figure 2. Central *Shariah* issues in financial statements.

In conclusion, the audit of financial statement to verify that they are following the *Shariah* involved many *Shariah* issues. It is essential to have the audit performed on financial statements in order for to ensure the transactions in IFIs carried out, recorded and reported in the manner compliant to *Shariah*.

CONCLUDING REMARKS AND DIRECTIONS FOR FUTURE RESEARCH

Shariah audit in financial statements represents an important facet of compliance audit in IFIs as financial statements are seen as the window to the IFIs overall operation, whether it reflects the application of *Shariah* rulings or not. Currently, each IFI has their own interpretation of what constitutes the audit scope for *Shariah* audit in financial statements. Furthermore, little research has been conducted and published to identify the ideal scope of audit for financial statements of IFIs. Firstly, there should be concerted effort by IFIs and stakeholders in identifying auditable areas relevant to the financial statements of IFIs. At current, the financial statement audit is more or less looking at the compliance level with financial reporting standards. Whereas, for the IFIs, there should be additional concern in identifying *Shariah* issues that arises from IFIs' reporting of Islamic financial transactions. Secondly, more researches and publications should be produced by both academician and practitioners identifying such issues so as to provide a balanced point of view theoretically and practically. Lastly, regulators should be able to draw on the findings from these findings to assist them in formulating guidelines and regulations for IFIs to uniformly practice. With such concerted effort from various parties, that is the IFIs, stakeholders and regulators, this would channel to the market that *Shariah* audit in the financial statements is an important exercise that requires contribution of ideas and input from various levels of participation. More importantly, the management of IFIs would be more confident in declaring in their *Shariah* Committee Report that the operations and financial statements of IFIs adhere strictly to the *Shariah* precepts. This in turn would foster greater confidence to the market that IFIs are truly *Shariah*-compliant.

REFERENCES

ACCA and KPMG (2010). Harmonising Financial Reporting of Islamic Finance. London, United Kingdom.

Asian-Oceanian Standard Setters Group (AOSSG) (2010). Research Paper: Financial Reporting Issues Relating to Islamic Finance.

Bank Negara Malaysia (2010). Concept Paper on Accounting and Regulatory Treatment for Profit Equalization Reserve. Kuala Lumpur, Malaysia.

Houghton, K.A., Jubb, C. & Kend, M. (2011). Materiality in the context of audit: the real expectations gap. *Managerial Auditing Journal* 26(6),482-500.

IFRS Foundation (2010). International Accounting Standard 2. Inventories. London, United Kingdom.

IFRS Foundation. (2010). International Financial Reporting Standard 7. Financial Instruments: Disclosures. London, United Kingdom.

Krueger, R.A. & Casey, M.A. (2000). Focus groups: A Practical Guide for Applied Research. 3rd edition. Thousand Oaks, California: Sage Publications.

PricewaterhouseCoopers (2010). Open to Comparison: Islamic Finance and IFRS.

Hanefah, M.M., Shafii, Z., Salleh, S., & Zakaria, N. (2012). Governance and Shariah Audit in Islamic Financial Institutions. Kuala Lumpur, Malaysia: Penerbit USIM.

Shafii Z. & Salleh S. (2010). Enhancing Governance, Accountability and Transparency in Islamic Financial Institutions: An Examination into the Audit of Shari'a Internal Control System. *The Journal of Malaysian Accounting Research Special Issue* 2010, Vol 9, No. 2, December 23-42.

Shariah Governance Framework. (2011). Bank Negara Malaysia. Kuala Lumpur, Malaysia.

Yaakub, N. I., Mujani, W. K., Jusoff, K., Hussain, W. K., Zainol, Z. A., Deuraseh, Z. A. & Jamsari, Z. A. (2011). Laws Governing Islamic Banks and Financial Institutions in Malaysia: An Overview. *Middle-East Journal of Scientific Research* 7(Special Issue of Diversity of Knowledge on Middle East), 87-92.

In: Contemporary Issues in Islamic Finance
Editor: Andrew C. Worthington
ISBN: 978-1-62948-905-6

Chapter 11

THE TRANSFORMATION OF RISK MANAGEMENT PRACTICES IN ISLAMIC BANKING

Yahia M. Baej [*] ***and Andrew C. Worthington***
Griffith University, Nathan, QLD, Australia

ABSTRACT

Like their conventional counterparts, Islamic banks are subject to various risks associated with their everyday activities that require proper management. However, the types of risk and their measurement and management may vary. The objective of this chapter is to compare several aspects of risk management in conventional and Islamic banks, including the concept of risk, type of risk, risk approaches to risk measurement and management, and capital adequacy. The findings reveal that unlike the conventional banking model, *Shariah* considers some conditions for risk to be acceptable, including the objective of taking risk, the value that taking risk would add to the economy, and the degree of risk taken. Consequently, a number of conventional risk measurement and management approaches are available to Islamic banks as they are also *Shariah*-compatible instruments. However, adopting and developing tools that serve unique risks associated with the nature of Islamic methods of finance is crucial. For example, alongside the implementation of international capital adequacy guidelines, there are special calculation guidelines available to Islamic banks issued by the Islamic Financial Service Board (IFSB) and the Accounting and Auditing Organization for Islamic Financial Institutions (AAOIFI).

1. INTRODUCTION

Risk exists in every aspect of life. Like most other financial institutions, banks are subject to a range of risks, including credit, market, operational and interest rate risk. It is then of importance for banks to manage these risks as failing to do so may lead to adverse

---

[*] Corresponding author: Department of Accounting, Finance and Economics, Griffith University, Nathan QLD 4111, Australia. Email. yahia.baej@griffithuni.edu.au.

consequences. The Islamic banking industry is no exception. For this purpose, a large literature is available relating to banking risks. Moreover, a number of models, approaches, and guidelines were developed over the last half of the 20th century and the beginning of this century to measure, report, constrain and manage the various types of risk faced by financial institutions including banking industry (Froot et. al, 1993; Stulz, 1984).

However, risk management in Islamic banking needs to be theoretically and practically developed as it is relatively new. A number of academic researchers, including Shaikh and Jalbani (2009), Khan and Bhatti (2008), Hassan and Dicle (2005), Marston and Sundararajan (2003) and Khan and Ahmed (2001) argue that the unique nature of financial activities in Islamic banks makes them vulnerable to specific risks on both the asset and liability sides, notwithstanding the other risks faced by conventional banks. This leads to the question whether conventional risk management techniques and guidelines can apply to Islamic banks given they may have a basis in activities prohibited by *Shariah* (Khan and Bhatti, 2008). As an example, Iqbal (1999) imputes the shortage of risk management tools in Islamic financial institutions to a lack of research in the area. Another issue is whether Islamic banks should follow the international bank regulation guidelines (such as the Basel Accord) or Islamic guidelines (AAOIFI and IFSB) in holding an adequate amount of capital.

This chapter investigates risk management issues in conventional and Islamic banks and their differences in terms of risk management behavior. Section 2 discusses the concept of banking risk. Section 3 undertakes the comparison of the risk measurement and management approaches and techniques in both types of banks. Section 4 addresses some aspects of capital adequacy.

2. Types of Banking Risk

Like all financial institutions, banks face various types of financial risk in their role of providing financial services (Santomero, 1997). According to Bessis (1998), banking risks are adverse impacts on profitability associated with several distinct sources of uncertainty. From the management viewpoint, financial institutions, including banks, face three basic types of risk. The first is risk that simple business practices could eliminate or avoid. These include applying effective standards to preventing inappropriate financial decisions, diversifying the loan portfolio, and hedging or asset–liability matching. A second type of risk is that transferrable to other market participants. For example, banks can transfer interest rate risk through swaps and other financial derivatives. Finally, some risks link directly with firm activities and therefore should be absorbed and managed within the firm (Oldfield and Santomero, 1997). In practice, banks tend to distinguish between credit, market and operational risks due to the importance of these types of risks as key drivers determining financial loss (Kupper, 2000). In addition to these risks, interest rate, liquidity and foreign exchange risk, as well as country and performance risk, are other examples of the primary bank risks (Bessis, 1998).

A number of studies have addressed the matter of individual as well as groups of risks in the Islamic banking system. An example is Al-Tamimi's (2002) empirical examination of commercial bank risk management practices in the United Arab Emirates (UAE). This study, which targeted both local and foreign banks, found no difference between Islamic and conventional banks in terms of the practice of risk management. In addition, credit followed by liquidity risk was the most important risks facing commercial banks. Moreover, the findings revealed that banks depended on managers using financial statement analysis to identify these risks.

Al-Tamimi and Al-Mazrooei (2007) also examined UAE national and foreign banks to understand how they practiced risk management techniques across the various types of risks and whether there was any difference between Islamic and conventional of banks risk management practices. Interestingly, the findings differed somewhat from those in the previous study, with foreign exchange risk, credit risk, and operational risk identified as the most important risks facing all UAE commercial banks. In addition, they found the two sets of banks, Islamic and conventional, differed in their efficiency with respect to risk assessment and analysis. Finally, they identified similarities in the identification and analysis of credit risk. A comparison between these two studies reveals that banks develop their risk management behavior as banking practices become more complicated.

In a conventional bank only analysis, Salas and Saurina (2002) combined macroeconomic and microeconomic variables to discern whether the determinants of problem loans in the Spanish savings and commercial banks using panel data over the period 1985–97. Salas and Saurina (2002) used several variables to explain credit risk, including the GDP growth rate, the indebtedness of family and firms, rapid past credit or branch expansion, inefficiency, portfolio composition, size, net interest margin, the capital ratio, and market power and found that savings and commercial banks differed substantially. The main finding was that after controlling for macroeconomic conditions, individual bank level variables strongly affected credit risk. Moreover, GDP growth exerted a strong negative effect on the expansion of loan losses. The latter reflects the importance of reinforcing control actions in dealing with a changing economic cycle.

A number of other studies have focused on the determinants of risk-taking and risk-shifting behavior in banks. For the most part, the existing literature suggests that the system of deposit insurance found in many countries exposes banks to moral hazard. Nevertheless, the empirical evidence provides conflicting results. For example, Duan et al. (1992) tested whether US banks use fixed rate deposit insurance as an incentive to shift their risk to the Federal Deposit Insurance Corporation (FDIC) using an option-based methodology and a sample of thirty banks over the period 1979–86 and by pricing the bank actuarial liabilities. The results showed that shifting risk neither is a common behavior among US banks nor did it increase following deregulation. In addition, Keeley (1990) and Marcus (1984) concluded that potential bankruptcy costs counterbalance risk-taking by bank management and shareholders due to deposit insurance given that in doing so they may lose the bank's charter representing valuable assets. Salas and Saurina (2003) followed a similar methodology to that in Keeley (1990) and confirmed the results for deregulation, market power, and risk behavior using a sample of 21 Spanish commercial banks over the period 1968–98. They concluded that the liberalization caused moral hazard as characterized by increasing competition. This in turn negatively affected market power, with firms with low charter values experiencing default risk owing to solvency problems.

Elsewhere, as Hahm (2004) has highlighted, financial liberalization and capital markets may account for Korean banking exposure to interest rate and exchange rate risk between 1994 and 1997. This study also indicated that interest rate policies combined with a dramatic decrease in the return worsened the banking crisis in that country. This suggested the upgrading of risk management practices and bank supervision in that country. In other work, Flannery and Sorescu (1996) studied the US bank debenture yields over the period 1983–91 and concluded that market discipline and government regulations limit risk taking in banks. This could partly explain the lack of relationship between deposit insurance and moral hazard behavior. These results are consistent with Ioannidou and Penas (2010) who examined the risk taking behavior of Bolivian banks before and after the introduction of a deposit insurance system. They found that while banks increased their risk taking afterwards, it was because of a decrease in market discipline not deposit insurance per se.

In other work, Alston et al. (1994), Wheelock and Wilson (1995), and Wheelock (1992) argued for a connection between deposit insurance and US bank failures in the 1920s and 1930s. A more recent study by Hovakimian and Kane (2000) found that capital requirements did not prevent large US banks shifting their risk onto the safety net. Niinimäki (2004) investigated the impact of competition on bank risk taking behavior. This study showed that deposit insurance has no effect on risk taking, but only if the bank monopolizes the market or there is competition between banks in the loan market. However, banks are obliged to take excessive risks if they compete for deposits.

Some other studies focused on the link between risk taking behavior, banking efficiency, and capitalization. For instance, Kwan and Eisenbeis (1997) used simultaneous equations to investigate the relation between risk taking, capitalization, and operating efficiency in a sample of 352 banking institutions. They found that efficient banks were less vulnerable to risk taking than their counterparts. The results also show that well-capitalized firms operated more efficiently. Similarly, Linbo and Sherrill (2004) examined efficiency versus risk in a sample of 866 large local US banks in 1998. They found that credit and insolvency risk affected profit efficiency, unlike liquidity risk or the mix of loans.

Islam perceives the protection of property or *Al-maal* as one of five necessities. Risk within its broad meaning (*Khatar* in Arabic), is therefore undesirable in *Shariah* as it contradicts this necessity. However, early Islamic jurisprudents divided risk taking into two main categories. The first is commercial risk, where the purchase of a commodity for making a profit by selling it with a reliance on the influence of Allah. Although this transaction is associated with a potential loss, it is necessary for trading purposes. The second category is the risk of gambling which falls into the Islamic term 'eating wealth for nothing'. *Shariah* strictly prohibits this category of risk (Al-Suwailam, 2006).

In addition, taking risk in *Shariah* (*Mukhatarah* in Arabic) is not an objective of its own. Rather, the main aim is to create economic value and increase wealth, which effectively legitimatizes risk. In other words, economic decisions are determined by the value they add which in turn defines the value of risk. We can discern this from the rule of *fiqh* '*Al-Kharaj bil Dhaman*' (Sabiq, 2006) which means that a person or an institution is entitled to revenue on accepting liability for losses. The *Shariah* approach of taking risk identifies extremes that distinguish between what is allowed and what is not. One is the prohibition of interest (*Riba*) which guarantees revenue without risk. The other is the prohibition of gambling (*Al-Maysir*), which involves significant risk taking with a generally very small chance of a win. In this respect, *Fiqh* scholars identify three conditions under which risk could be taken. Generally, risk is acceptable if it is inevitable, which means the value added of the economic activity is not possible without taking risk. Risk is also acceptable if it is insignificant, meaning the likelihood of failure is relatively small. The third condition is based on the first two, which is that the risk should be unintentional where the economic activities are taken because of the value they add not the risk they necessitate (Al-Suwailem, 2006). Figure 2.1 summarizes the various types of risk in financial transactions.

A zero-sum game refers to games where one party wins at the expense of another. Gambling is an example of such game. In contrast, a non-zero-sum game indicates positive-sum games where both parties gain or lose, following the outcomes of a project. A *Musharakah* or partnership is an example of a positive-sum game.

The above discussion briefly highlights the Islamic approach that Islamic banks adopt towards the types of risks and risk taking behavior. The differences in institutional infrastructure between conventional and Islamic banking systems determine each type's bank management behavior including risk taking patterns and the types of risk they face. This means that due to the nature of their activities, Islamic banks are exposed to categories of risks based directly on their investment activities notwithstanding other traditional banking risks. Empirically, Shaikh and Jalbani (2009), Khan and Bhatti (2008), Hassan and Dicle (2005), Marston and Sundararajan (2003), and Khan and Ahmed (2001) argue that the unique nature of financial activities in Islamic banks makes them vulnerable to unique risks on both the asset and liability sides, over and above the risks faced by conventional banks.

Khan and Ahmed (2001) detail some issues relating to risk management behavior in Islamic financial institutions with special reference to Islamic banking, along with the implications of Islamic jurisprudence (*Fiqh*) for future effective risk management and supervision. Using a questionnaire supported by field level interviews with Islamic bank staff in the UAE, Malaysia, Bahrain, and Egypt, Khan and Ahmed (2001) aimed to understand better some of the more important risk management issues. They found that Islamic financial institutions face some unique risks arising from the use of profit and loss sharing models. These risks are considered more serious than other types of risks faced by both conventional and Islamic banking firms. The results also indicated that the earnings on Islamic investments should be competitive or investors will choose institutions with higher returns, which might cause withdrawal from Islamic bank deposits. Khan and Ahmed (2001) also found *Murabahah* and *Ijarah* were less risky than other profit and loss sharing methods. In addition, although Khan and Ahmed (2001) found evidence of reasonable risk management processes, they recommended further improvements in the risk management instruments and processes, money markets, and regulation used in Islamic banking.

In other work, Marston and Sundararajan (2003) argued that *Shariah*-compliant financial activities and Islamic finance infrastructure generated risks that needed consideration at both the individual and macro levels. These risks were also studied by Makiyan (2002), who argued that special risks surround both profit and loss sharing (PLS) modes, such as *Mudarabah* and *Musharakah* contracts, and non-PLS contracts, such as advance payments (*Salam*) and lease financing (*Ijarah*), because such contracts give banks neither information nor guarantees it investment until the contract due date. They also argued that the lack of developed Islamic money market, the absence of a lender-of-last-resort (LOLR) facility for many Islamic banks, and the shortage of credit hedging instruments ensured that the Islamic banking industry operated with less profitability and more risk than conventional interest-based banks. Zainol and Kassim (2010) also examined the exposure of Islamic banks to rate of return risk and the effect of interest rates on the former with particular reference to the dual conventional–Islamic banking system operating in Malaysia. The main results of the study showed that Islamic banks are vulnerable to rate of return risk, as influenced by interest rates in a competitive market environment.

Investment risk is potentially one of the main distinguishing characteristics of Islamic banking. In general, 'investment risk' contains any risks involved in the use of Islamic banking products, and includes credit, market, rate of return, and trade risks. For example, Khalidi and Refai (2009) investigated investment risk in Islamic banks and theoretically concluded that Islamic banks were not necessarily riskier than conventional banks in this regard. Nonetheless, the choice of the types of products and services practiced by banks as well as the diversification of investment portfolio could enhance the ability of these banks to manage their investment risks. However, as investment risks carry a broad meaning, Ariffin et al., (2009) specified 'risk of trade and investment' as unique risks arise from the different structure of assets and liabilities in Islamic banks, namely, fiduciary and displaced commercial risks. The former occurs as a result of breaching *Mudarabah* contract while the later results when banks fail to pay a competitive rate of return on the investment accounts.

Another important risk in Islamic banks is compliance risk (also referred to as integrity risk). Basel defined compliance risk as "the risk of legal or regulatory sanctions, financial loss, or loss to reputation a bank may suffer as a result of its failure to comply with all applicable laws, regulations, codes of conduct and standards of good practice (together, laws, rules and standards)" (Basel, 2003, p 1). However, Elsafi (2010) included another meaning of the risk applied to Islamic banks, which is the risk of trading in *Shariah*-prohibited products and services such as alcohol products and *Riba* contracts.

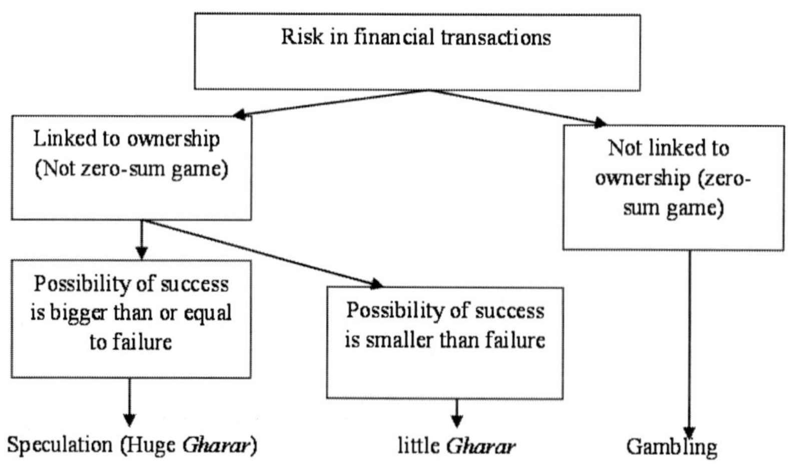

Source: (Al-Suwailem, 2006, p. 103).

Figure 1. Risk in financial transactions.

Elgari (2003) compared credit risk in Islamic and conventional banking industries by arguing that although Islamic banks had a relatively higher level of credit risk it was not obvious whether this risk derived from the Islamic banking model itself. Khan (2003) also stressed the importance of a risk management framework that covered Islamic financial instruments individually given their exposure to very different levels of risk. This study also analyzed the minimum capital required by Basel I and II in the light of Islamic finance modes.

Finally, Djojosugito (2008) identified the exposure of Islamic banks to legal risk arising from the divergence between *Shariah* requirements and law. In a related analysis, How et al. (2005) used a sample of 23 Islamic and conventional Malaysian banks from 1988 to 1996 to analyze the degree to which both types of banks were exposed to credit, liquidity and interest rate risks, finding that Islamic banks generally had relatively higher levels of all three risk types.

3. Risk Measurement and Management Issues

When discussing the risks face the banking industry, especially for the purpose of comparing conventional and Islamic banks, it important to focus on risk measurement and risk management tools and techniques and how such approaches and techniques differ in terms of theory and practice. It is also important to discuss the risk reporting system in both industry segments and whether they differ.

The literature of risk management in the banking industry shows that banks implement a variety of risk measurement approaches, including value at risk (VAR), earnings at risk (EAR), economic value added (EVA), the risk-adjusted return on capital (RAROC), simulation techniques, worst case estimates, maturity matching, duration analysis, gap analysis, credit analysis, and internal ratings systems. The literature also identifies a number of techniques that banks use to manage their risks, including securitization, futures, options and swaps, loan loss reserves, collateral arrangements, on-balance sheet netting, guarantees, and internal ratings systems (Santomero, 1997; Kupper, 2000; Longin, 2000; Lopez and Saidenberg, 2000; Khan and Ahmed, 2001; Stoughton and Zechner, 2007; Grundke, 2010; and Arrifin, et al. 2009). In practical approaches, a number of studies have tested these approaches and techniques in terms of their accuracy, appropriateness for application and evaluation through comparing between approaches and developing and adopting models for better risk measurement and management techniques. In this section, we review the risk management literature with an eye on comparing conventional and Islamic banks. However, we note that literature on risk management practices in Islamic banks is relatively underdeveloped.

In terms of conventional banking, Cocheo (1997) highlighted how Sanwa Bank, Los Angeles, helped the entire banking industry in California in identifying a common risk vocabulary. This study found that while other banks use massive glossaries to define their risks, Sanwa developed their own risk categorization around just nine points. In order to deal with the identified risks, they set up a three-way strategy including avoiding, transferring, and accepting risk. In another study of commercial banking risk management, which covered a number of US banks and other financial institutions, Santomero (1997) examined risk management system in light of four essential stages to implement an internal control of risk management in any banking system. These stages are: standards and reports; position limits or rules; investment guidelines or strategies; and incentive contracts and compensation. The study found that risk management approaches are more common in larger, more developed firms. However, this study again only dealt with only risk management in conventional banking.

In other work, Kupper (2000) argued that banks operate in a vicious risk cycle because of the uniqueness of banking crises. The study identified a number of risk management techniques that may be suitable to break out of this cycle. These techniques included the use of economic value-added (EVA) to measure the risk associated with shareholder value and employing stress tasting to understand the behavior of financial crises and the weakness of risk models in dealing with these crises. The case study bank in Kupper (2000) used similar techniques to manage their credit portfolio during the 1997 Asian crisis and to assess the impact of the 2000 Millennium Bug on their customers.

Meulbroek (2002) analyzed firm integrated risk management systems through illustrating a wide range set of cases. The author defined 'integration' as the calculation of total risk faced by the company as well as the mixed use of three basic risk management techniques: altering the firm's operations, implementing aimed financial instruments, and modifying the company's capital structure, with senior managers assigned a seven-category corporate framework to manage risk. A more recent study by Grundke (2010) used a comprehensive simulation study to examine the accuracy of integrated risk management approaches. This study showed that the appropriateness of the top-down approach it is not obvious due to factors that affect its performance, such as the definition of loss, the employment of a particular copula function, and the relation between risk types. The study also found that the total economic capital for poor credit qualities can be underestimated using such approach.

Another study by Wetmore (2004) used panel data to examine the change in the loans-to-core-deposits ratio as well as the relationship between this and market risk. The study targeted large commercial US bank holding companies between 1992 and 2000. The results showed that the coefficient of the market model equation changes over time. For the most part, these outcomes are consistent with evidence in the literature, including Elyasiani and Mansur (1998), Flannery, Hameed, and Harjes (1997), and Kane and Unal (1988, 1990). A negative relation was found between the change in the loan-to-core-deposits ratio and market risk before 1994 whereas a positive link was found afterwards. In general, the increase in the deposits ratio explains change in bank asset and liability practices.

Concerning the differences of risk and risk-taking concepts between conventional and Islamic banks, we need to consider risk measurement and risk management tools and techniques from the perspective of the Islamic principle of *fiqh*. In this regard, Khan and Ahmed (2001) argue that we can segment risk management practices into two parts. The first are tools and techniques consistent with Islamic principles of finance. GAP analysis, maturity matching, internal rating systems, risk reports, RAROC, internal control systems, and internal and external audits are some examples. The second part is the adaptation of other conventional bank risk-management techniques to suit *Shariah* requirements, and/or developing Islamic alternatives. Techniques not applicable to Islamic banks, as highlighted by Al-Suwailem (2006), represent zero-sum games and generate no real economic activities. These include financial options and futures, given that while most involve over-counter-payment (*Urbon*) conditions and therefore may be technically allowable, they also involve speculation and uncertainty.

Empirically, Khan and Ahmed (2001) assert that Islamic banks lack short-term financial assets and access to derivatives and the money market. For this reason, they expressed the need for more research to improve risk management procedures, techniques, and instruments that are consistent with *Shariah*. Shaikh and Jalbani (2009) compared the efficiency difference between conventional and Islamic banks in terms of managing risk. Based on the idea that Islamic banks are often heavily involved in equity investment, Shaikh and Jalbani (2009) calculated the return on equity and compared both sets of banks. The results showed that Islamic banks adequately managed their risk, also obtaining a reasonable return on their investments compared with their peers.

Khan and Bhatti (2008) highlighted that the Islamic banking industry is yet to manage fully its own inherent problems. They found that seemingly despite the substantial growth of Islamic banks in recent years, they still face crucial challenges represented in dealing with risk management strategies, corporate governance, and liquidity issues. They added that most risk management techniques used in conventional banks include activities prohibited by *Shariah* and therefore unavailable to Islamic banks. Iqbal (1999) attributed the shortage of risk management tools in Islamic financial institutions to the lack of research in the area.

Risk management techniques were also considered by some studies such as Hakim (2003), Hassan (2003), Sundararajan (2005) and Ariffin et al. (2009). Hakim (2003) studied the potential use of VaR for managing market risk, referring to the possible application of 'P&L at risk' in the Islamic banking context by analyzing profit-and-loss (income statement) data from the Al-Rajhi Bank in Saudi Arabia). Hassan (2003) also considered the possible use of VaR methodologies in Islamic banks, not just for ascertaining market risk, but also for other risks such as credit and operational risk. Likewise, Sundararajan (2005) presented a VaR proposed methodology for disclosing and measuring risks associated with profit sharing investment accounts (PSIA) in Islamic financial institutions at both the aggregate and individual bank levels. Finally, Ariffin et al. (2009) surveyed 28 Islamic banks in 14 countries as a means to understand their risk measurement and risk management techniques. The results showed that advanced risk measurement techniques—such as VaR, RAROC, simulation techniques, and worst-case estimates—were uncommon. On this basis, supervisory authorities were encouraged to play a crucial role in enhancing transparency in Islamic banking through a risk reporting system. Overall, the nature of the investment methods used by Islamic banks and the uniqueness of the relationships between banks and their customers appears to carry a huge amount of risk not found in conventional banks.

4. Capital Adequacy Issues

Islamic banks, by nature, face exposure to unique types of risks arising from *Shariah* investment methods and a commensurate lack of access to a number of conventional risk measurement and risk management techniques. This could infer the need for these institutions to hold a different (larger) percentage of capital than conventional banks. We should note that the current international capital adequacy framework issued by Basel Committee on Banking Supervision I and II, however, does not specify particular capital requirements for Islamic banking institutions. As a result, Islamic organizations such as the Accounting and Auditing Organization for Islamic Financial Institutions (AAOIFI) and the Islamic Financial services Board (IFSB) have proposed a developed framework for capital adequacy that tackles the specific issue of risk in Islamic banks.

Following the issuance of the first accord, the Basel Committee introduced a detailed framework for capital adequacy measurement and supervisory standards known as the Basel Capital Accord II (2004). This contains three pillars: minimum capital requirements, a supervisory review process, and market discipline. With the first pillar, banks must maintain a minimum of 8% of risk-weighted assets as capital, but the way in which risk is calculated differs completely from Basel II. Pillar 2 discusses the supervisory principles and review process. The third pillar includes disclosure issues. The committee issued a revised Basel II (2006) and implemented this in 2008. However, Jarrow (2007) argued that the proposed capital required under the revised accord to implement Value-at-Risk (VaR) does not practically fit with the market requirements. Through using the XYZ theory of regulatory capital, Jarrow (2007) concluded that Basel II rule should not replace other existing rules, such as FDICIA. Finally, maintaining banking capital aggregation by scaling the capital requirement was in line with theory. McAleer et al. (2010) analyzed the risk management strategies exist under Basel II standards and found that it could have worked well against market risk. However, Basel II was not implemented in US banks and was only just introduced in European banks during the 2008 financial crisis, as pointed out by Cannata and Quagliariello (2000).

Although the Basel Accord I and II worked as a rule to insure that banks have the ability to absorb the financial shocks by holding adequate amount of capital, Basel committee has been and remains amending its proposals and outcomes since 1987 as well as many models for risk approximation and measurement. This indicates the uniqueness of each crisis mentioned by Kupper (2000). The US Federal Reserve Board issued proposals on capital measurement and standards for banking industry, the so-called Basel Capital Accord I (1998), encouraging banks to hold a minimum of 8% of their capital adequacy ratio for financial safety reasons. In order to calculate such a percentage, assets have been classified into five risk groups: (0%, 5%, 10%, 20%, 50%, and 100%). However, one of the main concerns was that while long-term funding was weighted as 100% risky, financing over a period of less than one year was given 20% of risk. Such classification may have encouraged using the later fund at the expense of the former, which led to financial insatiability.

In terms of Islamic banking, Ariss and Sarieddine (2007) argue that the AAOIFI proposal, as it allocates only 50% of risk-weighted assets financed by investment accounts, lacks proper consideration of the asset side in the balance sheet. They suggest that Islamic banks should hold 100% of risk-weighted assets as capital instead of 50% to protect their investment funds due the increase of market risk over that of conventional banks. Conversely, Hassan and Dicle (2005) argue that Islamic banks need to comply with the Basel Accord guidelines in order to maintain their financial stability, manage their risk, and to be internationally recognized. Ariss and Sarieddine (2007) calculated the credit and market risks of the Dubai Islamic Bank as a case study. The findings showed that the bank holds an efficient amount of capital as recommended by international regulatory bodies and the UAE central bank. In addition, Islamic banks are found to be highly exposed to liquidity risk, a matter not previously addressed by the IFSB. A number of other studies have examined the Basel Accord guidelines for risk management and capital adequacy and their potential use in Islamic banking. This led to the introduction of the Accounting and Auditing Organization for Islamic Financial Institutions proposal (AAOIFI) in 1999, which was the first attempt to calculate the capital adequacy ratio (CAR) for Islamic banks. The proposed framework, however, did not take into account the risks carried by Islamic banks on the asset side of the balance sheet, pointed out by Ariss and Sarieddine (2007). The Islamic Financial Service Board (IFSB) (2005) proposed another set of guidelines for Islamic banking risk management, which aimed to complement the principles issued by Basel I and II. The fifteen proposed principles included risks associated with the nature of Islamic bank activities not addressed by either Basel Accord.

CONCLUSION

Islamic banking differs from its conventional counterpart most in that the former does not deal with interest. Rather, it involves investment activities permitted by *Shariah*. The bank management literature shows that while both conventional and Islamic are exposed to risks associated with their activities, there is significant variation across the two systems with respect to the types of risk and the way in which they are measured and managed. In general, the Islamic approach views risk (*Mukhatarah*) according to the objective of the transaction, the degree of risk taken, and the value the transaction adds to the economy. This effectively prohibits gambling and speculation, where there is often large risk involved with no economic value-added (zero-sum-games), and this corresponds with many of the tools conventionally available for risk management in banks, especially derivatives. However, many other conventional risk measurement and risk management approaches are, to at least some extent, available to Islamic banks as many are *Shariah*-compatible. However, due to the unique nature of Islamic banks, they are exposed to some unique risks that need to measured and managed differently. Overall, the literature shows that more attention needs to be given to risk management in Islamic banks for the purpose of developing new approaches and techniques to serve the unique nature of these institutions and the risks involved.

REFERENCES

Accounting and Auditing Organization for Islamic Financial Institutions AAOIFI, (1999). *Statement on the Purpose and Conclusion of the Capital Adequacy Ratio for Islamic Banks*. Manamah, Bahrain.

Al-Suwailam, S. (2006). *Hedging in Islamic Finance*, (Vol. *10*), Islamic Research and Training Institute. Jeddah, Saudi Arabia.

Al-Tamimi, H. & Hassan, A. (2002). Risk management practices: An empirical analysis of the UAE commercial banks. *Finance India*, *16*(3), 1045.

Al-Tamimi, H., Hassan, A. & Al-Mazrooei, F. M. (2007). Banks' risk management: a comparison study of UAE national and foreign banks. *The Journal of Risk Finance*, *8*(4), 394.

Alston, L. J., Grove, W. A. & Wheelock, D. C. (1994). Why Do Banks Fail? evidence from the 1920s. *Explorations in Economic History*, *31*(4), 409-431.

Ariffin, N. M., Archer, S. & Karim, R. A. A. (2009). Risks in Islamic banks: Evidence from empirical research. *Journal of Banking Regulation*, *10*(2), 153-163.

Ariss, R. T. & Sarieddine, Y. (2007). Challenges in implementing capital adequacy guidelines to Islamic banks. *Journal of Banking Regulation*, *9*(1), 46-59.

Basel. (2003). *The compliance function in banks*, (pp. 14): Basel Committee on Banking Supervision.

Basel, I, (1998). *International Convergence of Capital Measurement and Capital Standards*, (July 1988, updated April 1998)1. Retrieved from http://www.bis.org/publ/bcbsc111.pdf.

Basel II, (2004). *International Convergence of Capital Measurement and Capital Standards.* Retrieved from http://www.federalreserve.gov/boarddocs/press/bcreg/2004/20040626/attachment.pdf.

Basel II, (2006). *Core Principles Methodology - consultative document.* Retrieved from http://www.goodwinprocter.com/files/Basel/TheAccord.pdf.

Bessis, J. (1998). *Risk management in banking*. Chichester; New York: Wiley.

Cannata, F. & Quagliariello, M. (2009). The Role of Basel II in the Subprime Financial Crisis: Guilty or Not Guilty? *SSRN eLibrary*. Retrieved from http://ssrn.com/paper=1330417.

Cocheo, S. (1997). How Sanwa plans for overall risk management. *ABA Banking Journal*, *89*(1), 47.

Djojosugito, R. (2008). Mitigating legal risk in Islamic banking operations. *Humanomics*, *24*(2), 110.

Duan, J.-C., Moreau, A. F. & Sealey, C. W. (1992). Fixed-rate deposit insurance and risk-shifting behavior at commercial banks. *Journal of Banking and Finance*, *16*(4), 715-742.

Elgari, M. (2003). Credit risk in Islamic banking and finance. *Islamic Economic Studies*, *10*(2), 1-25.

Elsafi, F. (2010). *Risks of investment methods in Islamic and Conventional banks: a comparative Study. 14.* Retrieved from http://alazmah.wordpress.com

Elyasiani, E. & Mansur, I. (1998). Sensitivity of the bank stock returns distribution to changes in the level and volatility of interest rate: A GARCH-M model. *Journal of Banking and Finance*, *22*(5), 535-563.

Flannery, M. J., Hameed, A. S. & Harjes, R. H. (1997). Asset pricing, time-varying risk premia and interest rate risk. *Journal of Banking and Finance*, *21*(3), 315-335.

Flannery, M. J. & Sorescu, S. M. (1996). Evidence of Bank Market Discipline in Subordinated Debenture Yields: 1983-1991. *Journal of Finance*, *51*(4), 1347-1377.

Froot, K. A., Scharfstein, D. S. & Stein, J. C. (1993). Risk Management: Coordinating Corporate Investment and Financing Policies. *Journal of Finance*, *48*(5), 1629-1658.

Grundke, P. (2010). Top-down approaches for integrated risk management: How accurate are they? *European Journal of Operational Research*, *203*(3), 662-672.

Hahm, J.-H. (2004). Interest rate and exchange rate exposures of banking institutions in pre-crisis Korea. *Applied Economics*, *36*(13), 1409 - 1419.

Hakim, S. (2003). *A Value-at-Risk Framework for Islamic Banks.* Paper presented at the Islamic Banking: risk management, Regulation and Supervision. Jakarta, Indonesia.

Hassan, M. & Chowdhury, M. (2004). *Islamic banking regulations in light of Basel II.* Paper presented at the Proceedings of the Fifth Harvard Research Forum on Islamic Finance.

Hassan, M. K. & Dicle, M. F. (2005). Basel II and Regulatory Framework for Islamic Banks. *Journal of Islamic Economics and Finance*, *1*(1), 17-36.

Hassan, M. K. (2003). Value at Risk (VaR) Analysis*: An application of some Emerging Country Banks.* Paper presented at the Islamic Banking: risk management, Regulation and Supervision. Jakarta, Indonesia.

Hovakimian, A. & Kane, E. J. (2000). Effectiveness of Capital Regulation at U.S. Commercial Banks, 1985 to 1994. *The Journal of Finance*, *55*(1), 451-468.

How, J. C. Y., Karim, M. A. & Verhoeven, P. (2005). Islamic financing and bank risks: The case of Malaysia. *Thunderbird International Business Review*, *47*(1), 75-94.

Islamic Financial Service Board IFSB, (2005). *Guiding Principles of Risk Management For Institutions (Other than Insurance Institutions) Offering Only Islamic Financial Service* (pp. 32): Islamic Financial Service Board.

Ioannidou, V. P. & Penas, M. F. (2010). Deposit insurance and bank risk-taking: Evidence from internal loan ratings. *Journal of Financial Intermediation*, *19*(1), 95-115.

Iqbal, Z. (1999). Financial engineering in Islamic finance. *Thunderbird International Business Review*, *41*(4-5), 541-559.

Jarrow, R. (2007). A Critique of Revised Basel II. *Journal of Financial Services Research*, *32*(1), 1-16.

Kane, E. & Unal, H. (1988). Change in market assessments of deposit-institution riskiness. *Journal of Financial Services Research*, *1*(3), 207-229.

Kane, E. J. & Unal, H. (1990). Modeling Structural Temporal Variation in the Market's Valuation of Banking Firms. [Article]. *Journal of Finance*, *45*(1), 113-136.

Keeley, M. C. (1990). Deposit Insurance, Risk and Market Power in Banking. *American Economic Review*, *80*(5), 1183.

Khalidi, K. & Refai, G. (2009). *Investment risks in Islamic banks and ways of mitigation*. In B. Muafaq (Ed.), Encyclopedia of business and Islamic Finance.

Khan, M. M. & Bhatti, M. I. (2008). Development in Islamic banking: a financial risk-allocation approach. *Journal of Risk Finance*, *9*(1), 40(12).

Khan, T. (2003). *Credit Risk Management: A framework for Islamic banking*. Paper presented at the Islamic Banking: risk management, Regulation and Supervision, Jakarta, Indonesia

Khan, T. & Ahmed, H. (2001). *Risk management: an analysis of issues in Islamic financial industry*. In Islamic Research and Training Institute, (First ed.). Jeddah- Saudi Arabia: King Fahd National Library Cataloging-in-Publication data.

Kupper, E. F. (2000). Risk Management in Banking. *Gambrera M.* Retrieved from http://citeseerx.ist.psu.edu/viewdoc/download?doi=10.1.1.138.437andrep=rep1andtype=pdf

Kwan, S. & Eisenbeis, R. A. (1997). Bank Risk, Capitalization, and Operating Efficiency. *Journal of Financial Services Research*, 12(2-3), 117-131.

Linbo, F. & Sherrill, S. (2004). Efficiency Versus Risk in Large Domestic US Banks. *Managerial Finance*, *30*(9), 1.

Longin, F. M. (2000). From value at risk to stress testing: The extreme value approach. *Journal of Banking and Finance*, *24*(7), 1097-1130.

Lopez, J. A. & Saidenberg, M. R. (2000). Evaluating credit risk models. *Journal of Banking and Finance*, *24*(1–2), 151-165.

Makiyan, S. (2002). *Risk Management and Challenges in Islamic Banks*. Economics Dept., Yazd University. Iran.

Marcus, A. J. (1984). Deregulation and bank financial policy. *Journal of Banking and Finance*, *8*(4), 557-565.

Marston, D. & Sundararajan, V. (2003). *Unique risks of Islamic banks: Implications for systemic Stability*. Paper presented at the Islamic Banking: risk management, Regulation and Supervision, Jakarta, Indonesia.

McAleer, M., Jiménez-Martin, J.-A. & Perez Amaral, T. (2010). Has the Basel II Accord Encouraged Risk Management During the 2008-09 Financial Crisis? *SSRN eLibrary*. Retrieved from http://ssrn.com/paper=1397239.

Meulbroek, L. K. (2002). A senior manager's guide to integrated risk management. *Journal of Applied Corporate Finance, 14*(4), 56-70.

Niinimäki, J.-P. (2004). The effects of competition on banks' risk taking. Journal of *Economics, 81*(3), 199-222.

Oldfield, G. S. & Santomero, A. M. (1997). The place of risk management in financial institutions. *Center for Financial Institutions Working Papers.*

Sabiq, S. (2006). *Fiqh As-Sunah* (*fiqh* of the prophet's tradition) (Vol. 3). Saida-Beirut: *Al Maktaba Al Assriya*. (Arabic).

Salas, V. & Saurina, J. (2002). Credit risk in two institutional regimes: Spanish commercial and savings banks. *Journal of Financial Services Research*, 22(3), 203.

Salas, V. & Saurina, J. (2003). Deregulation, market power and risk behavior in Spanish banks. *European Economic Review, 47*(6), 1061-1075.

Santomero, A. M. (1997). Commercial Bank Risk Management: An Analysis of the Process. *Journal of Financial Services Research, 12*(2), 83-115.

Shaikh, S. & Jalbani, A. (2009). Risk Management in Islamic and Conventional Banks: A Dierential Analysis. *Journal of Independent Studies and Research*, 7(2), 67-79.

Stoughton, N. M. & Zechner, J. (2007). Optimal capital allocation using RAROC and EVA. *Journal of Financial Intermediation, 16*(3), 312-342.

Stulz, R. M. (1984). Optimal Hedging Policies. *Journal of Financial and Quantitative Analysis, 19*(2), 127-140.

Sundararajan, V. (2005). *Risk Measurement and Disclosure in Islamic Finance and the Implications of Profit Sharing Investment Accounts*. Paper presented at the Sixth International Conference on Islamic Economics, Banking and Finance, Jakarta, Indonesia.

Wetmore, J. L. (2004). Panel Data, Liquidity Risk and Increasing Loans-to-Core Deposits Ratio of Large Commercial Bank Holding Companies. *American Business Review, 22*(2), 99-107.

Wheelock, D. C. (1992). Deposit Insurance and Bank Failures: New Evidence Form the 1920s. *Economic Inquiry, 30*(3), 530-543.

Wheelock, D. C. & Wilson, P. W. (1995). Explaining bank failures: Deposit insurance, regulation. *Review of Economics and Statistics, 77*(4), 689.

Zainol, Z. & Kassim, S. H. (2010). An analysis of Islamic banks' exposure to rate of return risk. *Journal of Economic Cooperation and Development, 31*(1), 59-84.

INDEX

#

A

B

C

G

H

I

J

K

L

Q

R

S

T

U

V

W

Y

Z